RUGBY, RESISTANCE AND POLITICS

RUGBY, RESISTANCE AND POLITICS

HOW DAN QEQE HELPED SHAPE THE HISTORY OF PORT ELIZABETH

BUNTU SIWISA

The financial assistance of the Johannesburg Institute for Advanced Study (JIAS) towards this publication is gratefully acknowledged.

First published in Southern Africa by Jacana Media (Pty) Ltd in 2022

10 Orange Street
Sunnyside
Auckland Park 2092
South Africa
+2711 628 3200
www.jacana.co.za

ISBN 978-1-4314-3291-2

Cover design by publicide
Editing by Sean Fraser
Proofreading by Ali Parry
Indexing by Ali Parry
Set in Ehrhardt MT Std 11/15pt
Printed and bound by ABC Press, Cape Town
Job no. 003968

See a complete list of Jacana titles at www.jacana.co.za

CONTENTS

To all the people of Gqeberha / Port Elizabeth

ABBREVIATIONS AND ACRONYMS

AAM	Anti-Apartheid Movement
ANC	African National Congress
AZAPO	Azanian People's Organisation
BAAB	Bantu Affairs Administration Board
BAB	Bantu Administration Board
BCM	Black Consciousness Movement
BERBOC	Bethelsdorp Rugby Board of Control
CCIRS	Coordinating Committee for International Recognition of Sport
CEDF	Cape Economic Development Forum
CIR	Committee for International Recognition
CNETU	Council for Non-European Trade Unions
COSAS	Congress of South African Students
COSATU	Congress of South African Trade Unions
DPSC	Detained Parent Support Committee
ECAB	East Cape Administration Board
EPRU	Eastern Province Rugby Union
FNQ	Frans, Ngwendu, Qeqe
ICU	Industrial Commercial Union
IDAMASA	Inter-denominational Ministers Association of South Africa
IRB	International Rugby Board
KADRU	King William's Town African District Union
KWARU	KwaZakhele Rugby Union
MACWUSA	Motor and Components Workers Union of South Africa

NAHECS	National Heritage and Cultural Studies
NMBMM	Nelson Mandela Bay Metropolitan Municipality
NSC	National Sports Council
PAC	Pan Africanist Congress
PEARB	Port Elizabeth African Rugby Board
PEBCA	Port Elizabeth Black Civic Association
PEBCO	Port Elizabeth Black Civic Organisation
PEUTOF	Port Elizabeth/Uitenhage Taxi Owners' Forum
PEYCO	Port Elizabeth Youth Congress
SAARB	South African African Rugby Board
SACOS	South African Congress on Sport
SACRFB	South African Coloured Rugby Football Board
SACU	South African Cricket Union
SAIC	South African Indian Council
SANCO	South African National Civic Organisation
SAN-ROC	South African Non-Racial and Olympic Committee
SAP	South African Police
SARB	South African Rugby Board
SARU	South African Rugby Union
SASA	South African Sports Association
SASF	South African Soccer Federation
SASSA	South African Schools Sports Association
SEDRU	South Eastern District Rugby Union
TCB	Transvaal Cricket Board
TCU	Transvaal Cricket Union
TLC	Transitional Local Council
TYRU	Tygerberg Rugby Union
UBCO	Uitenhage Black Civic Organisation
UDF	United Democratic Front
UK	United Kingdom
UWC	University of the Western Cape
VERU	Victoria East Rugby Union
WASA	Writers' Association of South Africa
ZWIRU	Zwide Rugby Union

ACKNOWLEDGEMENTS

This book is the result of forces unseen and seen. At the beginning of 2020, begrudgingly and with my feet itching, COVID-19 hard lockdown sat me down to solely focus on writing this book. With the world shut at my face, confused and angry, I sat down and began one of the most enjoyable and satisfying journeys of writing this book. Were it not for hard lockdown, I doubt I would have written this book when I had. And I doubt I would have written such a fine, cohesive work were it not for the strength, resilience, clarity of mind and purpose I received from God.

But there were also earthly and seen entities who immensely contributed to the conception, shape and direction of this book. Perhaps let us start from the beginning. It all started with an unexpected phone call in August 2018 from an old friend, Dr Bongani Ngqulunga, the Director of the Johannesburg Institute for Advanced Study (JIAS) at the University of Johannesburg (UJ). He briefed me on the institute's and the university's flagship project he was coordinating, the 'African Biographies Project'. He had recruited a corps of South African scholars to research and write biographies of South Africans who have contributed significantly to our current dispensation of freedom and democracy from various fronts. In a way of recruiting me, he had proposed that I write a biography of a well-known ANC activist. Wetting my lips with enthusiasm, he had quickly interjected, 'But wait. I don't know if you've ever heard of Dan Qeqe from Port Elizabeth? What fascinates me about him is how a living black man had a stadium named after him at the height of apartheid.' And that was my entry point.

An old friend in Oxford during my student days once told me that a book is as good, and as bad, as its editor. I wish to extend here this saying to its publisher and staff. Bridget Impey of Jacana Media was eager about the book from the beginning. She gave me so much confidence in my own writing, validating me in areas I never thought I was good at. From the time she showed interest to now, it took over a year to turn the first draft into this book. There was a gruelling review process, wherein I took the book apart and put it together again; various editing phases that focused on granular aspects of the book. And through it all, and particularly through the editing prowess of Sean Fraser, I disentangled writings I never thought I could. And through the work, efforts and insights of Megan Mance, Kelly Ann Mawa, Shay Heydenrych and Kiara Myburgh, the book turned out this way.

I understood two fieldwork research trips to the Eastern Cape in March – April and October–November 2019. These were generously funded by JIAS and administered by the superbly able and efficient administrative staff there. I venture to single out Ms Emelia Kamena, who explained, assisted administratively and with the finances, and trouble-shot at snags during my fieldwork research trips.

Arriving in my hometown, Port Elizabeth / Gqeberha, I found a coterie of old family friends and acquaintances who were only too eager to help me. Mr Vuyisile (Ngconde / Togu) Kosana, an old family friend, made the grand introductions that opened gates to networks of people and institutions. But, most importantly, it was Mrs Pinky Nkanunu who introduced me, directed me, briefed me on opportunities and dangers to almost all the interviewees I interacted with in Port Elizabeth. Right to the most minute details of the contacts, she choir-mastered my interviews in Port Elizabeth. But it was mainly her enthusiasm for the project that kept me going. If it was not for her, this book would not have come out as lively as it is, at this time, without her.

I thank all the interviewees who gave of their time and energy to this book. I thank Crosby 'Winky' Ximiya; Mveleli Ncula; McKenzie Sloti; Thozamile Botha; Alan Zinn; Janet Cherry; Mkhuseli Jack; Lucky 'Coach' Mange; Mpumelelo 'Sbhidla' Majola; Silas Nkanunu; Phumla

Qeqe; Mpumelelo Qeqe; Sinazo Vabaza; Thembela Vabaza; Thando Manana; Gerald Majola; Jumartha Milase Majola; Kolekile Kwatsha; Keke Pemba; Ngconde Balfour; Mncedi Mali; Weaver Qeqe; Nqaba Mali; Ray Mali; Vusi & Nozuko Pikoli; Mthobi Tyamzashe; Lex Mpati; Stone Sizani; Joe Maboyisi Mahala Mbiza; Sipho Tanana; Thami Songongo; Themba Ludwaba; Amon Nyondo; Moki Cekisani; Barry Sinuka; Andile Nyembezi; Harold & Sheila Wilson; Dan Ngcaphe; Valence Watson; Cecil 'Doc' Somyalo; and Archie Mkele. Sadly, some of these wonderful people passed on during the write-up of this book – Silas Nkanuñu; Jumartha Milase Majola; Crosby 'Winky' Ximiya; and Sipho Tanana. May their souls rest in peace.

Thembile and Vuyo Matomela, the uncle and nephew duo, provided me with the right research perspectives and insights in the middle of my fieldwork research. It was a turn the research needed to take, at the right time that it needed to take. Thozamile Botha gave me his holds-unbarred critique of the first draft of the manuscript.

At the research institutes and libraries I worked in, I received the most enthusiastic help from staffers. At the offices of the *Herald*, *Evening Post* and *Weekend Post* – Black Tiso, in Port Elizabeth, a Mr Mabece helped me mine over 186 newspaper articles. At the National Heritage and Cultural Studies (NAHECS) at the University of Fort Hare in Alice, I am indebted to Dr Mike Maamoe, the senior archivist, and Lunga. At the King William's Town Archival Depot, a small corner unrecognised for its very rich material, I received the most patient care from its staffers. At the Port Elizabeth Archival Depot in Greenacres, they went out of their way to find documents for me although they had just relocated to their new offices.

I thank friends and my family in Port Elizabeth and Alice who went out of their way to link me with research contacts. I am particularly grateful to Didi Resha, Nambitha Stofile, Lukhanyo Ntuthu, Zukisani Resha, Lulama Mphalala and others I may have forgotten to mention. It was a whirlwind of research and writing, and I thank you all.

INTRODUCTION

Early on the evening of 8 September 1975, Dan Qeqe stared up at the headlights of all his cars flooding back at him. He had fetched them from his home in the upmarket suburb of Thembalethu in New Brighton, and driven them to the makeshift stadium in Veeplaas.[1] Much the same had been done by all the other car-owning officials, players and supporters of the four-year-old KwaZakhele Rugby Union (Kwaru). Their vehicles had joined Qeqe's to line the perimeter of the temporary stadium and light up the field with their headlights. The alpine-bright deluge provided adequate light for this night of a historic game of rugby.

The short and stocky 46-year-old Qeqe, commissioned by Kwaru's executive committee, had flattened the ground, planted the grass, built the grandstand, and fenced the ground using corrugated-iron sheets. Some of the panels were new, but many had been bought from scrapyards in the Port Elizabeth and Uitenhage areas. The stadium had turned out a seating capacity of 6000.[2]

But all the makeshift plans belied a soulful extravagance. The night's game had been preceded by a series of political and legal tussles that threatened to overshadow what the black people of Port Elizabeth held dear. This was set to be a feast of rugby, the significance of which reached far beyond the clear-cut simplicity of a single game. The effects were already finding expression in the brewing local and national politics and sociologies never before generated in modern sport.

Reeling from a ban on using the Zwide Stadium, a municipal sports ground, Kwaru had had to quickly find a new stadium for their game,[3] its tussles with the Port Elizabeth municipality ending in a bruising court loss for Kwaru. The ban had been instigated by Kwaru and the non-racial stance of the South African Rugby Union (SARU) in refusing to lend its players to the Leopards, the state-owned black rugby team of the South African African Rugby Board (SAARB), to play in the British Lions tour of 1974.[4]

The event of this night – a South Africa (SA) Cup Final match between Kwaru and the Tygerberg Rugby Union (TYRU) of Cape Town, simply known as Tygerberg – had special meaning, lending to a new sense of people's ownership, of community representation, black pride, the defiance of an oppressive political authority, all for the love of non-racial rugby. The SA Cup was sponsored by SARU. Having changed its name from the Rhodes Cup in 1971, SARU's premier SA Cup was sponsored by Atkinson Motors in Cape Town.[5]

Shebeens, taverns, dancehalls and various other entertainment centres in Veeplaas, New Brighton and other townships had closed for the night. Many had clamoured to the makeshift stadium. Others had turned on their radios in the comfort of their homes to listen to the Radio Xhosa broadcast of the game.[6] Rather than risk having to settle for uncomfortable seating or standing spots at the ground, many spectators had hurried to take their seats immediately after returning from work. Some had arrived promptly after completing their chores and other daily responsibilities.[7]

Mrs Jumartha Milase Majola, Qeqe's long-time friend and neighbour, and director of the Ivan Peter Youth Club in New Brighton,[8] had, along with Mrs Rose Qeqe and friends, prepared hot meals for the administrators and dignitaries. Abdul Abbas, president of the non-racial SARU, was in town, accompanied by senior SARU officials. Other sports and political struggle dignitaries had come from even further afield.

Methods of gate keeping and entrance-fee collection were as improvised as the temporary grounds. Qeqe and Kwaru officials, with hats in hand, made their way around the fence collecting money and, despite no visible gate, spectators dutifully paid their gate fees. Some of the money collected came in as donations from non-racial rugby lovers who had come from towns and cities of the Eastern Cape to watch the game[9] – all in support of continuing with the building of the new stadium. For other non-racial sports liberation activists, Qeqe's erection of a stadium made a clear and profound statement: 'that actually you don't need to have everything before you do things. Look at me, I'm doing it. I'm building a stadium'.[10]

The Kwaru executive committee, to be seated on the grandstand with Qeqe, who was not in the executive committee, moved around, finalising preparations for the game. Arthur Sipho 'Mono' Badela – president of Kwaru, charismatic, politically active, and a 'true blue African National Congress (ANC) man'[11] – turned up in a suit, as he almost always did. As a journalist on Port Elizabeth's *Evening Post*, Mono Badela had defiantly defined Kwaru's non-racial stand against the local and national state onslaught over the past four years.[11]

Seated on the grandstand was the rest of the Kwaru executive: vice-president Wilkinson M Maku, treasurer Newman Grawana, secretary-general Samuel Nghona, assistant secretary Bruce Mahonga, recording secretary Daliwonga Siwisa, match secretary Koks Mtwa, chairman Lawrence Jack, trustees Thomas Sullo and Morris Peta, senior selectors Sipho Nozewu (also coach) and Hamilton Madikane, and junior selectors James Mtanga and Zweli Wabana.[12]

Despite the festive mood, Qeqe, Badela and the Kwaru executive committee looked on pensively. This was going to be a record-setting game in various ways: not only to clinch Kwaru's playing prowess by winning the SA Cup for the first time, but also to redeem itself from a self-inflicted shame of the previous year's SA Cup Final match against Western Province. Perhaps as an act of desperation in a tough, neck-and-neck SA Cup Final in 1974 and in apparent protest at an award to Western Province of an easy penalty point right in front of the posts, Kwaru's Themba 'Sgabadula'[13] Ludwaba, a scrumhalf and flanker,[14] had sat on the ball mid play time, refusing to let Western Province kick the penalty ball to the goal post.[15] The 1974 final match produced no winner, and the trophy was shelved. In all likelihood, Western Province, which had had straight SA Cup wins since 1971,[16] would have won.

Ludwaba, regarded as an 'outstanding achiever,'[17] was an amazingly tall player, fiercely muscled, agile and a terror to any rival team.

Nonetheless, his mischievous antic on the field had cost Kwaru, ending with disciplinary action at the table of SARU administrators.[18] Qeqe and the Kwaru executive committee, sitting on the grandstand on match day in September 1975, were eager to redeem Kwaru's standing.

The ground's seating capacity of 6000 had swiftly swelled to about 20 000. Milling around the grandstand and all around the corrugated-iron fence, spectators erupted in awe and excitement at the 'Rolling Maul.'[19] This was the pinnacle of the Kwaru team's showmanship – a grand entrance akin to a long, fast-moving worm, with the ball moving fast from one player to the next. It was also executed as a winning movement towards scoring at a try line.[20]

Peter Mkata, part of the Rolling Maul, was Kwaru's premium favourite alongside Ludwaba. Mkata began playing for Kwaru in the early 1970s as a centre and fullback, but proved to be a brilliant fly-back. An elusive but direct runner, his excellence lay in tackling, well supported by his nimbleness and a brilliant sense of participation.[21] Also part of Kwaru's force was A Lefume, a scrumhalf (known as Zanemvula and nicknamed Kenya) from Ginsberg, King William's Town, and 'his performance at scrumhalf was noteworthy'.[22] Another crowd favourite was Wilfred Khovu, Kwaru's front-ranker.[23]

Qeqe himself – from New Brighton – had honed his rugby-playing skills and fitness from 1961 when he joined the Spring Rose Rugby Football Club. Welile Jeremiah 'Bhomza' Nkohla, another Port Elizabethan in the team and another of Kwaru's favourites, played club rugby in the Kwaru-affiliated Orientals Rugby Football Club. His well-rooted role in the team was as eighth man.[24] Ntonga 'Stix' Singata, Kwaru's flyhalf, was another popular player from the Kwaru-affiliated Walmer Wales Rugby Football Club.[25]

Tygerberg, of course, boasted its own star line-up. JP Jeposa was a well-honed and experienced hooker,[26] with Peter Jooste, one of the most experienced Tygerberg players, coming in as a lock.[27] Millen Petersen was a strong scrumhalf who was considered 'strong and sure',[28] particularly in his long, accurate passes. Another prominent Tygerberg lock who graced the field against Kwaru was Daniel 'Spook' September.[29]

As the game went on, at a neck-and-neck pace, Qeqe's tough

training and coaching regimen, placing a premium on physical fitness, stamina and endurance, gave the Kwaru team an edge over Tygerberg. However, in the second half of the game, it was Kwaru's Ntonga 'Stix' Singata who secured Kwaru's win with a final score of 15–9. Not long after Singata's winning try, the game was over. For the first time, SARU's youngest and first black affiliate had won the SA Cup. And, with Singata's score, Kwaru had redeemed itself.

The triumph of that night, however, huddled alongside the fear of what might have happened. Qeqe or Badela or any of Kwaru's executive committee members and administrators could have been arrested and thrown into jail for their defiance in playing non-racial rugby. Even worse, their actions could have been seen as a dastardly and daring appropriation of land in order to defy the laws of the state. Louis Koch, chief director of the Cape Midlands Bantu Affairs Administration Board, had already tried to sabotage the building of the stadium, but had failed against the fury and determination of Qeqe.[30]

Fortunately, the Security Branch did not, however, swoop in on them. Instead, the wild, uproarious cheers heralded an incredible feat, an achievement that had never been seen before in South Africa. This was a new phenomenon, the start of the journey of one community stepping beyond the crosscurrents of the social, cultural, political and sporting worlds. A new era of Kwaru rugby had been launched, one that sought to consolidate the organisation's iconic status as one of black pride, a culture of political defiance, and an expression of community cohesion. These attributes all coalesced around the amazingly selfless acts of Dan Qeqe.

That night, Qeqe, Kwaru's executive and all the players and administrators moved on to David Mbane's business premises, Melisizwe Butchery, for celebrations. Mbane, Qeqe's contemporary on the rugby field, had played for Eastern Province in the 1950s and 1960s,[31] as well as in the major African Cup competitions of that time.[32] In his playing days, he was considered 'the mobile and tough Eastern Province forward'.[33] But on that evening of Kwaru's victory, he was one of Spring Rose's administrators, a prominent businessman, and served with Qeqe on the Port Elizabeth Joint Bantu Advisory Board.[34]

Monumental gate takings of R11 578 had been further cause for celebration.[35] In the room above Melisizwe Butchery[36], Abbas named the makeshift stadium ground the Dan Qeqe Stadium. Standing to address the crowd, he said, 'I want you to adopt that name and leave it to the authorities to remove it even if by forcing us to play in the streets.'[37] And so, inadvertently, Qeqe had lived up to the meaning of his middle name, 'Dumile', meaning, 'famous'. At the height of apartheid, this black man had come to have an entire stadium, built on land literally appropriated by the people, named after him. This was the beginning of a journey of challenges, joys, fears, loss, pain and history-making for Dan Qeqe and the people of Port Elizabeth.

EARLY ONE MORNING IN 1989, slightly after 1 am, I sat hunched over a typewriter at the dining table. My face was already stinging from my grandfather's imminent hot slap.

'*Kunini*?' asked my grandfather in his trademark clipped, staccato voice, piercing anger glistening in his eyes. Love and wrath lived not in his mouth, but in his eyes. His *kunini* meant, in this case, 'how many times?' rather than the direct isiXhosa–English translation of 'how long?' I had no room to lie, nor to run. And my saviour, my grandmother, was fast asleep at the far end of the long passage.

I had been completely unaware of his presence, and by the time I caught sight of him hovering over me across the table it was too late. Caught up in the frenzy of the clacking, tap-tap, tap-tap-tap of the typewriter, I hadn't realised he had been there all along. Only when I pushed the carriage return lever, rattling on, to begin typing a new line, did I realise I had been caught red-handed. He had been waiting for me to spot him, for me to realise I had been caught in an act of theft. I was cornered in a nasty jive, with no room to spin a lie. The beast was right there in front of me, nestled in the embrace of my arms, and the imposing dining table blocked any swift exit.

'*Kunini*?' Leaning against the wall in his navy-blue bathrobe, his arms folded over his chest, he stared at me.

'Many times, *tata*. Many times,' I said.

'How many times have I told you not to touch this typewriter?' his voice rose.

'Many times, *tata*.'

My answer sought to placate, concerned only with how to save myself from the slap that was bound to follow. I gasped, the heat rising to my face in the knowledge that I had been bust. It had never entered my mind that my trysts with the typewriter would ever be found out. It had been close to a month since I had first embarked on these stolen moments. And I had grown too comfortable. I had mastered the safety drills: wait until everyone had gone to sleep, then close the door separating the living area from the master bedroom and the other rooms, aided by a door shutting off the long passage and separating myself from them. But I did not take into account that the loud typewriter, clacking and squelching, would bring him to attention on his way to take a leak at 1 in the morning.

'I told you many times, this typewriter is not mine. It belongs to Kwaru. It has been entrusted to me as the secretary of Kwaru. If it breaks in your hands, I will be responsible for its repairs. And the repairs will be expensive. Are you going to pay for them? No.' His voice had reached a distinctive bark. I was not yet out of the woods. This was only the beginning. My nabbed thief's play at appearing remorseful, coy, and responsibly attentive all in one breath was a delicate balancing act. It was in how I had to angle my eyes, dip and raise my head, and what – and how – I said in response that would count. And an indication of the outcome lay in measuring the cadence of his voice. At the height of his screech, I rested. I was still safe. But at the incline of his voice, teetering towards silence, and the shuffle of his feet, it was game over.

This was not the time to remind him I had told him that I wanted to be a writer, which was why he had caught me mindlessly typing out an extract from *Upbeat*, my favourite youth magazine, that of the United Democratic Front (UDF). I had resorted to theft simply because of his notoriety for saying 'no' to 99.9 per cent of my requests.

But those other requests were always momentary desires, hazy wants spurred on by fleeting triggers – of whole pork sausages all to myself, taking his car for a spin, travelling to see my biological father in exile in Zimbabwe. But writing, and writing on that typewriter, was something else altogether. It was a fixed, constant, unyielding need. I had seen him tapping away on it, his tongue clipped sideways between his teeth, clucking on the keys with two pointed index fingers. It had been a one … one, two … one, two, three … three, four … one … one … clack and tap.

He worked on it against the background of his personal library: *At the End of the Day* (a volume of Harold Macmillan's memoirs at No. 10 Downing Street), *Working for Boroko*, *Communism Today* magazines, an essay collection on pan-Africanism, a collection of interviews with African writers edited by Lewis Nkosi and published by Voice of America, Ngugi wa Thiong'o's *Matigari*, a host of other titles in the African Writers Series, numerous Shakespeare volumes, some Charles Dickens, George Eliot's *Silas Marner*, a DH Lawrence, Geoffrey Chaucer's *Canterbury Tales*, a scholarly biography of Julius Caesar, textbooks on English grammar, journalism and economics, a freshly printed and unbound draft copy of Benjamin Pogrund's *How Can Man Die Better*, a thick directory of African universities, and a slew of copies of George Orwell's *Animal Farm*.

I had marvelled at the spell his sentences had over me: relaxed, full-bodied, luxurious and languid in their completeness. My sentences were hurried, staggering, out of breath, panicky and, at times, incomplete. And, on that morning of the imminent hot slap, I did not tell him that that image had stuck with me. So, in the insistent presence of his notorious 'no', I decided to steal Kwaru's typewriter.

My resolve to be a writer had that year been further firmed up. Astonished, I came across my own name printed on the spine of a book. I saw it again capitalised and typed in bold in the top left corner of my isiXhosa Literature examination paper. My other elder grandfather, LK Siwisa (in isiXhosa, there is no 'grand-uncle' or 'great-uncle') from Ngqushwa/Peddie, had written *Ndibuzen' Amathongo* (Ask Me of Dreams), a collection of short stories. First published in 1950, its 10th edition of 1985 was that year one of the prescribed fiction texts for Standard Six (Grade Eight) in our region. And from then, I knew that my hope of making this writing enterprise work for me was a reachable dream.

'Put that thing away and go to bed!' It was over. That was the end of it. The hot slap had been withdrawn. I swiftly packed the typewriter back into its hard black plastic casing and tucked it away where I had found it, under a chair in the dining room. I went to bed, mighty glad that I had narrowly avoided a hot slap. That night, I firmly resolved that I would never touch that typewriter again, nor ever write again.

As I tucked myself into bed, I was less concerned about Kwaru. I didn't think about Kwaru simply because there was nothing to think about. Kwaru was part of the community furniture. Everyone talked about it. It was everywhere. For a long time, it never occurred to me that Kwaru was not a real word, but rather an acronym. It was a name I saw beneath an insignia of a lively and rather cheeky rhinoceros on my grandfather's green blazer. It was a name I associated with Dan Qeqe, a friend and associate of my grandfather's who came over to our house to engage him on adult business I couldn't care less about.

I never thought that the friendly, loud, talkative Dan Qeqe – the old man who dressed rather dourly, like a nondescript door-to-door insurance salesman on a lunch break, without a tie and jacket – was one of the wealthiest and most popular men in Port Elizabeth. I didn't associate him with the people's struggles. It never entered my mind that those adult talks had been shaping the political, cultural and sports liberation of the peoples of Port Elizabeth in profound ways.

It is my hope that this book will illuminate, in far-reaching ways, those conversations, those engagements on the journeys of Dan Qeqe and the struggles, joys and achievements of the people of Port Elizabeth. In whichever ways one views Qeqe's biography, it is a reflection of a social, political and sporting history of the people of Port Elizabeth, the Eastern Cape and South Africa. It is a reflection of the life and times of a man, with all the histories and contradictions that come with any individual and his community.

And it is now, in something of a gaping irony, that I return to an entity I swore to never have anything to do with 32 years ago. Now I find myself committed to a biography of Dan Qeqe – a history of resistance against the injustices of apartheid, and the road to triumph of non-racial rugby embedded in the struggles of Kwaru. This was a struggle only yielding to us now, following the spectacular success of Siya Kolisi, Solly Tyibilika and Mzwandile Stick (Stokololo). Back then, it was an impossible dream bulldozed into reality by Dan Qeqe and his associates in Kwaru.

Dan Qeqe is a living history. His life story stands on its own, but it is also a living history of Port Elizabeth and the Eastern Cape. His story has gone largely unnoticed, chronicled in scattered titbits of writings on the history of black rugby and the liberation of sport. Qeqe's story reflects the social and political history of Port Elizabeth and the region in a far more impactful and intimate manner than that of the city's political luminaries Govan Mbeki and Raymond Mhlaba. His life and times are embedded in the city's landscape, in popular memory of local anti-apartheid struggles.

The story of his life is a work of creativity – how he wrestled with the institutions he largely inherited in order to mould his destiny and that of his community. In many ways, he would not stand out as anyone of real biographical interest were it not for the embeddedness of the city and the region in him. The inverse equally holds true: the histories of the city and the region would not have come to pass as they have had it not been for his own contributions and sacrifices. He carried the multiple identities of various black social groups. His is the life story of what these social groups forged in him.

Despite the abundance of primary texts, oral histories and memories, Dan Qeqe's story remains untold in any cohesive published form. In writing his biography, I have come across staggering historical accounts within a vast array of sources. I recorded 36 in-depth interviews with his family, extended family, former associates in sports liberation, politics, and civic organisations in Port Elizabeth, Uitenhage, Fort Beaufort, Alice, East London and Pretoria, and even in Berlin, Germany. I could have effortlessly doubled the number of interviews had I not reached the opimum utility value.

From various archival depots in Port Elizabeth, King William's Town, Pretoria, Cape Town and Alice, I collected material on the history of sports liberation, of the politics of Port Elizabeth and the broader region, and of Qeqe's background in Fort Beaufort. The sources ranged from the National Archives of South Africa in Pretoria, the Mayibuye Archives at the University of the Western Cape (UWC) in Cape Town, the National Heritage and Cultural Studies (NAHECS) archives at the University of Fort Hare in Alice, the King William's Town Archival Depot and the Port Elizabeth Archives. I collected no fewer than 186 newspaper articles in Port Elizabeth and East London.

The conceptual framework for this biography demanded some sense of scholarly rigour, resting as it does between the socio-historical and humanistic tradition of biography writing. As a historical–sociological biography it seeks to conceptualise Qeqe as an individual, as well as a social and political being. It explores the significance of his subjective experiences through an analytic interpretation of his past through primary texts, secondary texts, oral testimonies and memories.

The humanistic tradition seeks to activate the reader's imagination, as they begin to better understand the multilayered depictions of Qeqe. It draws the reader into the text in an interactive manner. They unpack Qeqe's heroisms, the falsities, victories, setbacks, sacrifices, idiosyncrasies, limitations and inaccuracies. In that way, Dan Qeqe is inevitably revealed in many ways.

THIS WORK ON DANIEL Dumile Qeqe (1929–2005) is divided into three parts, the sense and logic of which are foregrounded in the understanding that, as much as this is a biographical study, it is also a stab at understanding the social and political history of the people of Port Elizabeth. And so it should inevitably be, considering that the sporting, civic, cultural and political obstacles Qeqe encountered in his life encapsulated the struggles and hopes of ordinary black residents of his community. Furthermore, the sequence of this book is chronological, revolving around key years. These are theme-centralising years, critical in the activities that shaped Dan Qeqe and those around him.

The partition, informing the separation of the different parts of the book, illuminates the themes that principally revolve around and thus shaped Qeqe's life and his community. Part One covers the history of black rugby in Port Elizabeth and the Eastern Cape, from the arrival of the British settlers in 1820 to 1971, the year in which the KwaZakhele Rugby Union (Kwaru) was founded. *Chapter 1: The History of Black Rugby (1820–1955): The Age of Innocence* examines the political, cultural and social forces that birthed and gave shape to black rugby in Port Elizabeth and elsewhere in the Eastern Cape. The years 1820 to 1955 cover what may be referred to as the 'innocent age' of the historical development of black rugby, before the politicisation of sport from 1955. Recognising local black clubs as the sprouting force of black rugby, this chapter examines the history of black rugby clubs in Port Elizabeth, Grahamstown and East London, and the cultural, intellectual and social forces that gave them definition. *Chapter 2: The History of Black Rugby (1956–1971): The Age of Politics* takes a closer look at the development of rugby in Port Elizabeth, and how individuals meandered through the harsh political and social environment facing them in those developmental years. More importantly, it gives a revisionist account that seeks to offer a sober assessment of how apolitical forces shaped black rugby, when dominant historical accounts tend to give too much credence to the overarching political influences over rugby and sport in general.

Part Two of the book covers both the biographical narrative of Dan Qeqe's life from the time of his birth in 1929 to the formation of Kwaru in 1971. *Chapter 3: Qeqe Begins (1929–1950s): The Roots* narrates Qeqe's personal history, from his formative years in Fort Beaufort, his schooling and early sporting experiences there and in Port Elizabeth. More importantly, it sheds light on some of the political contradictions he came to inhabit: the politically conservative, ethno-nationalist, black consciousness, and progressive community builder, and how they balanced and unbalanced him. *Chapter 4: Qeqe in Port Elizabeth (1950s–1971)* covers his teaching, his sport and his uneasy foray into entrepreneurship. It searches for the enduring influences around him, those that directed him toward political and social justice, and so helped carve his civic, political and sporting ventures.

Part Three covers the rest of Qeqe's adult life, from 1971 to 2006, the year he passed away. *Chapter 5: The Accidental Birth of the KwaZakhele Rugby Union: (1950s–1971)* gathers together scattered documented material, analytical secondary material, and new oral accounts on the formation of Kwaru. The founding of Kwaru exists only in widely dispersed forms, scarcely documented and, in many instances, only as oral accounts. The latter is perhaps most problematic in that it brings out a populist Kwaru modern history based on loyalties, and often incorrect understandings of the role and extent of political influences. So this section attempts to correct that historical narratrive, and also bring to the fore a more revisionist account of the role of Qeqe, his associates, both hostile and friendly, in the formation of Kwaru.

Chapter 6: 'Up Kwaru!' moves on to outline the far-reaching social, cultural, sporting and political influences Kwaru brought to bear in Port Elizabeth, in the Eastern Cape, South Africa and internationally. Equally, it examines how these developments led to the building of the Dan Qeqe Stadium by the people of Port Elizabeth, and named after a living black man at the height of apartheid. More importantly, *Chapter 7: Building eDan Qeqe* offers a fresh, new and profound take on how the stadium came to stand as a monument to defiance against apartheid, an iconic symbol of black pride, and instrumental in carrying out practical anti-apartheid struggle activities.

Kwaru collapsed from inside, and *Chapter 8: The First Implosion (1977) …* examines just how Kwaru managed to self-destruct, and the role Qeqe played in that. There is careful unpacking of the rather divisive oral historical accounts and documented history in order to make a sober assessment of the implosion of Kwaru. This chapter covers the so-called coup d'état of Kwaru's first executive committee, the forces that had led to that, and the organisational and political ambience that fostered this eruption from within. *Chapter 9: … and the Second Implosion (1982)* examines how the final implosion of Kwaru in 1982 stemmed directly from the remnants of that first implosion of 1977. It also examines how the political turbulence of the 1980s further cultivated the atmosphere of organisational chaos that eventually killed Kwaru.

The following two chapters narrate the political influences of Qeqe on the Port Elizabeth of the 1970s and 1980s. *Chapter 10: Qeqe and Port Elizabeth in the 1970s* takes a hard look at the contribution Qeqe made to the development of the education of the black child in the city, completely revolutionising the educational system and infrastructure. These were acts conceived through challenges and in isolation. The chapter also narrates the political sacrifices he made in a turbulent Port Elizabeth mired in the revolutionary upheavals of the Soweto of 16 June 1976, and the aftermath of the murder of Steve Biko. Similarly, *Chapter 11: Qeqe and Port Elizabeth in the 1980s* examines the contributions Qeqe made to the changing Port Elizabeth of the 1980s. The concluding chapter, *Chapter 12: Qeqe Rests: The Legacy* examines the last years of

Qeqe's life in the 1990s, his final contributions to the construction of a new, post-apartheid era, and the legacies he bequeathed Port Elizabeth, the Eastern Cape and South Africa in the arena of sport, civic life and politics.

PART ONE
(1820–1971)

1

THE HISTORY OF BLACK RUGBY (1820–1955): THE AGE OF INNOCENCE

'Try me, says PE's Dan'. So read the headline of the *Herald* of 13 January 1976.[1] A beaming Dan Qeqe stooped beneath the headline, complete in the white flannels of cricket wear, and a black cap. Posing with a cricket bat, the shadow of his home silhouetting his batting pose, the smile he wore belied his anger. 'Try me.' As reported by the *Herald*, Dan Qeqe had challenged Joe Pamensky:

> A Port Elizabeth ex-provincial black cricket player, Mr Dan Qeqe, has issued a single wicket cricket challenge to South African boss, Mr Joe Pamensky, following Mr Pamensky's remark on Tuesday that blacks 'don't seem to have the aptitude and ability' to become good cricketers.[2]

In print, it was an annoyance only captured by the headline's strapline: 'Qeqe throws Pamensky cricket gauntlet.' On that January morning of 1976, Mveleli Ncula, a former Eastern and Kwaru player, and former CEO of SA Rugby,[3] recalled in precise detail how Qeqe had hurriedly put together arrangements for the picture to accompany the press article. 'I remember, he called a coloured guy who used to come and take photos at Kwaru, to come and take that photo there … I mean, he had stopped playing long ago. He put on his white flannels and also this cap, and then, "Try me" … I remember that very well.'[4]

It was showmanship, a show of fury, responding to a racist remark made by Joe Pamensky, the South African cricket boss, at a lunch-hour talk to students at Rand Afrikaans University. To Pamensky, black cricketers had inherently inferior cricket skills compared to white cricketers, and there was nothing, he felt, that could be done about it. Such remarks had left enduring imprints on the black cricketers' socio-psychological perceptions of race and cricket. In 1978, a horde of coloured and Indian cricketers had moved *en masse* from their non-racial fold, the Transvaal Cricket Board (TCB), to the white controlling body, the Transvaal Cricket Union (TCU, all in the hope that they would play alongside famous white cricketers, like Graeme Pollock.[5]

Qeqe, then treasurer of the United Cricket Club in Port Elizabeth, had confidently continued that, 'Mr Pamensky's sweeping statement is shocking. I would like to challenge him to play me in a single wicket competition … He and I are the same age and even though I am at a disadvantage – as a youngster, I had no coaches and no nets – through inborn merit I will win.'[6] He also bemoaned the inadequate sports infrastructure in black township schools. At Newell, the oldest black high school in New Brighton, which catered for nearly 2000 students, there was a glaring absence of a cricket pitch.[7]

The racial segmentation – based on purportedly natural sporting abilities ascribed to particular race groups – is well documented in the proclamations of the apartheid government, and there were doggedly consistent assertions seeking to legitimise the ideological and policy bases for the existence of unequal sports platforms for South Africa's racial groups. For instance, the *Official Year Book for South Africa* in 1974 boldly maintained that:

> … from time immemorial the Whites, the Coloureds, the Indian community and the various Bantu peoples have administered and practised their sports separated at all levels of competition.

> Moreover, it is only comparatively recently that the Bantu peoples have shown marked interest in what may be called modern sporting activities. For centuries they have found their recreation in tribal activities, such as hunting, tribal dances – even faction fights.[8]

Douglas Booth and John Nauright further propounded on both colonialism's and apartheid's effects on the racial segmentation of sports abilities in South Africa:

> Notwithstanding sports traditional association with merit and the sports field as free from arbitrary social division, the apartheid state, and indeed its predecessor, applied formulas to the sporting realm and segregated blacks. Later, in propaganda, the apartheid state justified discrimination on the grounds that modern sport was alien to black culture.[9]

Pamensky's nakedly racist remark was nurtured by apartheid, 'a system unlike any other in the world whose every function turns on the pernicious factor of racism'.[10] Apartheid ensured white supremacy in sport through the overarching principle of separate development, best encapsulating apartheid's sports policy that '[the] first aim of the sports policy is given as "the maintenance of the white population in South Africa through and within the policy of separate development"'.[11]

When it came to modern sports, apartheid had anchored its discriminatory practices on three pieces of legislation: the Natives Urban Areas Act of 1923, as amended in 1945; the Group Areas Act of 1950; and the Reservation of Separate Amenities Act of 1953.[12] And it was particularly the Donges[13] policy proclamation in 1956 that began the politicisation and official racism of sports policies in South Africa.[14]

The genesis of Pamensky's racism, however, harkened way back to the nineteenth century with the reach of the British Empire. As Philani Nongogo noted, 'Institutionalised racism in South Africa and the country's sport did not start in 1948. It was preceded by colonialism and racism, which brought the colour bar policies,'[15] latching on to Victorian England's project – as instrumental agents of public schools and in church missions established in the colonies – of spreading the control of the British Empire.

Racism in nineteenth-century South African sport was not driven entirely by government, but rather by white colonial voluntary sports organisations. Colin du Plessis delineated how, separately, colonialism, imperialism and apartheid each outlined and established the framework of racism in local sport. Each political era offloaded its own burdens of racism on sport, with apartheid finally cementing the racist foundations laid earlier. Du Plessis argued that:

> Modern society has the inclination to credit Apartheid with the divisions of South African sport. Though the harsh policies and legislation of Apartheid undoubtedly added to sporting division, it was not solely responsible for segregating sport in South Africa – this would be giving Apartheid too much credit.[16]

Sport, race and the spread of control by the British Empire in its colonies were thus interrelated.[17] The economic priorities of the Victorian era, under the influence of both the French and the Industrial revolutions, placed a premium on maximising productivity. To achieve this, forms of social control and the regimentation of labour were required. Industrial employers therefore encouraged participation in organised team sports as a means of social control. It was thus a way of keeping workers from drinking, gambling and enaging in other social activities detrimental to maximising labour productivity.[18]

Through English public schools, the British Empire sought to groom white bourgeois leadership among schoolboys, a leadership that would be able to deal authoritatively with its working-class underlings. This class-based form of social control of the 'other' – taught on the sports fields – had, however, filtered through to the need for the control of 'other' racial groups in the colonies. In the absence of the class system to which they were accustomed in Britain, the mandate in the colonies had metamorphosed from one of class to race. Du Plessis remarked:

> It is on the sports field where the young middle-class Briton learns how to govern not only himself, but also those that were 'destined' to be under British rule. And the young middle-class imperialists were taught these values and morals on the flowing green grass of

> the English public school, which would be expanded to the colonies of the Empire. This class-specific social indoctrination would lead to the division of society along class lines and subsequently along racial lines when applied to the colonial context and to the interaction with the so-called 'other.'[19]

And so it was that racism in nineteenth-century sport preceded state-sanctioned racism. In this colonial setting, sports organisations found expression in inter- and intra-ethnically divided groups.[20] Sport in colonial South Africa thus shaped formations of social identity, imagined communities, invented traditions and cultural hegemony.[21] These served to 'create loyalties and social identities within different classes and conflicts between them that would permeate and persist in the decades that followed'.[22]

It was in the Port Elizabeth–Grahamstown districts of the 1800s that the foundations of black rugby were laid. Between 1820 and the 1870s, particular political events – and the social permutations they engineered – unwittingly forged the emergence of black rugby: the arrival of British settlers in Grahamstown in 1820, and the conclusion in 1879 of the Frontier Wars. All the while, the British were steadfast in their determination to consolidate the control of the British Empire in South Africa.

The end of the Frontier Wars in 1879 came with a devastating defeat for amaXhosa. Confronted by loss of land and thus livelihood, many amaXhosa families were compelled to seek livelihoods as labourers in cities and towns in the Eastern Cape. This augured well for the grand project of the British Empire of consolidating its control over the Eastern Cape, and maximising economic benefits from the area and its people. This form of control over the African population also meant cultural assimilation into everything British, bringing with it not only new urban settlement, but also cultural identity permutations for Africans, which inevitably meant the passing of colonial institutional values to new hybridised forms of urban black identities.

Team sports were a crucial element of the Empire's assimilation project. Wittingly or unwittingly, it gave rise to new urban black identities in which black rugby sprouted. Attesting to the enduring impact of colonial institutional values on modern sport in South Africa, Tarminder Kaur and Gerard Akindes pointed out that:

> Contemporary Africa and sports are tied to the colonial past of the continent. Introduction of 'modern' sports in Africa is intrinsically connected to Europe's colonial project and the agents thereof, including the army, the school system and the religious missions. Regardless of governing ideologies, modern sports played an important role in simultaneously separating and incorporating the colonisers and the colonised into racial, social, material and political folds.[23]

The arrival of the British settlers in Port Elizabeth in 1820 introduced the game of rugby to Africans.[24] Having, for the most part, settled in and around Grahamstown, some of the settlers finally returned to Port Elizabeth, with the mandate of constructing the city's harbour. This all formed part of the Empire's trade mission to link South Africa to its international trade routes. And so British engineers, technicians and mechanics flooded into Port Elizabeth. During their lunch breaks, they relieved the stress of work by means of informal games of social rugby,[25] and it was on these occasions that they requested their African co-workers to join them.

These observer–participants quickly picked up the rudimentary rules and regulations of the game, resulting in an unintentional pattern of learning for Africans. This pattern subsequently spread among other racial groups equally unfamiliar with the game of rugby. History would repeat itself in a similar initiation experience later when, at the end of the South African War (1899–1902), Afrikaners were first exposed to rugby in prisoner of war (POW) camps on St Helena, and in Ceylon, India and Bermuda. There, some 24 000 POW Afrikaners observed and learnt the intricacies of rugby.[26] Dean Allen explained:

> At a time when the Empire advanced its interests under the banner of development and civilization, the progress of indigenous communities still lay in the assimilation and incorporation into 'things' British. Sport, and team games in particular, were an integral part of this assimilation process.[27]

To the British, this was a gravely important element of social development and cultural assimilation, laying the foundations of the Empire's control of its colonies. Officially, and among white people, the first game of rugby was played in South Africa on 23 August 1862. Chronicled in the *Cape Argus*, it had been organised by Bishop's College Canon George Ogilvie, and played between teams of officers of the Eleventh Regiment and a Civil Service XV at Green Point in Cape Town.[28]

By the mid-1870s, rugby union matches in the Cape Colony had become commonplace.[29] By then, however, rugby had also caught on among the African population. By then, too, of course, the end of the nine Frontier Wars in the Eastern Cape had had significant ramifications for the new permutations of African urban resettlements. The Mfengu, Gcaleka and other amaXhosa sub-ethnic groups carried with them the inter-ethnic hostilities and subsequently transposed them to their new urban settings, resulting in sporadic clashes in and around Port Elizabeth.

And so it is in this milieu – the quest to end inter-ethnic clashes, the burgeoning of a black intelligentsia and the proliferation of churches and schools – that the first black rugby clubs were birthed. A buoyant and politically conscious black middle class, fast becoming embedded in the new urban communities,[30] had been '[growing] in numbers, confidence and assertiveness,'[31] a new black elite hewn out of a layer of teachers, ministers, law agents, clerks, interpreters, storemen, transport riders, blacksmiths, telegraph operators and printers.[32] And by the end of the 1880s, the first black cricket clubs, benefit societies, mutual improvement associations and templars organisations had emerged in Port Elizabeth.

The formation of rugby clubs in the black communities of Port Elizabeth and Grahamstown was premised on the cross-fertilising influences and values of public schools, the Church, the black intelligentsia and the middle class. The need for Africans to systematically control and come up with an organisational conduct of their own thus became political. To do this they appropriated organisational systems of sports control by utilising the educational skills and values, and the influence of the Church, to take control of them by their own means and for their own ends. This need became even more apparent after the passing of the Natives Land Act of 1913, as well as other disempowering legislative framework and policies.

With the advent of the Union Government of 1910, Africans felt an even greater need to adopt new forms of resistance to colonial rule. These included adopting Western education, instituting formal political organisations, converting to Christianity, and adopting modern sports in order to respond to repressive legislation and policies.[33]

AWARE OF THE VALUES OF reconciliation and camaraderie inculcated into the game of rugby, stewards of black Wesleyan Methodist, Presbyterian and Ethiopian apostolic churches were mandated by their superiors to form the first black rugby club in Port Elizabeth. As suggested earlier, this was geared at, among other factors at play, discouraging inter-ethnic hostilities, mainly expressed through bloody stick fights.[34] Port Elizabeth's first black rugby club, the Union Rugby Football Club, was thus formed in 1887 in what was then known as KwaMpundu, currently the upmarket suburb of Mill Park. Having been founded by Messrs Mjo and Magaba and others, Union's first fields were located in KwaMpundu, as well as Maxambeni, now Richmond.[35] It is speculated that Josepie Orie Cedrass from Uitenhage, a founder member of the Eastern Province Rugby Union (EPRU) in 1886, might have played a significant role in the formation of Union RFC.[36]

The black intelligentsia had a marked effect on the organisational outlook of Union RFC, with professionalism filtering through to formal, precise organisational forms and procedures set in place for the club. These came in the form of formal meetings, minute-keeping, official correspondence, and the training of coaches, captains, linesmen and referees.[37] Church stewards subsequently passed on the mandate to form other black rugby clubs in the region.

Initially, Union adopted the red, white and blue of the Union Jack.[38] Later, however, it changed the colour of its jersey to white only, on account of public taunts that the prominent red on its jerseys bore a striking resemblance to the red jerseys of the jailed convicts. As a result, the club became popularly known as 'Whites', but retained Union as its formal name.

Rugby's rootedness in Port Elizabeth's black communities was further reinforced by the equally cemented Church, with the position of Christianity in the townships feeding the sport's immersion into black communities, lending to rugby an animated black existence. The public school system and church rooted rugby, lending it an organic black existence in Port Elizabeth and Grahamstown. Rugby in Port Elizabeth came to represent the community from which it came. Du Plessis remarked that:

> Although sport shares many of the characteristics of a culture or society, it is important to know that it is not external and shares these from within. It is not removed or independent of society; it does not stand on its own at a distance. Sport is not *like* society; it *is* society … It is a fundamentally ingrained part of societal context and in the same breath it has an influence in the societal context in which it finds itself.[39]

The Church did not, however, assume only a spiritual and character-building role; it also acquired a symbolic role as a shaper of the institution. All meetings and matches were opened and closed with formal prayers, and there were no matches on Sundays because members were expected to attend church services.[40]

And so it was that the Church carried with it the social, symbolic and cultural associations of the new urban black identities into rugby. It was particularly the links between black rugby and black church leadership – often served by the same members in their executive committees – that lay the foundation for community ties with black rugby clubs. This often found expression in the colours and symbolism churches used. Thami Songongo explained this rugby–church nexus as follows:

> But there around the time when Spring Rose was born; the Easterns; St Cyprian's; you know, the Green Bucks, you will discover that those people were Christians … Out of that church, let us produce this club. Hence, if you observe the … rugby clubs of Port Elizabeth are aligned to church colours … The Easterns you are talking about, that red and black, is from Wesleyan [Methodist

> Church]. St Cyprian's, that black and white, is of St Cyprian's [Church] in Korsten. Spring Rose is from the Ethiopian Church [green and white]. In fact, even the co-founder, Skefile, is a member of the Ethiopian Church.[41]

Some Union members then helped form, in 1890, the Winter Rose Rugby Football Club in Grahamstown, under the leadership of black graduates from St Philip's Mission School and the Kaffir Institute. Popularly known as *Indlov'Enebatha* – 'an elephant with knock-on knees', with an elephant on its insignia – it had a reputation as a teachers' rugby club,[42] its two main founders being Fana 'Bush' Manana and Reverend Walter Tsotsobe.[43]

By 1894, the mandate of spreading the formation of black rugby clubs using the Union format had proved to be successful. The Orientals Rugby Football Club was founded in 1894 in Port Elizabeth, in the KwaMpundu area. It fell under the founding leadership of C Masoka, C Ngesi, G Nyathi, P Zozi, T Gwele, M Dwui, Z Ngcakazi, P Daniels, J Mavava and D Sesanti.[44]

In the same year, a group of players who worked at St Andrew's College in Grahamstown, mainly as waiters, were inspired by watching the school's white first team rugby matches and consequently formed their own rugby team. Reverend White, a prominent staff member at St Andrew's, was moved enough to help them in their organisational efforts. They named their club Lily White, after the reverend's daughter.[45]

Some players who had formed Lily White had come from Winter Rose. This was to be the beginning of an enduring feature of black rugby clubs – splits and breakaways. Nine years down the line, in Grahamstown in 1903, a group of players formed the Wanderers Rugby Football Club. And then, in 1905, another group broke away from Winter Rose to reconstitute themselves as the Eastern Rugby Football Club in Grahamstown.[46] When a group of players were confined to the second team of Winter Rose, they rebelled, convinced that they were better than the first team. Disgruntled, they then challenged the first team to a rugby match. On defeating the first team 3–0, they formed their own rugby club, the Eastern Rugby Football Club.[47] The new club adopted a rhino as their insignia, an indication of their former link to Winter Rose, whose insignia was an elephant.[48]

The first president of Eastern RFC was Mr Mjakamu, and it was in his house in Grahamstown that the first club meeting was convened. Mr Dumo became its first captain, and was also selected to play for Eastern Province. In 1907, Easterns won the Chithumzi trophy against Wanderers. Another championship trophy game against Winter Rose held in Port Elizabeth ended in a draw.

By the end of the nineteenth century and into the first quarter of the twentieth in the Eastern Cape, rugby had rooted itself in urban black communities. 'By the late nineteenth-century some Blacks had adopted rugby as an element of their identity.'[49] It had become a way of life for communities. Dr Manona, one of the pioneers of black rugby in Grahamstown, commented that rugby 'humanised people's lives, making life in the township worth living'.[50] Black communities had in fact come to embrace rugby, owning it, taking care of their own ground facilities. Milton Roxo, one of the founder members of the Eastern RFC in Grahamstown, commented:

> Clubs struggled to generate enough funds to buy balls and jerseys. Facilities were also a problem, the fields were in poor condition … and one field, the eGazini field, sloped so badly that when players were tackled to the ground, they often rolled down the slope. Cleaning the fields of the stones and gravel was a community effort and they would clear them with their own farming equipment.[51]

In Grahamstown, rugby clubs had become a community's pride, both in the uniform and colours of club identities. Curnick Mdyesha, Milton Roxo's cousin, a president of Wanderers in 1945 and later a prominent executive member of SAARB, noted: 'Women wore headgears, blouses and skirts … the colour of their clubs. For men, blazers, ties and shirts showed colours of their clubs. The general public would parade their best clothes in the colours of their clubs. Ordinary citizens would put on their best clothes for the day.'[52]

In Port Elizabeth, the Morning Star and Park Rovers clubs were formed closely on the heels of the Orientals.[53] In 1907, the Spring Grove Rugby Football Club was formed in Bedford under the initial leadership of W Notyoba, A Koboka, S Sitoto, H Koka and William Xhayimpi Tube. Named after an area of Bedford, this was where most of its players hailed from.[54] In 1908, the club was registered as a second-league team, and the following year, W Gelo, C Lamani and Charles Z Futshane in Grahamstown decided to change the name to Spring Rose Rugby Football Club.

Box 1: List and Founding Dates of Early Black Rugby Clubs and Unions (1886–1954)

- Western Province Coloured Rugby Football Board – Cape Town – 1886
- Union Rugby Football Club – Port Elizabeth – 1887
- Winter Rose Rugby Football Club – Grahamstown – 1890
- Orientals Rugby Football Club – Port Elizabeth – 1890
- Lily White Rugby Football Club – Grahamstown – 1894
- South African Coloured Rugby Football Board – Cape Town – 1897
- City & Suburban Rugby Union – Cape Town – 1898
- Wanderers Rugby Football Club – Grahamstown – 1903
- Eastern Rugby Football Club – Grahamstown – 1904
- Spring Rose Rugby Football Club – Port Elizabeth – 1907
- Swallows Rugby Football Club – East London – 1911
- Early Rose Rugby Football Club – East London – c. 1912
- Walmer Wales Rugby Football Club – Port Elizabeth – 1928
- African Bombers Rugby Football Club – Port Elizabeth – 1954

The trend caught on, particularly in East London, with the city founding Swallows Rugby Football Club,[55] its first black rugby club, in 1911, when AS Magalela, M Kotobe, J Dweru and WB Rigala got together after playing an informal rugby match to form Swallows. Following Union's crusade to spread the formation of black rugby clubs in the Eastern Cape and beyond, between 1900 and the 1920s, black rugby clubs mushroomed. One of the founders of Winter Rose, Fana 'Bush' Manana, subsequently took rugby to the Transvaal, and by 1924, when he had become a Johannesburg resident, he formed the Occidental Rugby Football Club in Orlando East. In 1927, the club was renamed the Olympics Rugby Football Club.[56]

Dr WB Rubusana was consulted on the drawing up of a constitution and the new Swallows fielded players who were mostly domestic, hotel and city workers. Soon after, Dr Rubusana played a central role in the founding of Swallows' sister club, Early Rose Rugby Football Club. It wasn't long, however, before more black rugby clubs emerged in the East London area, among them Home Sweepers, Tembu, Bush Bucks, Black Lion and the Young Wonders. Affiliated to the East London Native Rugby Union, later renamed the Gompo Rugby Union, they played their matches at Rubusana Park, a closed field fenced with zinc.[57]

Between the 1920s and 1950s, the black intelligentsia of New Brighton further advanced the indigenisation of rugby in Port Elizabeth, at the same time shaping new black identities in townships, as well as political agendas and mobilisation. For instance, SM Bennett Ncwana – who in the 1920s was editor of the Industrial Commercial Union's (ICU) newspaper, *The Black Man*, and in the late 1930s published *African Continent* – lived in New Brighton for many years.

AZ Tshiwula, organiser of the Council for Non-European Trade Unions (CNETU), and considered a rabble-rouser member of the New Brighton Native Advisory Board, edited *Ndavela* for railway workers in 1948. He, along with Jimmy Pemba, WW Mabija and G Soya Mama, who all lived in New Brighton, provided regular coverage for *Imvo Zabantsundu*. Also, the lesser-known son of DDT Jabavu, Wilson Weir Jabavu, who also lived in New Brighton, was a full-time journalist and press photographer, and was an elected member of the New Brighton Native Advisory Board.[58]

The proliferation of black rugby clubs continued under these influences from the 1920s to the 1950s. In 1928, the Walmer Wales Rugby Football Club was established in Port Elizabeth, its name inspired by the visit of the Princess of Wales to the city in 1925.[59] By the mid-1950s, there were 11 black rugby clubs affiliated to the Port Elizabeth African Rugby Board (PEARB).[60] Others were to follow over the years. African Bombers Rugby Football Club was founded in 1954.[61] Fabs – an acronym for Fort Beaufort, Adelaide, Bedford and Stutterheim – was a team of mostly migrant labourers, fielding players from those areas. Butcher Birds Rugby Football Club was also formed during this time.

A curious spin-off sprouted from the black intelligentsia's initial project of discouraging inter-ethnic conflict, with ethnic loyalties and subsequent skirmishes giving way to the loyalty of prominent, middle-class families to clubs. Thembile Matomela noted, 'The fraternal ministers' association idea of starting a rugby league paid dividends, as clubs were not formed around tribal lines, but interestingly had family ties.'[62] This soon translated into an enduring variable in the recruitment system of rugby players.

In East London, for instance, the Makhwabe family was linked to Black Lion. The Qinga family was associated with Winter Rose, while the Mandleni family was linked to Swallows,[63] and in Port Elizabeth, the Matomela family was traditionally associated with Union.[64] These family-club links were part of an elaborate urban–rural divide and work–housing recruitment system. In East London, how certain families attached themselves to particular rugby clubs followed a recruitment system based initially on drawing players from places of rural origin, and subsequently placing them in employment at particular places of work.

The chain of recruitment for East London-based players began where workers were employed. The objective was to offer players from neighbouring rural areas employment opportunities first, and then housing in the townships. As Ntobeko Gaca noted, 'The recruitment strategy by most rugby clubs was to offer players with first employment and then accommodation.'[65] As a result, 'a good player would arrive in East London on Monday and by Friday he would [be] a Swallows player'.[66] And so, in East London, Swallows recruited players who worked at Baker King, Moberg, Cyril Lord, Chloride and Five Roses, for instance.[67]

The boundaries of recruitment were thus clearly delineated among the East London-based clubs. Winter Rose identified with Stutterheim. Swallows was linked to the townships of East London and, as a result, its players were popularly known as *abafana base skom*, or 'township guys'. Wallabies was linked to the township area of West Bank. Tembu Rugby Football Club recruited from the abaThembu people in Umtata. Black Lion was associated with amaGqunukhwebe people from the Middledrift and Alice areas. Spring Rose (of East London) recruited from the Peelton area, located just outside Bisho. AmaGcaleka from Transkei were associated with Bush Bucks.[68]

Similarly, in Port Elizabeth, black rugby had its own recruitment system for good players resident outside the city. As with East London-based clubs, this was premised on twinning employment with housing opportunities by tricking the pass system. Dan Qeqe in fact used this method to recruit players for his club, Spring Rose. Thozamile Botha, however, argued that there were discernible differences between the recruitment systems of Spring Rose and Union, the latter – led by Mvelo Norris Singaphi and his associate, Pat Cossie, principal at Newell High School – having the advantage in that they occupied senior positions in the PEARB's administration. And they were also teachers, which afforded them further points when it came to recruitment.

Botha argued that Union relied on recruiting players from neighbouring rural areas, whereas Qeqe and his associates in Spring Rose recruited from neighbouring towns and cities. Botha argued:

> Thus, Union's strategy for recruiting from the rural areas and hoping to buy players with jobs was essential at a certain point, but it was not sufficient to stretch over time with growing political awareness. Meanwhile, Qeqe's broad strategy focused on education and the industry sector had a staying power albeit not without institutional support which Union through Singaphi had.[69]

However, Botha's understanding of this urban–rural divide in the recruitment system is not reflected in historical oral accounts. Instead, evidence suggests that the black rugby clubs recruited the best players they could find outside Port Elizabeth, from both rural and urban areas, using the most enticing jobs and housing as bait. Moreover, with Qeqe's roots in Fort Beaufort and in the wider Victoria East Local Council area,[70] he was most adept at recruiting players from these areas. Ncula explained this scheme in some detail:

> I was playing for Easterns. The Easterns was not doing well. And we decided that we are going to recruit people from outside PE. But then the stumbling block was the permit to come and stay here in PE in the first place. Then if you had the permit, you had to secure a work seeker's permit ... They'll get a person who's not related to that player, to secure a permit to stay in his house, as a cousin or whatever. Then, they'll get somebody in Ford ... to secure a work seeker's permit for that person. That's exactly what I did at Cadbury. We recruited players from all over Fort Beaufort, Jamestown, and so on. Then, there's an old man called Zinto,[71] uTat' uZinto (Mr Zinto). He was working for the administration. *Wayesisibonda* (he was a headman). So he used to get us the work permit. And all these were some of the strategies Dan Qeqe used.[72]

One of the most popular strategies was to arrange marriages of convenience. These were orchestrated with Port Elizabeth-based single women to facilitate housing and employment. Gerald Majola recalled an anecdote of an arranged marriage for his uncle, a rugby player, encouraged by his father, Eric Majola, who played for Spring Rose and was Qeqe's closest friend. It was arranged for his uncle to marry his family's live-in domestic help, who hailed from Debenek, a rural village located just outside King William's Town.

> Zwayi was a relative from my father's side of the family. So, he had been looking for a house for a long time, and could not get it, because he was not married. My father said, 'No, *maan*, take NoRoom here. Go and marry NoRoom. Go together and sign. NoRoom, go with Mzwandile, go together and sign.' So, in that way, Mzwandile got a house. So, these are the things that they were doing ... They were living separately ... It was something that did not exist at all.[73]

The school–family–rugby club nexus thus articulated the profound historical influence of rugby on communities, as well as placing a system similar to that of American high-school football recruitment. Particular high schools, attached to an unbroken heritage line of rugby-playing families, became historically aligned to specific rugby clubs. There were no exceptions to these rigidified alignments, and cross-recruitment generated acrimonious conflict within families and among rugby clubs. Mpumelelo 'Sbhidla' Majola explained:

> In the past, what used to happen was that they looked into families … In particular, they looked for sports talents in the families. Now, it was the principals themselves who searched for such talents. We didn't even look for schools to enrol at … But the significance of this was that, when you were going to enrol at a high school, when you were about to graduate from Johnson Marwanqa Higher Primary School, where we went to school, what used to happen was that they recruited you to their high school. So, in my case, Pat Cossie came to my house, and said this boy, Sbhidla, is going to Newell. And then for Thozi, Thozamile Majola, Gerald Majola, Principal Mesatywa said that he was taking them to KwaZakhele High School. Mesatywa was accompanied by Dlangi[74] [Dennis] Siwisa. This is what I am saying, at the end of the day, it was kind of a recruitment system, because from Newell you played for Spring Rose, do you understand? Or Pat takes you to play for Whites [Union Rugby Football Club]. So, they recruited that way.[75]

However, Songongo, a former Spring Rose and Union player, vehemently refuted the existence of this school–club–family recruitment system, maintaining that:

> And what you are talking about the recruitment of players from certain schools, it is not that it was fixedly determined that a certain club was permanently associated with a particular school. No. No. This school-based recruitment is a new trend, do you understand? Now, it is clear that we adopt certain schools, because, maybe, from this school there's, maybe, two or three good, brilliant players they want, do you understand? And you can ask from one of the

> people who told you that, as to which particular club recruited from schools? He will tell you. You could also ask these people …[76]

Songongo was working class, and did not come from a prominent, middle-class family for which the recruitment system was biased. It was not that the recruitment system nakedly discriminated against players from working-class families. In fact, from the nineteenth century and right through to the first half of the twentieth century, the bulk of rugby players came from working-class and poor backgrounds. Many of the founder members of black rugby clubs were working men. And the majority of players also came from struggling, working-class families. However, with the founding of black rugby clubs mainly resting on the black intelligentsia and the black churches and schools they controlled, the recruitment system was bound to bias prominent, middle-class families of Port Elizabeth, Grahamstown and East London.

WITTINGLY OR UNWITTINGLY, black rugby came at the interstices of sorrowful, hopeful and intriguing historic variables. It came at the meeting of various South African political eras, giving birth to a political act inherently innocent. And yet there was nothing innocent about the history of black rugby. Its rise and journey from the early nineteenth century to the middle of the twentieth century has been a captivating political journey.

The end of the Frontier Wars, the urban resettlement permutations for Africans and the transposition of inter-ethnic hostilities into them, the Victorian concepts of race and the spread of the influence of the British Empire in South Africa, how racism in sport unfurled in nineteenth-century South Africa, the influence of public schools and church missions, and the emergence of the black intelligentsia all contributed to the rise of black rugby.

These were all political variables, bound to give birth to a political act – black rugby. The black intelligentsia, black churches and black schools all contributed to the indigenisation of rugby. In turn, black rugby consolidated and affirmed new urban black identities. In constantly resisting colonial rule and apartheid constrictions, black rugby 'humanised' people's lives in the townships. It made their lives in the townships that much more tolerable, as Milton Roxo attested.

The indigenisation of rugby came as a result of variables and processes in South African history that were hostile to the welfare and interests of African people. How Africans, the black intelligentsia and the passage of time subverted these hostile variables and turned rugby black remains a truly significant portion of South African history. The development of black rugby from the nineteenth century did, however, churn out one enduring self-destructive pattern of black rugby: splits and breakaways. These were petty and apolitical, but were often shrouded in bitterly political atmospheres which tend to explain definitive moments in the continued rise and fall of black rugby.

2

THE HISTORY OF BLACK RUGBY (1956–1971): THE AGE OF POLITICS

The mid-1950s introduced two key elements pivotal to the history of black rugby in Port Elizabeth. The first was that Dan Qeqe was at the pinnacle of his active rugby-playing career. Scrutiny of the significance of this creates a greater understanding of the development of not only the history of black rugby in Port Elizabeth, but more particularly how local rugby club rivalries significantly shaped black rugby. This is a critical perspective, often misunderstood, especially when it comes to the second element: the apartheid government's politicisation of sport in general. Often, these are collapsed, giving politics an unduly overarching influence over certain dynamics concerning black rugby. This erroneous understanding offers a politically sensationalist view of the history of black rugby in the second half of the twentieth century in Port Elizabeth.

Qeqe began playing rugby in 1954 as a hooker in the Spring Rose Rugby Football Club. This was to be his enduring position, most probably because of his short stature, a characteristic many noted that he had inherited from his father, Vleikop. Qeqe was recruited by Wilson F Ximiya when he began teaching at Cowan Secondary School in New Brighton. 'He commenced his teaching career at Cowan Secondary School in 1954, and was recruited by the stalwart and coach, Wilson Ximiya, to play for the Spring Rose Rugby Football Club.'[1] In contradiction, however, Booley notes that Qeqe, in fact, started his rugby career in 1949, playing for Spring Rose as a hooker.[2] Ximiya had been instrumental in the development of sports in Port Elizabeth, occupying playing and administrative positions in the Fort Beaufort Cricket Club, and in the SAARB.

Throughout the 1950s and up until the mid-1960s, Qeqe played club rugby for Spring Rose, and provincial rugby for the Eastern Province. Regarded as an average hooker, he was nevertheless considered a strong player. Thami Songongo, a younger Spring Rose flyhalf who defected to Union, remarked: 'He was not so, he was not very good at playing, because he had a lot of rivals in the position of hooker. But he was strong.'[3] This is a view shared by many of Qeqe's contemporaries as well as younger players.[4] Ray Mali added that fairness and clean playing were some of Qeqe's trademarks in both his rugby and cricket career. Stick fighting from his rural background might have brought a character-shaping role to this playing philosophy, Mali argued. He maintained that:

> He comes from that background, hence, in his sporting activities and his make-up, he was one of the cleanest players. He used to play hard, his rugby, play his cricket hard, but very clean and fair. Coming from that background of stick fighting, because there are those unwritten laws and rules, that you cannot beat your opponent when he is down.[5]

Qeqe was, first and foremost, a Spring Rose player. It was there that he expressed his love for and commitment to rugby most, displaying a loyalty to club rugby that, arguably, surpassed his commitment to the provincial game. 'He loved rugby a lot, and especially loved Spring Rose, a lot, a lot!'[6] remarked Joe Maboyisi Mahala Mbiza, an East London-based former Springbok player in SAARB.

At provincial level, Qeqe played for the Eastern Province in the position of hooker, along with his closest friend and legendary hooker,

Eric 'Kokie' Majola. Alongside him in the team were also Barry Sinuka of Union and Melody Madikane.[7] However, in 1957, Spring Rose did not select any of its representatives to play in the Eastern Province Bantu Rugby Union's President Giants Championships.[8] This was played at Umtata at a time when Spring Rose had had a fallout with the the leadership of the PEARB over administrative and fixture-related issues.[9]

The Eastern Province Bantu Rugby Union team of 1957 comprised Wilkinson Maku, Chief M Zinto, S Lebakeng, HT Madikane, S Sokutu, ST Sali, GM Xotyeni, AL Dwesi (who played for Union and was a member of the PEARB administration), Mvelo Norris (vice-captain, as well as president of Union and chairman of the PEARB), and GD Nazo.[10] A number of these players were set to feature prominently, in one way or another – in support or in hostility – in Qeqe's sporting–civic affairs in later years.

In the early 1950s, the fortunes of Spring Rose were waning – until the return of Qeqe, Majola and Mokononyane to the club. Until the trio rejoined the club following the completion of their studies at Healdtown in Fort Beaufort, the club suffered a streak of losses in the PEARB championships. As Sinuka noted, 'Spring Rose improved its performance upon the return from school of Eric Majola and Qeqe and Mokononyane. That's when the performance of Spring Rose improved. Otherwise, teams that were prominent then were the Union and Eastern.'[11] Amon Nyondo also noted: 'The revival, the rise of Spring Rose as a major force was also contributed to by those two gentlemen. On the field of play, they were stars, Qeqe playing hooker, Majola playing flyhalf. Both went to play for Eastern Province African rugby as well.'[12]

In 1955, the Eastern Province Bantu Rugby Union's championships were played in the Western Native Township in Johannesburg. In later years, they were held in Port Elizabeth. In 1957 and 1958, when Spring Rose was absent because they had withdrawn from the PEARB, they were held in Umtata and in Mowbray, Cape Town, respectively. Spring Rose participated in the championships played in Queenstown 1959, the year they returned to the PEARB.[13]

Between 1953 and 1960 particularly, Qeqe played consistently at both club and provincial levels. In 1953, his Spring Rose won the championship in the PEARB league, with Union as first runner-up. The following year, Orientals won, with Union featuring as first runner-up. In 1955, Spring Rose took the championships league trophy, with Union following as first runner-up. In 1956, Union won, beating Spring Rose in the final knockout,[14] with a 6–3 score.[15]

It was in that year that Spring Rose boycotted the fixtures and broke away from the PEARB, forming their own union with other clubs. They played at the grounds of Pendla and Johnson Marwanqa primary schools. Songongo recalled, 'Yes, they formed a rugby union that played at Pendla Primary School. It was called the South Eastern District. They formed a board there, they played there – in '57 and '58.'[16] Sinuka also recalled that 'Spring Rose was not in active play in '57. In '58, Spring Rose was not in active play again, it did not participate in that tournament.'[17] In 1959, Spring Rose returned to the PEARB in the knockout championships.[18]

A year later, in 1960, Spring Rose went on to win the PEARB championship trophy. Qeqe played hooker in the first team, his team mates including S Marwanqa, SX Peter, W Nyangayibizwa, W Mgana, MV Gwaqu, M Mokononyane, CZ Matutu, Eric Majola, Sipho Nozewu and Baba Jali.[19] Again, some of these names were set to feature prominently in Qeqe's sporting–civic ventures later.

Although the previous decade – the 1950s – seemed to be characterised by Spring Rose's continued fighting against the leadership of the PEARB administration over fixtures-related concerns, this friction did not, however, filter down to adversely affect relations between the players of Spring Rose and Union. Attesting to this, Sinuka remembered that:

> There in Spring Rose, there were good chaps. There was Lemisa, who was my friend and a utility back of Spring Rose. There was Themba Salamntu, who was a centre of Spring Rose, and he was good, hot … We had Lebakeng there, Cwethe [his clan name]. We played our fixtures at the Showgrounds. We used to separate from each other at the gate, there at the Showgrounds when we entered, when there was a match between Spring Rose and Union. We had

> all our things, and we would go to the Red Location, to Themba Salamntu's house ... You see, this was a match between Spring Rose and Union, to prove that we got along with Spring Rose players.[20]

Sinuka recalled one particular friendly game in which Union and Spring Rose players played together against a coloured team at the Adcock Stadium in Port Elizabeth. They played with, notably, Ketile Mcatha, a Spring Rose frontrunner.[21] It is clear then that Spring Rose's serial conflicts with the leadership of the PEARB did not necessarily affect inter-club collegiality at the players' level. When conflict resolution failed, Spring Rose's chief tactic was to break away from the PEARB. As Songongo witnessed, 'So, here along the way, they have been splitting up, splitting up, splitting up, do you understand? And when they [Spring Rose] want to split, they fight with the board [PEARB]. They fight with threatening to split.'[22]

One of the major causes of the conflicts between rugby clubs and their affiliating unions was the awarding of championship trophies. This was a major gripe.[23] What had begun in the 1890s as breakaways and splits among the clubs themselves had now escalated into clubs splitting from their mother bodies. By the 1950s and 1960s, this had also become a tradition beyond Port Elizabeth. In East London, Winter Rose, founded in 1933, experienced its own split, as did Tembu and Boiling Sea rugby football clubs.[24]

Conflict between Spring Rose and the PEARB continued throughout the 1960s. At stake was the performance of black rugby. Sinuka remarked, 'The quality of the performance of black people's rugby was very high. It was very good, to the extent that when we started playing, we got into a scene of high performers, here in the Eastern Cape. And then, when we got into it, we raised the quality of performance.'[25]

Also at stake were the integrity and effectiveness of the PEARB. The PEARB had a reputation for administrative order and stringent adherence to its constitution – principles and values that had been central in effectively running the affairs of black rugby clubs in Port Elizabeth.[26] Since the end of the nineteenth century, the Church and early black intelligentsia, by maintaining administrative order and adherence to the union's constitution, were pivotal to the high-calibre performances of black rugby in Port Elizabeth. However, by the 1950s and into the 1960s, as sport became politicised, the PEARB had garnered a reputation as an apartheid stooge manned by apartheid black collaborators and old-guard administrators.[27]

This, however, is a historically incorrect perspective. Although the politicisation of sport had generated binary positions of pro- and anti-apartheid sports bodies, pro-state and later non-racial positions, the officials within these sports bodies were not necessarily neatly divisible between these binaries. Many of those officials popularly considered to be part of anti-apartheid and non-racial sporting bodies had contentedly served in native collaborationist bodies with their rivals in the so-called pro-state or pro-apartheid sporting bodies.

Gripes over championship trophies – central to so many of the conflicts between rugby clubs and their affiliating unions – were caused by disputes over play-time squabbles. So it was that by 1970 and into 1971, Qeqe's Spring Rose was involved in an elongated play-time squabble involving Wilfred Khovu. Khovu had joined Spring Rose as a front-ranker in 1964. In 1969, he played for the SAARB, and between 1958 and 1961, for the Eastern Province African XI as a cricketer.[28]

In 1970, he earned a penalty point against his own Spring Rose, but Spring Rose steadfastly refused to acknowledge the penalty, in effect rebelling against the PEARB's decision. Songongo clearly remembered the incident and its effect on the club:

> Khovu. He was given marching orders, and he refused to leave. Now, rugby rules, referee rules, stipulate that if you refuse to leave after being sent off, every time you touch a ball, it's a penalty. Every time you scrum, it's a penalty. Every time you handle a person, it's a penalty, because you're not part of the game, you have been sent off.[29]

Thembile Matomela also pointed out that Qeqe's Spring Rose carried this unresolved disciplinary issue with the PEARB into the 1971 rugby season, effectively muting its voice in the PEARB.[30] Booley noted that, on refusing to be disciplined, a match involving Spring Rose subsequently ended up in a scuffle.[31] Qeqe's Spring Rose was thus, in effect, flagged for disciplinary infringements. But it continued to play in fixtures nonetheless.[32]

This was a time when the petty, non-political squabbles of Port Elizabeth's black rugby landscape came to a head yet again – just as the politicisation of sports in general in South Africa was reaching its own boiling point. 'You hear me *mos*, I am not talking to you about politics at that time,'[33] Sinuka noted in our conversation, marking a clear bifurcation in the timeline between the era of non-politicised black rugby and that of politicised black rugby. And in the meeting of the boiling heads of petty, administrative squabbles with the oncoming tide of the politicisation from both non-racial and government positions emerged a historic novelty on the landscape of black rugby in South Africa.

In 1956, the Minister of the Interior, Dr Eben Donges, delivered a speech that, in many ways, officially politicised South African sport in general.[34] It brought South African sport under the stringent apartheid policy of separate development, allocating different platforms, resources and opportunities for each racial group. In the previous year, the non-racial movement had begun, forming the Coordinating Committee for International Recognition of Sport (CCIRS). Later, it simply called itself the Committee for International Recognition (CIR).[35]

Box 2: Defining Rugby Bodies and Tiers

South Africa's black rugby history is littered with many names and acronyms of rugby bodies, forming and splitting and breaking away many times within a very short time. Also, many of them exist at different tiers (local, union, provincial and national), causing even further confusion. This explanation then serves as a definitional way of clearing such confusion.

Rugby bodies were formed at local club level. A cluster of rugby bodies in one area constituted a union. It represented, jurisdictionally, rugby clubs in a particular local area. A union could potentially represent five or more clubs, with a democratically elected administrative leadership – in other words, a president, vice or deputy president, secretary, match secretary, treasurer and selectors. A maximum of two delegates from each club represented the club at union meetings.

A union then affiliated to a provincial body, ascribing to the same ideology. At times, unions affiliated directly to a national body, depending on what structures particular sports codes had available to them. Loose, non-affiliated unions were not eligible to play fixtures against clubs of other bodies. In rugby, they affiliated to SARU, which in turn affiliated to a national sports body, the South African Congress on Sport (SACOS). But affiliation was guided by ideology.

The PEARB affiliated to the South African African Rugby Board (SAARB), the double 'African' signifier indicating a racially demarcated black rugby body. It was separate from the whites rugby board, the South African Rugby Board (SARB), and for coloureds, the South African Coloured Rugby Football Board (SACRFB). SARB was formed in 1889, while the SACRFB was founded in 1897.

Many rugby clubs in the Western Cape moved over from the SACRFB to SARU. A definitive stamp of SARU's commitment to non-racial rugby came through the Malmesbury Declaration of 8 July 1970, particularly through the third of its four points, which indicated an assured move towards embracing non-racial sports ideology. It pointed out that 'The federation's objective will be the promotion and advancement of its players to the extent where they will be included in South African representative teams on the basis of merit.'[36]

The CIR, intent on selecting national sports teams on merit, was succeeded by the South African Sports Association (SASA) in 1958. It was founded by a group of weightlifters in East London, led by Dennis Brutus, and formally launched in Durban in 1959, with Alan Paton acting as patron.[37] In April 1960, police raided SASA's offices, seizing its archival material. Some of SASA's leadership, including Dennis Brutus, were subsequently forced into exile.[38] The Association was forced to dissolve in 1963, and in its place the South African Non-Racial and Olympic Committee (SAN-ROC) was formed. This body was equally hounded by the police, and resurfaced overseas, with support from the Anti-Apartheid Movement (AAM).[39]

The government, adamant on implementing its policies of separate development in all sporting codes, increasingly harassed non-racial sports organisations throughout the 1960s, continuing to insist that each racial group administer its sport separately. This was despite the creation of a new Department of Sport. In 1965, Prime Minister John Vorster – against the background of a debate surrounding the inclusion of Maoris in the All Blacks team of New Zealand – pointed out that, '[inside] South Africa there will not be mixed sporting events, irrespective of the proficiency of the participants. On this there can be no compromise, negotiations or abandonment of principle.'[40]

In the 1960s, the politicisation of the black rugby scene came under the leadership of SARU. The latter came out of the SACRFB in 1966, consequent to personality clashes and long-term disputes over regional Kimberley–Cape Town power bases and leadership clashes. The leadership of the SACRFB, based in Cape Town, had grown disenchanted with the distance and leadership style of the board's leadership of Cuthbert Loriston, based in Kimberley.[41]

Grumblings around the politicisation of rugby were first heard in 1965, when the SACRFB's president, John Kerster, declared the board's discontent with the racial tag matches between Africans and coloured rugby teams under the Rhodes Cup. At the Rhodes Tournament held in Port Elizabeth in 1965, Kerster pointed out that, '[the] days of racial tournaments as such are fast coming to an end, sooner than some of us might think, and we shall be compelled to reorientate our ideas about this biennial Rhodes Tournament and seek an outlet for our activities in a much wider field where there are no racial tags whatsoever'.[42]

SARU, as a national non-racial rugby body, fell under SACOS, the formation of which came about three years after the Malmesbury Declaration in 1970. This followed an incident concerning the

Johannesburg municipality withdrawing its permission for the South African Soccer Federation (SASF) to use a playing ground – one that it customarily used – on the grounds that 'the Federation was playing mixed sport'.[43] Following this 'overt act of racism',[44] on 6 September 1970, the SASF convened a conference of non-racial sports organisations in Durban. Represented at the conference were the SASF, SARU, the South African Amateur Swimming Federation, the South African Lawn Tennis Union, the South African Table Tennis Board, the South African Amateur Athletics and Cycling Board of Control, the South African Amateur Weightlifting and Bodybuilding Federation, and the South African Hockey Board.

The conference set up the Ad Hoc Committee for Non-Racial Sports Organisations, made up of sports liberation cadres who would dominate non-racial sport liberation for the next two decades. This committee comprised figures such as Morgan Naidoo, V Nair, Reg Munoo, CM Bassa, D Ramlall, Norman Middleton and NM Pather. Some of the key resolutions of the conference convened in Durban in 1970 included:[45]

- To work for international recognition by making sincere overtures to white-controlled national bodies to work with non-racial bodies;
- To attempt to solve the problems confronting non-racial sports through the lack of facilities and adequate sponsorship;
- The practice of applying for 'permits' to play sport should be stopped. This action was considered degrading and humiliating; and
- That all national sporting codes of the country come together under the Federation of South African Sports Organisations.

The landscape of black rugby had changed significantly post the Second World War. From the late nineteenth century to the 1930s, black rugby in Port Elizabeth and in the Eastern Cape had remained under the control of the black intelligentsia, with attendant influences of the Church. Racism and politics nevertheless hovered over black rugby, shaping the attendant bodies, and marking racial boundaries among and between sports bodies outside of the realms of government control, policies and proclamations.

However, by the 1920s, rugby had become immensely popular, fostering the transfer of the custodianship of black rugby from the black intelligentsia to communities. With this ownership of black rugby, those principles and values of unity and integrity came to have a looser hold over black rugby. A by-product was the deepening of the culture of splits and breakaways at intra- and inter-club tiers, and between clubs and their affiliating bodies. Many of these were fuelled by petty, on-the-field squabbles, which in turn led to administrative disputes.

Unfortunately, with the incoming tide of politicisation, these affiliating bodies came under binary – either pro- or anti-apartheid – bodies. The politicisation of the landscape of rugby and other sports thus threw a blanket of political interpretation over conflicts in black rugby. This has, unfortunately, gone down in history, lending either hostile or heroic political hues to otherwise innocent but destructive non-political conflicts. However, the net result of all of this is that the unity and integrity of black rugby had begun to deteriorate.

PART TWO
(1929–1971)

3

QEQE BEGINS (1929–1950S): THE ROOTS

The life of Dan Qeqe is not a rags-to-riches story. It is not one of a poor black boy's unrelenting wrestle with all manner of challenges in his rise to prosperity. It is rather a narrative of cushioned beginnings, and of a journey from prosperity to wealth. Key in his meteoric rise is how societal it was, how he was able to develop a firm grasp of historic black glories. Nothing of Dan Qeqe was for himself, nor forged solely for family prosperity. He was always conscious of the community and society from which he emerged and within which he moved. Even those cushioned beginnings inculcated in him a sense of community consciousness.

The Qeqe name is writ large. The family's fortunes and fame preceded and ran concurrently with those of Dan himself. But, more interestingly, the significance of the Qeqe name is regionally divergent. In the Fort Beaufort–Zwelitsha–King William's Town region, it is a name that is well know, its strength lying principally in its fecundity – one of those somewhat commonplace, ubiquitous surnames known for their firm roots in the area. It subsequently spread on account of the successes of the family's business entities. Today, many of these businesses have long been sold and subcontracted out, leaving billboards carrying the Qeqe name dotted here and there. Here, it is now a name only dimly reflecting its former glory, its weight remaining in somewhat faded black entrepreneurial adventures.

In the almost three-hour drive to Port Elizabeth, on the other hand, Qeqe invokes a sum of living glories. It is a totality of splendours that mirror a journey of a people and of a city to freedom and democracy. Qeqe is in the city's architecture, echoing the vast political and social histories of Port Elizabeth and its people. And yet, quite perturbingly, in his hometown in Fort Beaufort, the name Qeqe only rises in the memories of many of its uninterested residents in the name of a stadium. But in Port Elizabeth, the name carries the memory of the life and times of only one Qeqe that matters: Daniel Dumile Qeqe.

Born on 6 August 1929 in eDrayini, a village in Fort Beaufort, Daniel Dumile Qeqe came into a prosperous, polygamous farming family. His father, Vleikop Molose Qeqe, was born in the village of Chwaku, near Middledrift, a small town located about 30 kilometres from Alice.[1] Vleikop's father, Mkhencele Qeqe, and his mother, Sirityi (her surname), of the Sukwini (her clan name), also hailed from Chwaku.[2]

In Fort Beaufort, Vleikop was a well-off farmer. By Dan Qeqe's own account, 'My father, Vleikop Qeqe, was a semi-farmer. He had two plots, each the size of a rugby field, on the river and he ploughed other plots on a 50/50 basis. He grew mealies, beans, winter wheat and pumpkins. We had close to 100 head of cattle and goats and sheep.'[3] Mncedi Mali, Dan's nephew, maintained that his grandfather, Vleikop,[4] would hire land from white farmers, and generate revenue by means of agricultural production. 'They were not under the control of whites … They used to hire, to lease land, working on land, and generate money out of it,'[5] Mali explained.

Keke Pemba, Dan Qeqe's contemporary in Port Elizabeth, who had visited the Qeqe family home in the late 1940s, also attested to Vleikop's wealth of livestock. He remembered that 'Dan's father had livestock, sheep. He had a lot of sheep there.'[6] McKenzie Sloti,[7] another nephew, also pointed out that Vleikop was '…a very well-known man in Fort Beaufort, with a lot of livestock, and was also involved in the transport business'.[8]

Vleikop's farming was a reflection of the economic character of his area. The priorities of the Victoria East Local Council, the local government authority of the time, reflected that. The council's budget placed a premium on agricultural maintenance and associated land-development concerns. In 1929, the chairman of the Victoria East Local Council submitted a proposal for additional expenditure 'essential' for the district areas.[9] For dipping tanks, the council had allocated £75, £30 for grants (agricultural shows), and £80 for road repairs.[10] In the same year, it budgeted £250 for 'Construction and Repair to Dipping Tanks.'[11] In the following year, it budgeted an expenditure estimate of £230 for dams, windmills and irrigation.[12]

Vleikop, though a prosperous farmer, was illiterate but was nevertheless said to be a headman for his area[13] – although there is no documented evidence of that ever having been the case.[14] This, perhaps, might be expected, considering how contentions over the legitimacy of chieftaincies had become highly politicised. In the Eastern Cape, particularly during the first half of the twentieth century, the contesting of chieftaincies between white local authorities and black rural residents rapidly developed into heady conflicts.

By the 1940s, pernicious white power gnawing away at the authority and authenticity of chieftain rule in the Victoria East Council territories[15] had reached its peak. A circular from the Native Affairs Department in 1940, addressing *Succession to Native Chieftainship*, declared that:

> Sub-section (7) of section two of the Native Administration Act, No. 38 of 1927, confers upon the Governor-General authority to recognise or appoint any person as chief in charge of a tribe. No descendant or other relative of a deceased chief has, therefore, a definite legal right to succeed to the chieftainship…Indeed, to adopt any other policy would be to court disaster …[16]

This declaration also ensured that any attack of the government's supplanting of authentic traditional chiefs with pliant ones would not arise again, as it had with Dr Walter Rubusana. In response to Dr Rubusana's trenchant critique on the recognition of the chieftaincy of Chief Bonyoti Qasana in the Victoria East Local Council area, raised in

Imvo Zabantsundu in late 1930, the Chief Native Commissioner wrote: 'I beg to state that the Government is not prepared to recognise Bonyoti Qasana as a Chief, and Dr Rubusana should be advised accordingly.'[17] Further pronouncing itself on this, the Assistant Native Commissioner had, in October 1930, expanded on the government's position:

> While Bonyoti may be looked upon as a chief by his people, he cannot claim to be the Chief of the Imidushane. Gushipela is their chief and has been recognised as such by the Government ... An application for the recognition of Bonyoti as a chief was made as long ago as September 1925, but the Government definitely declined to accede to the request ... I see no reason why the decision then given should be departed from, and to do so would be opening the door to the Government being inundated with applications of this nature.[18]

The Qeqe family is of the Mbona clan, part of the amaJingqi sub-ethnic amaXhosa. They are from a long and proud lineage directly descended from Chief Maqoma. However, there is no clear indication of the official recognition of the chieftaincy of amaJingqi in the list of recognised chiefs in the Ciskei area.[19] However, it is highly probable that, among these chiefs, amaJingqi were under Chief Justice Mabandla of the amaBele in Alice. This suggestion is based on the fact that, in 1973, Qeqe campaigned on behalf of Chief Mabandla for a seat in the Ciskei General Assembly.

By February 1959, there were 68 chiefs and headmen officially organised under the jurisdiction of King William's Town and, in June 1959, 18 chiefs and headmen under the jurisdiction of Keiskammahoek.[20] These magisterial districts covered representations in King William's Town, East London, Sterkspruit, Middledrift, Alice, Whittlesea, Keiskammahoek, Port Elizabeth, Humansdorp, Fort Beaufort, Stutterheim and Cathcart.[21]

It is not clear why Vleikop does not appear in the list of officially recognised headmen. This might have been the result of political challenges traceable to their direct lineage to Chief Maqoma. It could also have been a technical matter relating to territorial and subject delineations. Perhaps a specific life-altering incident in the extended

Qeqe family may explain the absence of Vleikop's name in the list of headmen for the Fort Beaufort area in the archives of the 1920s to the 1950s. Mncedi Mali's father, closely related to Vleikop, who also lived and worked on a white farmer's land in the Fort Beaufort area, had apparently assaulted the son of a white farmer. Mali relayed this incident:

> He beat up a child of a white man. This child of the white man, when school was done for the day, his father would go and help out my father and mother at the fields. This son of this white man now acted as my father's foreman by force, and my father beat him up. The son of the white man ran away to get a horse. My father ran into the forest, carrying a rifle. My grandmother said, no ways! Let us not wait, let us move out. They gathered their cattles and moved out to another place. They found a place without a school. And then my father could not complete his schooling.[22]

This eventually led to the family's self-banishment from an area in which they had long lived. The move, of course, had long-term repercussions, leading to Mncedi Mali losing out on an opportunity for education. These skirmishes with white power over land and economic inequalities, in fact, characterised relations between black farmers, tenants and white farmers in the area. To many in the Fort Beaufort and the wider Victoria East Local Council environs, these conflicts resulted in progressive encroachment on their livelihoods. These forms of defiance reminded them of Chief Maqoma's gallant defence of the same territories against British colonial incursions in the nineteenth century, and thus left formidable impressions on the memories of Dan Qeqe, moulding and embellishing his ideology of black consciousness and black pride which was to drive many of his non-racial and anti-apartheid activities.

Vleikop had 18 children,[23] comprising 13 sons and five daughters.[24] Sired from the 'smaller house'[25] of the younger of the two wives, Nontsuku (nee Bazi), Dan Qeqe was the second-last child. From his senior wife, MamQoma, Vleikop had 10 children. In the 'smaller house', he had eight.[26] Vleikop's first child, Hontoti, a son, was born between 1905 and 1908; he was then followed by another son, Gxamesi, and then a daughter. These were followed by Velile (son), Desile (son), Komndeyi (son), Bhiza (son), Tobhiya (daughter) and Mute (son).[27]

From the younger wife, he had Ndwe (son), also known as Lace, who was followed by Nene (son). Then he had Nontose (daughter), Behe (son), Sotshisa (son), Kleintjie (son), America (son, born in 1924), Dan Dumile (born in 1929) and Wridge (son, born in 1931).[28] Vleikop's younger brother, Mzayifani, also had a polygamous family, with two wives. Passing away at a younger age, Vleikop took over the maintenance of Mzayifani's two wives and their children.[29]

In Fort Beaufort around the time of Dan Qeqe's birth, infant deaths in black families were commonplace, and it remains peculiar that the large Qeqe family was unaffected by this scourge. Born nine years earlier than Qeqe in Fort Beaufort, Raymond Mhlaba[30] lost three brothers and two sisters to infant deaths.[31] Perhaps the Qeqe's family's prosperity, fortified by the already well-established businesses in Port Elizabeth of Qeqe's maternal family, provided resources that helped to avert infant mortality.

It was only in 1931, in Fort Beaufort, that the Victoria East Local Council[32] decided to extend health services to its black districts in the hinterland. Writing to the chief of the Native Affairs Commission based in King William's Town in 1931, the council was concerned that:

> In consequence of the abnormal death rate of infants and small children in parts of the district due to ignorance and a lack of hygiene, the members of the Council were asked to meet the Victoria Hospital authorities at Lovedale. The Medical Superintendent stressed the need for the appointment of a district nurse and appealed for the co-operation of the Local Council. It was suggested that the nurse should be appointed by and come under the control of the Local Council.[33]

The rollout of the suggested health scheme involved the appointment of a 'native nurse' by the Victoria Hospital in Alice. Her jurisdictional areas of care were to include Middle Tyume,[34] Upper Tyume, Gaga, Sheshegu, Ely and Roxeni, and her role was to 'give advice to expectant mothers, and to mothers regarding the care of infants and child welfare'.[35] Receiving a salary of £110, the nurse was to be 'provided with a cart and horse or some other transport'.[36] The costs of medicine were estimated to be about £10 per annum.[37]

A sturdy oneness binds the Qeqe family, and this unity remains to this day a distinctive and palpable feature of the extended family. In listing Vleikop's children, both families in Fort Beaufort and Port Elizabeth often misplaced names, unsure of who came from the 'big house' and who from the 'smaller house'. Names are tossed back and forth, bouncing from one house to the other, with some sense of confusion. And then there is almost a nonchalance, a sense of unimportance attached to any inaccuracies in making these house allocations.

This oneness was established on the back of small but not insignificant family customs, such as dining. They all ate with one spoon, sharing, passing the spoon on among themselves as they scooped up from the shared dish or plate. Mali recalled that:

> One thing that was central in their character-building was one spoon. They all ate sharing one spoon … One spoon. If they came over to my house at the Sukwini, at the Mali household, they came and found us eating with one spoon … Even now, we are united. Even now … It comes from our grandfathers, from our fathers and grandfathers.[38]

Conforming to the expectations of a rural upbringing at the time, none of Vleikop's children from either house attended school, but neither were they completely illiterate. Dan became the only exception. It was the wish of Dan's mother on her deathbed that, of all her children, Dan be sent to school. In singling him out, she even forsook her last-born, Wridge. The basis of that decision is still considered a matter of whimsy, although the subtext is that of some kind of spiritual foreknowledge of what lay ahead for Dan specifically.

'It is said that his mother selected him, and said that, from all my children, from this one, I want a teacher … She perceived it … Elderly people perceive things. Dan had shown signs of his greatness at a tender age,'[39] Mali explained.

Qeqe's daughter, Phumla, also pointed out much the same:

> All of them were not educated. But the mother, before she passed away, she asked her husband, my grandfather, just to let him go to school … He kept that promise. Baas Dan was the only one of the 19 who was educated … It's the mother. Why the mother? I don't know. That was the wish of the mother. Maybe she spoiled him more than the others, do you understand?[40]

AND SO IT WAS THAT Dan attended primary school at Dorington Community School in Fort Beaufort,[41] while still tending his father's livestock. It was also at this time that Qeqe first played sport with white and coloured children, his initial foray into non-racial sport. He fondly recalled playing cricket, rugby and soccer without any racial restrictions.[42] He also assumed secretarial duties for his illiterate father, assisting him in carrying out his responsibilities as a headman.

Sloti further explained that, 'DDQ, as a primary school-going child, became his father's secretary, because letters came to the headman. DDQ then read those letters, reading them for the people, because during that time older people had not been to school.'[43] Mali added that, 'He was a headman, a land buyer, and Dan used to read for him. Even the letters that arrived for him, Dan used to respond to them.'[44]

It was this intimate relationship with his father, consumed by community affairs, that built Qeqe's public service character. He inherited from his father the love for community welfare. Vleikop lent a supportive hand, for all manner of assistance and services, to his community. Often, this extended to total strangers, going beyond the call for short-term help.

Mali remembered an enduring instance in which Vleikop helped out a father and son in distress. They were complete strangers passing through. Vleikop, unaware of their itinerary but concerned about them, intervened. He requested his wife to prepare meals and a room for them to rest for the night, so they could continue with their journey the following morning. Mali recalled that:

Figure 1: Qeqe Genealogy (Family Tree)

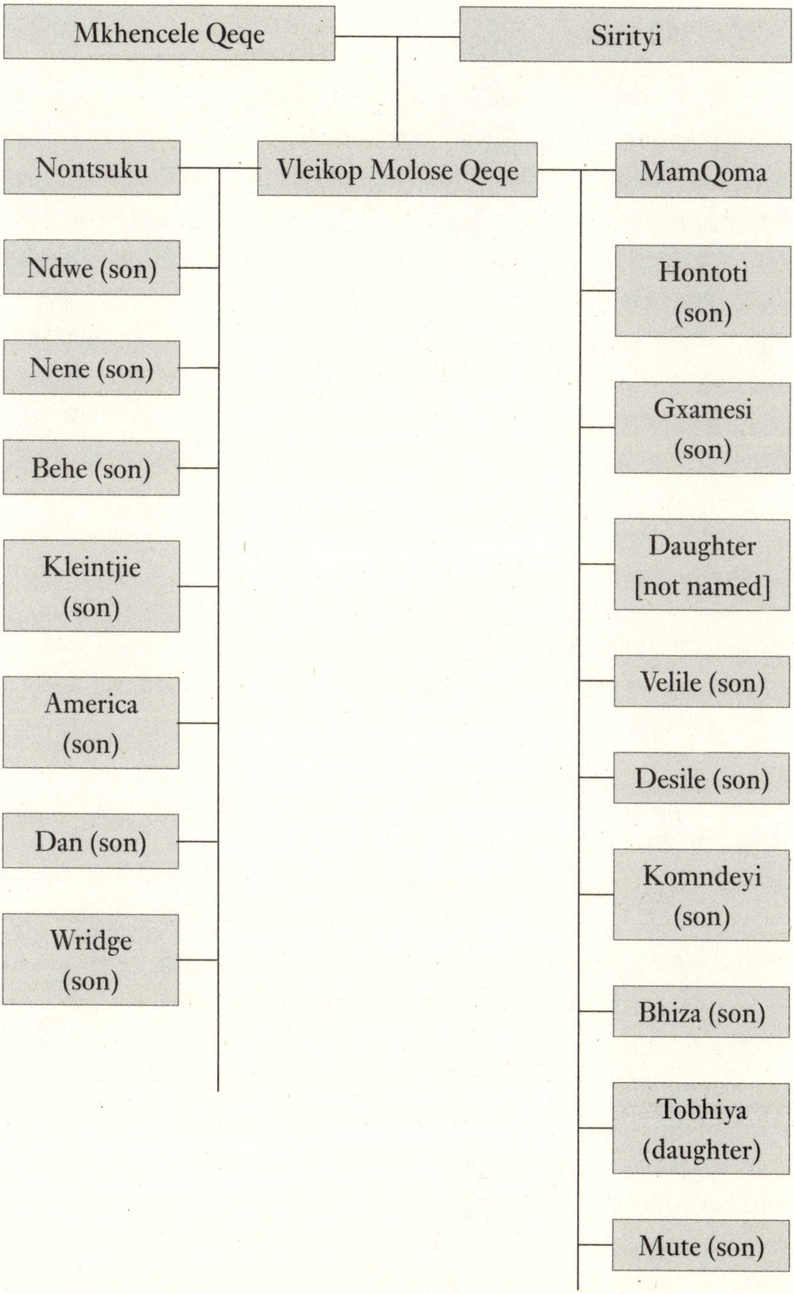

> This old man looked like a rag, and you wouldn't allow him into your house, going with this little boy with dirty and hardened feet. This old man and his son slept over. By sunrise, the old man had passed on … He had died.

The family gathered together, and buried the old man at Drayini. The little boy remained with the Qeqe family and went to school there. He undertook his ritual passage to manhood in the Qeqe family, overseen by Gxamesi, Dan Qeqe's elder brother from the senior wife. 'He grew up there, went to school there … He didn't know who his parents were, *mos*. He was a little boy. He got to know about his background after he became a man. He then left, apparently in search of his roots, and vanished.'[45]

Phumla also remembered her grandfather as a generous man who gave to the public freely and abundantly. Of the incident, she recalled:

> There was even a person who was travelling, I don't know, to Grahamstown, from Alice, somewhere … He slept over and died there … And then there was this son. He was raised at Bhiza's.[46] He is that dark-skinned man … He is that man, *maan*; he used to work at the bakery, living at Ncwana [Street][47]… He is dark-skinned with a rough face.[48]

Upon completing his elementary education in Fort Beaufort,[49] Qeqe moved to Port Elizabeth at the end of 1953, to enrol at Newell High School. At that point, Newell High School's principal was Reverend George B Molefe, a Presbyterian minister. Newell was the only high school in New Brighton.[50] All the other post-primary schools there and at KwaZakhele Township were secondary schools, offering classes up to Form 3, the current equivalent of Grade 10. There, he lived with his maternal uncle, Ngwehlathi Bazi, a prosperous businessman who owned a big trading shop in New Brighton's Red Location.

The family of the younger wife (Dan's mother) supplemented Vleikop's prosperity. The Bazi family, which came from Qoboqobo (Keiskammahoek), in essence, became the backbone of the Qeqe family wealth. This became particularly apparent when Vleikop lost much of his land and wealth following the implementation of apartheid laws on land ownership.[51] Mali explained:

> The Qeqes are nephews and nieces to the Tshawes through Molose's wife, their mother, this woman from the Bazi family. The Bazis are the first rich people in Port Elizabeth, along with the Maetles. Indeed, that man from the Bazi family was rich. He was rich! America inherited his riches from that woman, their mother. Lace, the elder brother, inherited his riches from there.[52]

It is on record that Ngwehlathi Bazi, affectionately known as 'Uncle Willy', 'in Red Location, was one of the first few black businessmen in what became New Brighton. He had a store and transport business.'[53] Illustrating the Bazi family wealth, Keke Pemba recalled visiting Qeqe in Fort Beaufort sometime in the late 1940s, travelling 'in a [Dyanasour?], which was black and automatic, belonging to Cheapline's[54] father, driven by a coloured man called Vos, driving for Cheapline's father.'[55] That a black man at that time was chauffeured by a coloured man in his employ was some indication of the level of his wealth.

At that time, Pemba recalled seeing in Qeqe a provincial uncouth who often hung around the Bazi trading store, wielding a knobkerrie. Pemba reminisced:

> I got to know him before he became a man, before he underwent his rite of passage to manhood … He came here from Fort Beaufort. We were young men then. [This] boy [was] wearing a pair of short pants, and he fastened farther up his calf those handkerchiefs that looked like duster cloth. He carried a knobkerrie there, at the shop owned by Bazi. We used to stand away from him, because he carried a knobkerrie. We feared that he would beat us with it.[56]

Of his arrival and schooling in Port Elizabeth, Qeqe said that, 'I came to Port Elizabeth to Newell High School in Standard 7 and matriculated there in 1950. There were not the funds for me to become a lawyer, so I decided to take up teaching instead and completed my diploma course at Healdtown training college in 1953.'[57] Qeqe admitted, however, that his first career choice had been law. But, due to financial constraints, when his father lost a substantive part of his wealth due to the impact of apartheid laws on his livelihood,[58] he could not afford university studies.

Between 1951 and 1953, Kolekile Kwatsha, who also became a prominent businessman in New Brighton, had also studied at Healdtown. He remembered Qeqe for his keenness for sport, recalling that, 'I knew him from then, because he was there at the boarding school … Now he played a lot of sports. We, as young chaps, we played in the junior teams, you see? I knew him then, seeing him at Healdtown, in Fort Beaufort.'[59]

And that was when he mischievously engaged in his love for stick fighting, while boarding at Healdtown in Fort Beaufort. Mali remembered the young Qeqe sneaking out of school for stick-fighting sessions in his village. 'Hey, my man, my man, my man, he and this one called America were very good. I've seen Dan sneaking out of Healdtown, coming over here for stick-fighting sessions. Ask me, what if he had sustained serious wounds?'[60]

At Healdtown, he was made head prefect, under the principal, Mr FM Maqhula.[61] It was here, too, that he consolidated his friendship with Eric Majola, one that anchored a life-long relationship between Qeqe and the Majola families in Port Elizabeth. Having initially met at Newell High School, Qeqe and Majola trained together as teachers at Healdtown, which is also where they honed their cricket and rugby skills. For Qeqe, this began with his involvement in the administration of the Fort Beaufort Cricket Club.

It was during this time, too, that he fathered his first child, a daughter, Nomasomi Penina Maka. She was born on 29 December 1953, at Dorington in Fort Beaufort.[62] Her mother was Noma Faith Ngoqo, born on 7 October 1933. Nomasomi was raised by her grandparents, the visually impaired Gideon and his wife, Novenisi (who died at the age of 102), in Fort Beaufort. Gideon, whose maternal line was of the extended Soga family, was a prominent community leader, political activist and well-known lay preacher in the Presbyterian Church of Dorington, Fort Beaufort, at the time of Nomasomi's birth. To that extent, Nomasomi's home at 112 Dorington became a 'church mission'.[63] Ngoqo was a founding member of the ANC, attending its inaugural conference in 1912, and had also travelled to Salisbury,

Southern Rhodesia, on political business.[64]

Nomasomi grew up in this fertile home environment, shaped by political debates and activities, education and Christian evangelism. Her middle name, Penina – reference to a rare rock – was given to her by Reverend James James Ranisi Jolobe, a prominent Presbyterian Church minister. Jolobe, then 51 years old, was already an acclaimed poet, his collection of poems, *Umyezo*, having been published in 1936; he had also published a Xhosa–English–Afrikaans dictionary,[65] and was a prominent, although quite conservative, politician as well as a member of the New Brighton Native Advisory Board in Port Elizabeth.[66] It was happenstance that when Qeqe's first child was born, Reverend Jolobe was in town visiting Gideon Ngoqo.

Qeqe did not, however, continue the relationship with the mother of his first daughter. It is not clear how long he was romantically involved with her, or whether theirs had been a formidably strong relationship. What is clear, though, is that, on completing his teacher's diploma, he left Fort Beaufort and returned to Port Elizabeth with Eric Majola, taking up a teaching position at Cowan Secondary School in New Brighton, under the principal, Mr Qunta.[67] In 1954, before he married, he sired another child, a son, Michael Qeqe. As with his daughter, Nomasomi, sired out of wedlock, he later adopted Michael, and they both lived with him.

It was then, in the early 1950s, that Qeqe met and married Rose Nonyameko Mbolekwa from East London. At that point, she was working as a nurse at Livingstone Hospital in Korsten, Port Elizabeth. While courting Rose, he introduced her to Eric Majola's wife, Mrs Jumartha Milase Majola (nee Moyake), who was teaching at Pendla Primary School in New Brighton with her husband. Meeting Qeqe and his then girlfriend through her husband, Mrs Majola recalled:

> He came with her to our house, because we were already married by then. He then said, 'You see, you are going to befriend this woman …' In that way, I befriended Mrs Qeqe, Rose Nonyameko … We became friends that way. It was like we were sisters. When they were off-duty, going out, the teacher, Qeqe, would pick his lady from Livingstone Hospital, and bring her here to my house, and we

> would enjoy a cup of coffee together. And again, they would go back together … When they got married, we used to exchange suppers – one Sunday we would eat at his place, and the other Sunday they would eat at my house. That is how strong our friendship was.[68]

Qeqe married Rose in 1955,[69] and together they had four children. His son Mpumelelo was born on 6 December 1956 and his daughter Phumla on 31 July 1958 and, four years later, they had another daughter, Belinda, born on 18 September 1962. Two years later, Boniswa was born on 19 July 1964.[70] During his marriage, Qeqe sired six more children out of wedlock. Nomabhesiniya was born in Fort Beaufort sometime in the 1950s, as was Barbara. And then, in the 1960s, he had four more children with two women in Port Elizabeth. With one of them, a woman whose surname was Tshiki, he had a son and a daughter. The son, Malixole Tshiki, committed suicide, but the daughter survives. The other two children were sons from another woman in Port Elizabeth in the 1960s.[71]

FIGURE 2: DAN QEQE FAMILY (UNVERIFIED)

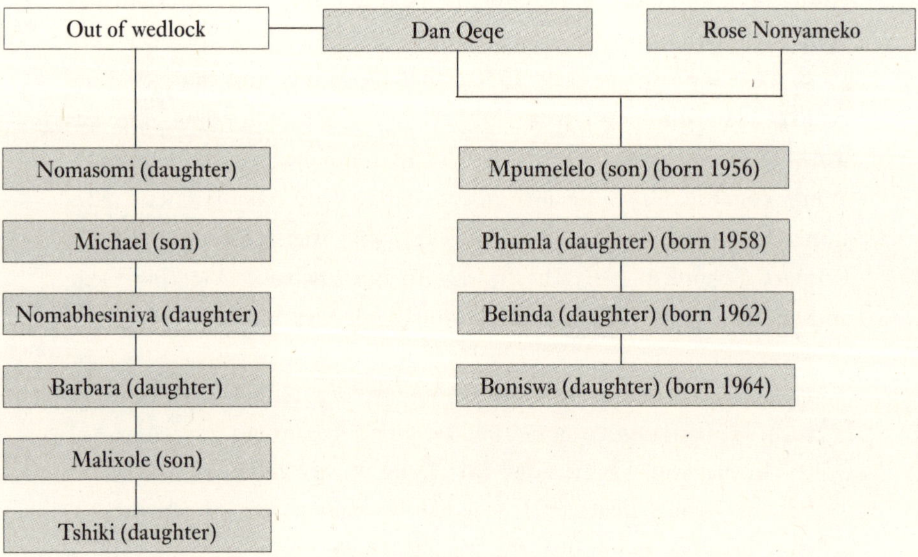

It was while he was teaching at Cowan Secondary School that Qeqe received a promotion, becoming principal of the new Ford Lower Primary School in New Brighton.[72] He also continued training the Spring Rose Rugby Football Club, consolidating his sports administration skills.[73] This was the time when his rugby career flourished, at both club and provincial levels. He played for Spring Rose as a hooker, representing the club in the annual championship trophies organised under the aegis of the PEARB. At provincial level, he played in the Eastern Province Bantu Rugby Union, again in the position of hooker. In cricket, he played for the Fort Beaufort Cricket Club, while his friend, Eric Majola, played for the New Brighton Cricket Club. It is said that although they were best friends, they did not talk to each other during the summer cricket season, when the Fort Beaufort and New Brighton cricket clubs – the derby black cricket clubs in Port Elizabeth – competed fiercely against each other.[74]

Dan Qeqe's roots germinated in Fort Beaufort and Port Elizabeth, providing him with a rural background steeped in the traditions of a polygamous family. The effect of this on his life went beyond family, stressing the importance and value of unity. It also rooted him deep in the history of nineteenth-century wars fought against British land dispossession. As much as this provided Qeqe with an enduring, life-long attachment to his native land and ethnic kinship, it also inculcated in him a sense of black pride and black consciousness. The milieu of non-racial sport and of black political activism he had witnessed provided fertile ground for much of his sporting, civic and political life. It was a background that, in many ways, prepared him for much of his activity in Port Elizabeth in the 1960s.

4

QEQE IN PORT ELIZABETH (1950S–1971)

Following the implementation of the Bantu Education Act, Qeqe resigned from his teaching position and, after six years as principal at Ford Lower Primary School, decided to join his younger brother, Wridge, in the transportation business. Publicly, he articulated his resignation on political principle. This was his way of protesting against the implementation of the Bantu Education Act. As he put it, he abhorred how the Bantu education system was expected to reduce the quality of the black child's education.[1] Sloti, however, refuted Qeqe's public postulation, arguing that his resignation was purely for financial reasons. Sloti drove home the point:

> No, no, no, no. What made Dan leave is remuneration in teaching. It is because the salaries that they received were inadequate. When he saw his younger brother's wages in the transport business, in the truck that he had, delivering paraffin and furniture, he decided to join his younger brother. That is why he quit teaching.[2]

At a time when teaching was one of the core middle-class professions in black communities, Qeqe's colleagues endeavoured to sway him back to teaching. To them, it was a more dignified profession, commensurate with his education and middle-class status. Entrepreneurship was apparently lowly, unsteady and risky. Many of Qeqe's colleagues who were also teachers, such as Eric Majola, Wilson Ximiya and Mokononyane, did their best to convince Qeqe not to leave the profession for somewhat risky entrepreneurship. However, Qeqe was determined to leave. He had firmly made up his mind. [3]

The Bazi family's reputation and capital provided entrepreneurial opportunities and expertise for the Qeqe brothers from an early age. Hanging around and lending a hand at the Bazi trading store provided Qeqe with basic business management skills and expertise. The Bazi family's connections and resources helped set up the Qeqe brothers in ventures in Zwelitsha, King William's Town and Port Elizabeth. Working in partnership, Dan's elder brothers, America and Ndwe (aka Lace), ran businesses in Zwelitsha and King William's Town, while Dan and his youngest brother, Wridge (aka Natuma), began a prosperous transportation business and petrol station in Port Elizabeth.[4]

Dan's partnership with Wridge was successful mainly because of his younger brother's own success. Wridge was wealthier than his elder brother, Dan. Attesting to this, Mali pointed out that Wridge had become prosperous before Dan, and remained wealthier than him for quite a long time. 'He was very, very rich. Even Dan was beneath him.'[5]

With the addition of a second vehicle, their transportation business expanded. Kwatsha, then a fellow entrepreneur, also noted that, 'Dan Qeqe then, as a man in business, developed tremendously.'[6] With the growth of the business, Qeqe enlisted the assistance of his wife. Soon thereafter, they opened a petrol station, a garage located at the entrance of New Brighton, a site that was given to them free of charge by an advisory board headman, a Mr Sali,[7] who was inspired by the hard work of the Qeqe brothers.

Some maintain that Qeqe's forays into entrepreneurship were motivated by his long-term goal of community development. As a teacher, he always envisaged himself as a community builder, a goal that would be enhanced by the financial muscle his businesses would be able to provide. Harold Wilson, a former executive member of SACOS, a historian of non-racial sports liberation, and also a former school principal in Bethelsdorp, Port Elizabeth, was privy to Qeqe's vision.

He had relayed his vision to Wilson when playing cricket on Sundays in the 1950s.[8]

Soon, Qeqe began to see the direct role entrepreneurship was to play in the social transformation of his New Brighton community. It was to be a role that reassessed and challenged the notion of black business people as beneath the class and dignity of the black intelligentsia. When the Rio Cinema burnt down on 18 October 1952,[9] Qeqe – using his resources and networks – became one of the central players in the rebuilding of it. Kolekile Kwatsha remembered, 'Yes, he was there with Wridge Qeqe. And then this matter concerning Rio Cinema happened. We got into Rio, because Rio got burnt down, *mos*. We got into that, and rebuilt Rio Bioscope.'[10]

In the 1950s, Rio Cinema had been run by Mr R Brand, under his company R Brand & Co. Brand was, however, killed during the 1952 Defiance Campaign riots, and soon thereafter the ownership and management of Rio Cinema was taken over by a number of black people in the Eastern Cape. Some of the prominent figures included Mr Nduna from Grahamstown, Mrs Masangwana, Mrs Madikane, Dr Peteni from King William's Town, Dr Mahlangeni and Mr Jolobe.[11] However, the enterprise soon encountered formidable management challenges, and was brought under judicial management. Judge Cecil 'Doc' Somyalo, then a practising attorney with Dumile Kondile, whose offices were located upstairs from the Rio Cinema, was directly affected by the judicial management of the building.

A Mr Pitje, a businessman from Pretoria, then bought the shares, and began running the cinema before the matter of judicial management was conclusively resolved. Despite this development, Somyalo and Kondile's lease nonetheless remained unfavourably affected, and they received an attorney's letter demanding that they vacate the premises. Apartheid laws did not allow black lawyers to rent offices in town, which meant that they effectively ran out of options when it came to leasing office space. And the Anglican Church in New Brighton, their last viable option, did not have space for them in the township either.

A gap, however, appeared when Somyalo approached Mrs Masangwana. She revealed that Mr Pitje had not yet actually bought the shares. Pitje's intention, Somyalo gathered, was to use the revenue he was generating from showing films at Rio Cinema to buy the ownership shares. As a way to save their office, Somyalo and his associates then decided to buy the shares and run the cinema themselves. As he put it, 'So, as a last resort, we never wanted to run a business. We decided, man, our salvation, to be able to stay up there, [for] our offices to remain there, let's buy this thing, fresh.'[12]

Realising that they did not have the money to buy the shares, Somyalo and Kondile thus approached Qeqe. Somyalo relayed:

> But we didn't have the money, so we got hold of Dan Qeqe. And he said, look, this is the way to approach this venture, we approach these people, they are business people. Dan Qeqe organised a few friends, Frans, Mantuntu, and KK, and then Ponono ... And we decided, let's organise, get some money, get our resources together. I think it was about R64 000 shares, shareholding. That was a lot of money. [13]

With the shareholders Dr Bokwe, Dr Rwairwai and Mr Moyake, and under the efficient management of Mr Fezile Sobikwa, the Rio Cinema was run effectively and profitably. To Somyalo's 'great surprise', 'it ran well ... It was the only cinema in the township at the time, and it would be packed, you know?'[14]

Community development and politics had natural interstices. And the Dan Qeqe of the 1960s to the 1970s was fashioned by the local political influences that defined the Port Elizabeth of the 1950s. Equally, it was these public influences that crafted a public Qeqe, coming into his own as he forged a life of community service. The Port Elizabeth of the 1950s was heaving with insurrectionary political activity, of labour militancy and local anti-apartheid mobilisation.

From the 1940s, Port Elizabeth had witnessed a spike in the militancy of African labour, particularly with the rent boycotts of 1945 and 1946, the dockworkers' strike of 1946, the laundry workers' strike of 1948, and the three-month New Brighton bus boycott of 1949.[15] The Defiance Campaign of 1952 had also exerted further strain on the Port Elizabeth Council, which was particularly determined to stem any recurrence of the riots consequent to the Defiance Campaign, led by the ANC. In Port Elizabeth, the campaign was led by Dr Njongwe and Raymond Mhlaba, who had resigned as an elected member of the New Brighton Native Advisory Board the previous year.[16] And so tensions came to a head.

Despite the abiding revolutionary ambience, Qeqe came under the influence of a reformist black intelligentsia, and this old guard nurtured him in his sporting life and teaching career. It was this middle-class black intelligentsia, firmly placed in local state collaborationist structures, that in turn assured its own bourgeois status in Port Elizabeth. This, too, was a black intelligentsia more attuned to short- to medium-term practical solutions with a provincial lens.

This old guard – of Lamani, Ximiya, Molefe, Jolobe, Ntshinga and others – for much of the 1940s, 1950s and 1960s, shaped Qeqe's political and community development outlook. More particularly, it oriented his life of community service, and so it was through their influence, particularly that of Ximiya, that he joined and served on the Native Advisory Board.[17] The board had changed its name from the New Brighton Native Advisory Board to the Port Elizabeth Joint Bantu Advisory Board, with Qeqe joining in 1964 and serving on the board for the next 13 years.

Theirs was not an outlook or method of community service entirely without value, as has been widely claimed in much of South Africa's leftist historical critique. Many of these reformist methods of service were driven by particular local events and incidents that required local responses. One such incident, which had an abiding influence on how Qeqe's predecessors in the community of New Brighton approached community service, took place in December 1952.

On the evening of Tuesday, 2 December 1952, Alfred Z Lamani chaired a marathon five-hour meeting, running from 8 pm to 1 am.[18] In his capacity as chairman of the Bantu Social Centre, Lamani had called the meeting to deliberate on the report of the eight elected members of the New Brighton Native Advisory Board who had resigned. It sought 'to hear reasons of their resignation from the Advisory Board of New Brighton and to devise ways and means of how to co-operate with the City Council of Port Elizabeth in future'.[19]

The eight members had been elected by registered residents of New

Brighton to sit on the advisory board, as opposed to the nominated members.[20] The board held one ordinary meeting once a month, but for special meetings – in the event of extraordinary circumstances or emergencies – the chairman, or in his absence, the superintendent of New Brighton, had the discretion to convene a special meeting. As stipulated in the rules and regulations of the board:

> The Chairman may at any time, upon being satisfied of the necessity of so doing, call a special meeting of the Advisory Board, but no business shall be transacted at any such meeting except such as the meeting may have been specially convened to consider.[21]

The abrupt resignation of the board's eight elected members was one such emergency, and one that had sprung up entirely unexpectedly. Lamani, appointed in 1944 by the Bantu Administration Board as the first sports organiser and social worker of New Brighton, had been trained at the Jan Hofmeyr School of Social Work in Johannesburg, run by the American Missionary Board under the leadership of Reverend Ray Phillips.[22] At that time, Lamani was already an administrator of Spring Rose Rugby Football Club,[23] and had been instrumental in escalating it to a first-league club.[24] Affectionately known as 'Diesel',[25] he was well known in and outside Port Elizabeth as a very cunning man. '*Mfondini, ingengo maqhinga*!' – 'My man, what a very crafty man!'[26] Dan Qeqe's nephew, Mncedi Mali, distinctly remembered his character.

The eight members – PP Mati,[27] Wilson F Ximiya, AA Tsekelitsa, J Tsikila, WF Tuta, WM Stemele, S Sigetye and H Mabamba[28] – had all resigned in protest at not having been consulted by the Native Affairs Commission in the appointment of a Social Welfare and Employment Officer. The meeting's overriding fear was that the immediate (and principal) task set for the appointee would be to address 'hooliganism and juvenile delinquency in New Brighton', which would in turn invoke the implementation of harsh apartheid laws such as had never been experienced before.[29]

It would entirely overturn Port Elizabeth's 'liberal' character,[30] leading to the city council's adoption of apartheid's new social and labour restrictions. Already recently implemented in Kimberley, East London and Uitenhage, 'Port Elizabeth is next in the order of programme,'[31] they feared. The meeting boldly protested that:

> The residents feel that the appointment of such an officer is tantamount to the introduction of the unwelcome introduction of the Registration of Service Contract and permit to seek work with all the accompanying evil regulations to which the residents are in no uncertain terms opposed.[32]

Setting up a Labour Bureau meant that an African would be required to produce a permit in order to seek work, or a document that declared that he was registered with the Labour Bureau. Accompanying that would be a presentation that a resident was up to date with his Native Poll Tax payment. The delegates to the meeting also dreaded the 'vigorous application'[33] of section 17 of the Urban Areas Act, and 'the rounding up and mass arrests by police of all unemployed youths in the Village'[34] to be drafted to mines and farms.

State provision of sport and recreational facilities was sorely needed in New Brighton. As expressed in the December 1952 meeting, 'The meeting feels that the provision of social and recreational facilities and the augmentation of the present social and recreational facilities; inadequate as they are, is a crying need at New Brighton.'[35]

Lamani and the meeting pleaded that, 'The residents feel that such a step instead of restoring things to normality between the residents and the liberal Council of Port Elizabeth, this would definitely restrain relationship.'[36] Much earlier, there had been clear indications that the state was heading towards the centralisation of the organisation of black labour. These practices had been steadily streaming through state institutions since the advent of the Union of South Africa regime.

From the 1920s, the Union Government had deliberated on various means of systematically organising black labour in a centralised manner. One such attempt had occurred in 1925, coming at the end of the conference of representatives of Juvenile Affairs Boards. Convened on 26 September 1924 in Pretoria, conference Resolution (a) on 'Native Policy' carried that:

> As the unemployment of natives which would be extremely undesirable, unjust, to the native, and injurious to the potential productive power of the country, the Government should be recommended to survey systematically the available fields of employment for natives, and to adjust policy so as to divert natives into such fields.[37]

The abandonment of the so-called 'liberal' character of Port Elizabeth was to completely change the social and economic relations between the city and its black residents. *EBhayi*, the geographic grid of the black townships of Port Elizabeth – which in isiXhosa means 'a blanket', invoking comfort – began to lose its original metaphorical meaning. *EBhayi* was popularly considered a haven that offered a blanket of 'solace, strength, and warmth'.[38] The term is taken from the song titled '*eBhayi*', composed by Snowy Radebe in the 1940s, celebrating the absence of the state's repressive labour and social laws and regulations in Port Elizabeth. The stanza most emblematic of *eBhayi*'s 'liberal' blanket-warmth character summed up popular sentiment of the time:[39]

Wakufika eBhayi	When you arrive in PE
Noba uvel' eQonce	Even from King William's Town
Wakufika eBhayi	When you arrive in PE
Pha eBhayi pha	Here in PE, here
Lingaphel' ixhala	Your anxiety disappears
Uvel' ubone	Then you can see
Kuzolile eBhayi pha	It is quiet in PE

The 'racial hatred in the Union is largely due to the uncompromising attitude of the Nationalist Party Government in its dealings with the African people, and this has given the Communist agitators an opportunity to flood cities like Port Elizabeth with Communist propaganda,'[40] the Cape Town-based proprietors of a new magazine, *New Africa*, wrote to the Native Affairs Commission in 1952 when applying for funding. They went on to note that, 'It is our firm conviction that the remedy for all problems lies in a return or resuscitation of the old Cape liberal policy, which Port Elizabeth in its dealings with the African people, has persistently followed.'[41]

This protestation notwithstanding, the Native Affairs Commission moved ahead, tightening its grip on labour practices and social laws, with conservative, working-class Afrikaners and their families deliberately lured to employment opportunities in Port Elizabeth. The objective was to effect a mass move of Afrikaners to Port Elizabeth in order to augment and embolden the National Party voting bloc in the city.[42] The white local authority, comprising local capital and rate payers, which had moved for the creation of black townships in the first decade of the twentieth-century,[43] were also decisively pushing for an apartheid Port Elizabeth Council.

Consequently, the council immediately sought to implement new influx-control provisions in sections 10, 11, 12 and 14 of the Natives (Urban Areas) Consolidation Act, No. 25 of 1945. Most significantly, it introduced the Labour Bureau,[44] with the Native Affairs Commission moving to remove 'Natives' who 'had shown to be leaders in the riots'.[45]

In the late 1950s and 1960s, residents of New Brighton had to produce residence certificates, and visitors had to report their presence to the township superintendent.[46] Native Tax Cards had already been introduced in the city in 1949,[47] but on 3 and 4 May 1956 the Native Commissioner of Port Elizabeth arranged for a hall – normally used as a bioscope, and leased from Mr Soobramanyan Chetty[48] – in order to issue residents of New Brighton with reference books. He instructed that, 'With reference to the above matter I have to inform you that it has been arranged to issue Reference Books to Natives at Veeplaas during the period 3rd May 1956 to 8th May 1956.'[49]

CONSEQUENT TO THE CITY'S embracing of apartheid, as predicted by the fears at the meeting of 1952, the black leadership of the New Brighton Native Advisory Board began to execute new, official chicaneries – small, accumulative incidents designed to undermine local apartheid restrictions on social and lived realities of the people of New Brighton. With the exception, perhaps, of Reverend George B Molefe on the board – who remained a co-operative collaborationist, a model and principled 'Native' leader to the end – other members, such as Lamani and Ximiya, carried and passed these deceptions over to a young Dan Qeqe, who had joined the New Brighton's Native Advisory Board in

1964, then reconfigured as the Port Elizabeth Joint Bantu Advisory Board.[50]

Many of these activities related to the recruitment of players from neighbouring towns, cities and rural areas to play for Port Elizabeth's rugby clubs, as well as the subversion of locally enforced apartheid laws on housing and employment. Qeqe and the board members often took proactive measures to safeguard New Brighton's welfare, particularly in the field of education.

It was particularly Wilson F Ximiya, who had taken Qeqe under his wing, who trained Qeqe in community social work and mobilisation in Port Elizabeth. As Ximiya's son, Crosby 'Winky' recalled, '[Qeqe] learnt all the things which my father used to do for the community of Port Elizabeth.'[51] He 'would assist, like my father used to do, in making people to have the permits and the rights to be registered in Port Elizabeth.'[52] They executed these deceptions in sly but profound ways in order to make the lives of New Brighton residents more tolerable. And, in doing so, they inadvertently influenced the course of black social struggles in Port Elizabeth, adding yet another layer to the tactical defiance against apartheid. This defiance came from inside the belly of a state body, a 'dummy institution', ordinarily relegated to a sell-out, collaborationist status.

By the time Qeqe joined the Port Elizabeth Joint Bantu Advisory Board, he was already a prominent businessman. Behind him also was an outstanding record of sportsmanship in both the rugby and cricket codes, at club and provincial levels. He was an active administrator for Spring Rose and the Fort Beaufort Cricket Club, and an influential administrator in rugby structures at provincial level. As a former schoolteacher and principal, as well as with all these other educational, sports and community accolades, he was thus a prime candidate for recruitment into the native advisory boards.

Native advisory boards had always sought upstanding and well-educated, black middle-class men to sit on the councils. As model members of their communities, they wielded the appropriate amount of influence over their communities. Local councils also banked on the conservative outlook that came with their status, aware of what they could potentially lose if the status quo were to be upturned. In this way, Qeqe – then a 35-year-old married man with a family and a bonded house – was an appropriate appointment. The Port Elizabeth Council viewed him as a prime candidate for effecting their agenda of social order and balance in New Brighton. In doing so, he joined other community luminaries on the board: Ximiya, Lamani, Reverend Molefe, Reverend Jolobe, David Mbane, AL Dwesi and Mvelo Norris Singaphi.[53]

A popular argument setting out the state's objective in creating the native advisory boards is that they wanted to wedge a black middle-class as a buffer between the local state and the black working-class masses. Thozamile Botha reasoned:

> Now you would notice that many of these advisory councillors, as I said earlier, were also business people. They were very involved in business. So, part of the strategy of the Kochs and the Cravens and the Louis Luyts was to use, create business opportunities for these sports leaders and community leaders. To create business opportunities [so as] to create this middle class during that period, a middle class which would be a buffer between the apartheid state and the masses. To neutralise them, so the struggle would not be between the government and the people, but it would be these people who would become the target, which became the case, by the way. Because we started then focusing on the Singaphis, and the Mpondos, the people who became the front of the community councils, and representing in the township those administration boards.[54]

Louis Koch was the chief director of the Cape Midlands Native Bantu Affairs Board; Mvelo Norris Singaphi was also a Native Advisory Board member, a rugby administrator, and a former black Springbok player;[55] and AS Mpondo was a long-time member of the Native Advisory Board and one of the city's prominent businessmen.[56]

Although attuned to the sensitivities of the impoverished in New Brighton and to matters of social injustice, Qeqe at that time was politically conservative, an outlook measured on ideology. Although he believed in and touted strong principles of black consciousness and pride, he did not embrace this as its ideologue. He also did not publicly wear the Charterist or pan-Africanist values of the ANC and the Pan-Africanist Congress (PAC) of Azania. Most valuable to him was the platform available to him to carry out social justice in the most practical manner, often in piecemeal form. And the Native Advisory Board was one such platform. His daughter, Nomasomi Penina Gxasheka (nee Maka), pointed out that in the 1960s, on account of his board membership, members of the New Brighton community came to his house in droves. They sought his help on housing, services and welfare matters, and he often helped them from his own pocket.[57]

The New Brighton Native Advisory Board has offered history a rather strange legacy when compared to typical native advisory boards. In the 1950s and 1960s, it sat between a chequered reputation, and a bona fide instrument of community representation, surviving in a landscape of severely curtailed consultative powers. These were characterised by paternalism, and an often outwardly corrupt patronage system. Urban geography scholars such as Paul Maylam are decisively judgmental about the legacy of native advisory boards. He noted that, 'All case studies show that the advisory boards were powerless bodies. Even their advisory role was generally not taken seriously by municipal councils.'[58] Some, such as Kwatsha, considered it an entity that 'connected people … where people got together to deliberate on matters concerning New Brighton'.[59]

What is astonishing, though, about the legacy of New Brighton's Native Advisory Board is its quiet resilience in the physical memory of New Brighton. All streets bearing the names of the members of the board have survived the post-apartheid excising acts against segregation and apartheid memories. Almost all the eight members of the Native Advisory Board who had resigned at the end of 1952 are remembered in New Brighton's street names. They include the majority of those elected and nominated to the board from 1909 to 1952,[60] who also had primary schools named after them. This resilience may perhaps serve as a recognition of the board's ambivalent position – not quite anti-people, nor necessarily anti-establishment.

Not widely acknowledged, though, is how members of native advisory boards journeyed through complex and contentious politics

– an expedition of experiences riddled with contradictions: often altruistic, but also corrupt and opportunistic. In the 1930s and 1940s, they stridently clashed with the township superintendent, mainly over corrupt practices in the allocation of housing and the awarding of trading licences. These clashes were led by such board members as Wilson Weir Jabavu and AZ Tshiwula.[61]

On his recruitment by Dan Qeqe, Mrs Nozuko 'Girlie' Pikoli's[62] father hesitantly joined the Port Elizabeth Joint Bantu Advisory Board in the mid-1960s. 'He was a bit reluctant because, I would say my father belonged to, I would say he was quietly political, but belonged to a strain which is more PAC,'[63] she pointed out. His reluctance to join the board was both an echo of black popular perceptions of the board's 'dummy' pliancy in the face of apartheid restrictions. Though Qeqe was acutely aware of these flaws, he nevertheless saw fit to wage local welfare struggles from certain strategic vantage points offered by the board.

Members of the New Brighton Native Advisory Board thus used what opportunities they could to lessen the effects of local state repression. As Sidney Tarrow argued, 'Contention increases when people gain the external resources to escape their compliance and find opportunities in which to use them.'[64] Board members used systems, laws and regulations of repression to erode the system of permits and repression. To Thozamile Botha, the usefulness of the New Brighton Native Advisory Board was to wield influence over rugby through the control of resources and population regulatory systems. As he put it, 'They had to participate in the Bantu Administration Advisory Board which controlled resources, and take control of the administration of the popular sport in the black communities – rugby.'[65]

Lamani, Ximiya, Molefe and Qeqe honed these acts of defiance through their positions on the board. Lamani chaired the General Purposes and Finance Committee, while Ximiya chaired the Welfare and Recreation Sub-Committee, with Qeqe heading the Public Transport and Traffic Committee. Reverend George B Molefe chaired the entire board, and occasionally headed the sub-committee on education.[66] However, the chairs of these sub-committees were not fixed to particular board members. They rotated, consistent with changes in the membership of elected and nominated members that were reviewed annually.[67]

Notable among the four nominated members of the board in 1952 was Reverend George B Molefe,[68] who carved out for himself quite a significant community activist and education-building profile in New Brighton in the 1940s and 1950s. In many ways, he preceded Qeqe in that role. Some of the beneficiaries of Reverend Molefe's mobilisation of educational funding were the then Newell High School pupil, Reverend Makhenkesi Arnold Stofile, and the uncle and father of Mrs Nozuko 'Girlie' Pikoli.[69]

Having worked together on the board since 1964, it is difficult to ascertain how Reverend Molefe's politically conservative outlook might have influenced Qeqe during their time serving together. Conservative politics was a Molefe trait, one that is evident in the black conservative institutions and ideas that inspired him towards public service. Making a plea to Dr Thomas Jesse Jones of the Phelps-Stokes Foundation in 1939 for inclusion on a study tour of the social conditions of the Native Indian and the Tuskegee Institute while studying at the Union Theological Seminary in New York, he wrote:

> I would very much like to go as I long wished to study the social organisation and religious beliefs of the Red Indians and to compare them with those of my own people – I refer to the Bantu people, in South Africa. I would be very grateful indeed, Dr Jones, if you would be so kind in this connection.
>
> The tour would also mean very much to me in that I would learn more about the land, and the Negroes as well when we visit Tuskegee and Atlanta.[70]

Advising Molefe on what platform and path of public service was best to choose following the completion of his studies at the Union Theological Seminary, Charles T Loram of Yale University's Graduate School steered him towards progressive trade unions. However, Loram, well acquainted with Molefe's affinity towards political conservativeness, noted that, 'Of course you will by your very nature be a cooperator and among the many fine South Africans, black and white, who are working for and with the Bantu, you will find advisers, colleagues and friends.'[71]

Perhaps Loram had already gleaned Molefe's inclinations towards co-operating with the state from Molefe's previous proclamations and activities. In 1936, four years before he first took his seat on the New Brighton Native Advisory Board as a nominated member,[72] he clearly postulated this position at the Natal Missionary Society Conference. Its ninth objective in 1936 was, 'To co-operate with Joint Councils, Missionary Conferences, and other bodies working for Native benefit.'[73] With John Langalibalele Dube also in attendance, and Chief Albert Luthuli in the organisation's active roll,[74] among others, Molefe pointed out that, 'All social activities should be under the church.'[75] On education, he noted, 'I have left out education as I feel that the Education Department is the best man to look after that. They are doing missionary work in that connection, thus giving the missionaries the opportunity to devote their whole time to the spiritual task.'[76]

Also preceding Qeqe in pursuing community development in New Brighton and one who may well have influenced him through the Native Advisory Board was James HE Ntshinga. Ntshinga was elected to the New Brighton Native Advisory Board in 1938, and served for many years, particularly as its chairman of the Chiefs' Committee.[77]

Ntshinga was born in Grahamstown, but had completed his elementary education in Port Elizabeth. In 1910, after having worked in the mine offices, and active in sports and social life in New Brighton, he joined Knight Central Mine in Germiston, Johannesburg, as a clerk interpreter. In 1916, he participated in the First World War through the Red Cross Forces, earning a promotion to First Orderly.[78]

Having moved back to Port Elizabeth at the end of the war, he went on to found the Blind and Crippled League in 1935, becoming its president. The following year, he became a member of the Vigilance Committee of New Brighton. Most notably, Ntshinga led the executive committee of the Bantu Benevolent and Welfare Society. The society's mandate incorporated the administration of the Adcock Homes, which assisted 125 indigent people, each receiving one meal a day for six days a week.[79]

However, the Bantu Benevolent and Welfare Society relied on financial assistance from local capital and the white political class of

Port Elizabeth. In a letter addressed to the Chief of the Bantu Affairs Commission on 17 September 1968, Ntshinga blatantly admitted that the society was 'supported down the years to the present day by City Councillors and ex Mayors of Port Elizabeth, as a Bantu effort to take care of the needs of our under-privileged people'.[80] The financial management of the affairs of the society also relied on the judgement and decisions of a white honorary treasurer appointed to its board. The society's constitution clearly stipulated that 'the Executive Committee is empowered to invite a European person who is a not a member of the Organisation to act as Honorary Treasurer, until such time as a capable Bantu person can be appointed as Treasurer'.[81]

Increasing implementation of repressive laws in New Brighton produced equally consistent counter tactics – such as evasions and subversions – and sometimes even outright defiance from some of the board leadership. The city council and other apartheid-implementation machinery at council level were thus a deliberate, in-built institutional contradiction. As Maylam noted:

> But there is a danger in viewing control in teleological, monolithic, functionalist terms – creating a picture of a powerful state agency ever tightening the screws of control with growing effect, in the service of the dominant class. Such a picture is, paradoxically, because controls have been steadily tightening through the course of the twentieth century. But also misleading, because the whole apparatus of urban segregation and apartheid has been *riddled with contradiction and dysfunctionality*.[82]

So Qeqe forged his public service through the Native Advisory Board. Throughout his time on the board, through the networks he built, and with his working knowledge of the governance of Port Elizabeth, he learned effective ways of subverting oppressive systems for the benefit of the black communities of the city. These were to come in handy in devastatingly effective ways in his sporting–civic ventures. Also, these years of service not only earned him a sound reputation, but also provided him with the knowledge and courage it took to advance local infrastructure for the education of the black child.

PART THREE
(1971–2005)

5

THE ACCIDENTAL BIRTH OF THE KWAZAKHELE RUGBY UNION (1950S–1971)

'Well, let me say, 1971, it was something that was, you can't call it, you can't call it an event … It was never, it was never an event.'[1] This was how Sipho McDonald Tanana described the events in 1971 that led to the birth of the KwaZakhele Rugby Union (Kwaru). Key to Tanana's postulation was that events over the past two decades had built up to this point. 'When the conflict started, there were other preceding issues that led to the conflict that we didn't know about. The break-up happened then because of that.'[2] Dan Ngcaphe, a former Kwaru player and now principal at Ndzondelelo High School in Zwide Township in Port Elizabeth, affirmed as much.

East London-based Tanana was the Border region chairman of the state-sponsored, multiracial SAARB, as well as the former president of the South African Federated Chamber of Commerce and Industry. He remained unrepentant about his past as a leading multiracial sports proponent, and held firmly to his conviction that 'Kwaru has never had an impact'.[3] To Tanana, Kwaru's legacy was rather 'destabilising various clubs and unions, at one time getting to universities, black universities. Kwaru has never, you can't say it had an impact on these provinces.'[4] By this, he meant that it never had any meaningful impact beyond Port Elizabeth. And yet Tanana displayed an idiosyncratic political ambivalence in his commitment to multiracial sport and the Ciskei government as one of its senior civil servants. He was arbitrarily arrested three times by Sebe's Ciskei government for his sometimes contrary political views.[5]

Tanana and Ngcaphe's views thus capture the core essence of how Kwaru came to be, born at the tail end of long, drawn-out inter-club rivalries and clashes with the mother body, the PEARB. Many of these had found expressions in breakaways, club splits and administrative conflicts. And all of them were non-political, if not downright petty.

Kwaru came right after the untimely death of Eric Majola in June 1971. As a legendary double Black Springbok flyback and member of Spring Rose,[6] his almost mythical status, both in rugby and cricket, but more especially in rugby, was well known throughout South Africa. By the 1960s, he was a commanding and sellable icon, appearing in the Wilson's Three-X Mints advert. 'Wilson's Three-X Mints are my favourites – I use them always, both on the field and off – says Eric Majola.'[7] Majola radiated in the advert, his face centred next to the caption, while a picture of him batting in a white cricket uniform hovered above his head. This was a rare status for a black sportsman at the height of apartheid.

Eric Kolekile Majola was born in the old Village of New Brighton, and attended higher primary school in the Red Location, and high school at Newell with Dan Qeqe.[8] Playing for the cricket XI at the age of 15 years, he accomplished himself as a batsman, and took part in the Kaffrarian Cricket Tournaments played annually during the December school holidays. At the 1950 tournament in Kimberley, he was selected, along with Matthews Mokolonyane[9] and Lent Maqoma,[10] to represent Eastern Province. He first played for Spring Rose during the school holidays of 1951.

Majola ushered in a new era of flyhalf skills in African rugby.[11] Mbiza, who played with Majola and Singaphi in SAARB,[12] fondly remembered his playing expertise and popularity:

> We valued him highly. We valued him very, very highly in rugby. Yho! Yho! Yho! Yho! When we went to District Six, Coloureds there wanted to see him, 'Where's Majola? Where's Majola? Where's Majola? Where's Majola?' And Majola was on the other side. He was the shortest one amongst us all. Then the Coloureds spoke Afrikaans, saying, 'He's so small, man.' He was small. He looked small. You would seriously underestimate him. But let him get into the field, and you're in trouble. You're in great trouble![13]

One of his sons, Gerald Mongezi Majola, the former CEO of the South African Cricket Union (SACU) who played non-racial cricket and rugby in the late 1970s and 1980s, remembered his father's unsurpassable rugby skills:

> In rugby, I was the captain of the SA Schools in 1978. And I was a flyhalf. Even then, people used to come, flocking … during those days, people used to leave work to come and watch school rugby. And people were raving about my rugby, and there would be one person who would say, 'No, my son, you could be good, but you would never reach your father's level.' You know, you play, you'd think you've played the best game, and these guys would just tell you, 'You're not half your father's game.'[14]

Songongo, a Whites modelled his rugby-playing style as a flyhalf on Majola, recollecting that he played in 'an era dominated by Eric Majola, Norman Ntshinga. So when you were at school at that time, you wanted to play in the position played by Eric Majola. Even when you dodged an opponent, you impersonated him, the way he moved and swayed around an opponent.'[15]

By the 1960s, Majola's outstanding flyhalf skills had earned him international attention, to the point that he was recruited to play for a team in the United Kingdom (UK). However, unable to take his family along, he turned down the offer.[16] And so his sudden passing away not only disturbed Qeqe, but rocked the black Port Elizabeth rugby fraternity to the core.

Majola died in a car accident on Commercial Road in Port Elizabeth in June 1971. Many rugby clubs affiliated to the PEARB felt strongly that, out of respect and admiration, rugby fixtures scheduled for the weekend of his funeral should be cancelled. Qeqe and many other members of the PEARB's affiliate rugby clubs strongly insisted on the cancellation. Booley accounted:

> In 1971 an event of small beginnings had great consequences for SAARB rugby. Spring Rose, a club chaired by Dan Qeqe and belonging to PEARB headed by Norris Mvelo Singaphi, applied to the board for the postponement of a Saturday fixture, because several players wanted to attend the funeral of one of their former team-mates, the great double Springbok Eric Majola.[17]

Singaphi, however, stood firmly against popular sentiment, and the request was officially turned down.[18] This, of course, flies in the face of the narrative that has gone down in popular pro-Qeqe and pro-Kwaru oral history, which has given Singaphi personal ownership of the decision to cancel the fixtures. Such a historical narrative puts Singaphi at the incendiary centre of this dispute.

Singaphi was a bold and authoritative figure. In populist oral history of old black rugby circles, he is passed off as mostly villainous, a counter-revolutionary and selfish figure. Mthobi Tyamzashe, former secretary-general of the National Sports Council (NSC), and director-general in the Department of Sport and Recreation in President Nelson Mandela's administration, described Singaphi as disagreeable and aggressive. He 'used to go into meetings with a monkey, and wielding a sjambok'.[19] Ray Mali remembered Singaphi as a man who 'was ready to fight all the time'.[20] He was also considered opportunistic, 'always looking for a quick buck. He can be swayed if he was going to get something from it.'[21] Somyalo remembered him as a man who 'always had issues',[22] and that 'he was all over. He was a person who was impressionistic, and had a penchant for going into ventures that made quick money.'[23]

But these particular understandings of personalities in social history do not lead to a comprehensive appreciation of what really transpired in 1971. As a result, there is now a rather binary, villainous Singaphi versus a lionised Qeqe behind the populist–mythical story of Kwaru's birth. It is a dualistic account that has, regrettably, cast in stone the myth that has been passed around in Port Elizabeth. It becomes then important to question some of these populist Kwaru modern histories, now cemented in the guise of urban pseudo-folklore. Rather, as Ama Binney reflects on the legacy of Kwame Nkrumah, we need a critical contextual approach, a slant that should fuse understandings of ideology, political performance, events, personalities and agencies.[24]

Accounts of the reportedly monkey-accompanied and sjambok-wielding Singaphi versus the heroic Qeqe are not pertinent and helpful in gaining a factual understanding of how Kwaru came to be. André Odendaal points out that Kwaru unintentionally snowballed into a political movement and symbol.[25] It became 'the most successful African provincial rugby body in the Republic'.[26] Nonetheless, its formation, coming at the back of 'many years of internal disputes, some of which ended in court',[27] are neither correctly nor comprehensively historicised.

At that meeting in June 1971, it was Mono Badela, then secretary of St Cyprian's, who came up with the proposal to cancel fixtures scheduled for the Saturday of Majola's funeral. Badela had sat next to Singaphi when he raised his hand, making the proposal. Songongo, who had attended that meeting, provided this witness account:

> Now, the chairman of the meeting, Singaphi, says he hears all these arguments. But now the crucial point is that, because Majola is a Springbok, matches should be cancelled? What if I die? What if that man dies, and that man dies? Those are also Springboks, are you going to cancel [fixtures?]. It was said, but no, he is an exception. He is the one who asked, 'How is he an exception, because I, Singaphi, I've played more tests than him? He has only played two tests for South Africa. I've played more tests than him.' He then mentioned others. He said, and then he stood, and said, 'I won't cancel [the fixtures], but the clubs involved, they should decide what to do with their fixtures. For instance, I am related to the man, I am going to the funeral.'[28]

Amon Nyondo, an advocate of the High Court of Port Elizabeth, a former Young Collegians Rugby Football Club, Kwaru administrator and long-standing non-racial sports proponent, commented on that 1971 meeting:

> [It] was said that Mvelo Singaphi was saying, there are many people that have been dying in the past. There are many people that are going to die in the future. Why must we call off the fixtures because of Eric Majola? And the majority of people were saying Eric Majola is no ordinary player, he is our leader, he is our star, for all of us. Remember that the man was even the South African African Rugby Board flyhalf. Yes. So, they were saying, this is no ordinary player. And the issue is, Mvelo Singaphi milked that down, to say, he is another player, like all the others that have died, and there are other players that are going to die in the future. We are not going to call off the fixtures … What I'm saying, the issue is that we are dealing with a rivalry element between Whites and Spring Rose. That was the overriding sentiment. And the net result, the net result, is the fixtures went on. And then, those clubs that did not want the fixtures to go on, did not go to play.[29]

Indeed, the death of a star player in the PEARB was not new; there were existing procedures and protocols that had been followed for many years. Barry Sinuka recalled the precedence and past protocols:

> It was not the first time that we had experienced the death of a star player like Eric … No, we had experienced deaths of a lot of star players. I think there was a Spring Rose chap, a flanker, Louis Mbelekane, I think. When he died, the matches carried on. We attended funerals of sportsmen. You get into the field, bow your head for that time, finish, and resume playing.[30]

Singaphi, then also a member of the SAARB, played interracial tests against the South African Coloured Rugby Federation between 1950 and 1967. He was regarded as a 'brilliant wing with a split-second side-step'.[31] During that time, he was a Black Springbok in the SAARB team of the South African Bantu Springboks. So, indeed, his experience as a Springbok player in test matches was vaster and longer, preceding Majola's rugby career. However, a distinctive difference between Singaphi and Majola was their playing abilities. Majola's skill was undoubtedly far superior to Singaphi's, and with far more thrilling showmanship, drawing accolades from many rugby lovers across racial lines.

Songongo added that, 'I was in that meeting. My club, the one Singaphi was president of, also decided not to go and play. I went to the funeral, and Singaphi was also there in the funeral.'[32] He went on to explain Singaphi's strength in rugby club and union meetings, as well as his proficiency in the constitutions of the PEARB and affiliated rugby clubs. 'You see, Singaphi, where he defeated a lot of people in debates, especially in rugby meetings, when he argued, he argues on a constitutional point, and you cannot argue against [the] constitution. That is the only area he defeated them. He was that type of person.'[33] Sinuka also affirmed Singaphi's proficiency on constitutional points:

> Mvelo properly pursued the constitution. I used to play together with Singaphi … Mvelo was alright. He was alright, but he had a problem with his temper, just like everyone else. He was alright. And he knew the constitution and the laws very well. He used to follow the constitution and the laws of whatever institution he was in.[34]

Odendaal pointed out that Kwaru was formed when the clubs that wanted to attend Majola's funeral refused to accept the PEARB's disciplinary measures for refusing to abide by SAARB's decision.[35] Booley relayed that, on the Saturday of the Majola funeral, Spring Rose did not honour their fixture against St Cyprian's. The following Saturday, Spring Rose played a fixture against Whites. The match was, however, stopped early because of fighting.

At the following meeting of the PEARB, Qeqe's Spring Rose refused to face disciplinary measures. That refusal followed the bitterness of the Wilfred Khovu debacle of 1970.[36] When Khovu earned a penalty point for Spring Rose, his club had refused to acknowledge the penalty. In its refusal, they were supported by nine first-division rugby clubs affiliated to the PEARB, namely Easterns, Fabs, St Cyprian's,

Wallabies, Butcher Birds, Park Rovers, Walmer Wales, Orientals and African Bombers. Only Whites and the reserve league clubs remained in support of the PEARB.[37] The rugby clubs affiliated to the PEARB were Easterns, Fabs, St Cyprian's, Wallabies, Butcher Birds, Park Rovers, Walmer Wales, Orientals, African Bombers, Spring Rose, Unionand Vultures.[38] Understandably, Whites – the oldest black rugby club in South Africa – remained in support of the PEARB's decision because it was under the chairmanship of Singaphi.

The KwaZakhele Rugby Union (Kwaru) was then formed on the back of this breakaway from the PEARB, moving away from the mother body, along with nine of the affiliate clubs that supported it. Kwaru's main objective was to find a home – a rugby union to affiliate to. Lucky 'Coach' Mange, then a Spring Rose player, maintained that Kwaru's overriding preoccupation was affiliation rather than political conscientisation. As he put it, 'It was not that we saw the light. We were not politically conscientised … it's just that we wanted a place to play.'[39]

Soon after Kwaru broke away from the PEARB, it immediately returned to request affiliation,[40] following serial rejections from the Eastern Province Rugby Board and the national SAARB. These were all tiered racial rugby boards, capacitated by the same ilk of administrators. So a similar interconnection of rugby officials who had rejected them at district and provincial levels rejected them at national level. As Nyondo related, 'The South African African Rugby Board, the Eastern Province African Rugby Board, the PE Board of Mvelo Singaphi thought, we will shut the door on these Kwaru boys. Where will they go? They'll come back to us, and ask for our mercy. That was not to be.'[41] Mono Badela had heard via SARU's president, Abdul Abbas, that SARU's vice-president, Fred Hufkie, was visiting Port Elizabeth to attend a wedding. And so it was that Hufkie and Badela's *alma mater* connection as former Fort Harians readily facilitated Kwaru's affiliation to SARU.

Odendaal pointed out that contentions over corruption and the maladministration of the PEARB were behind the long-standing conflicts.[42] Booley maintained that the majority of senior officials in the 12 rugby clubs affiliated to the PEARB were 'grossly dissatisfied' with the administration of the PEARB leadership.[43] Odendaal maintained that it was the leadership of 'old timers', such as Singaphi, Curnick Mdyesha and WL Dwesi, behind the PEARB's corruption and maladministration.[44]

Singaphi was not, however, an 'old timer'. Although he was slightly older than Qeqe and Majola, they were more or less contemporaries. Singaphi had played rugby for the Eastern Province and SAARB less than a decade before Qeqe and Majola. He had also been a member of the Eastern Province Bantu Rugby Football Club, and his team had won the NRC Trophy in the 1947 SAARB Tournament held in Kimberley.[45] Between 1950 and 1967, more or less the same period in which Qeqe played competitively,[46] Dwesi also played rugby. He was remembered as an agile, Cradock-based scrumhalf, 'with strong blindside breaks around the scrum'.[47] Singaphi and Dwesi were thus not old-timers to Qeqe, as Odendaal contended.

It was, instead, petty club rivalries and playtime squabbles that generated non-political administrative conflicts, the sum of these informing all the bitterness and acrimonious differences between the PEARB, SAARB and affiliating rugby clubs. Ngcaphe similarly explained:

> When Kwaru broke away from Eastern Province, it was not because Kwaru wanted to play non-racial sport. And anyone who says so is lying. Kwaru did not break away from there because they wanted to play non-racial sport. Kwaru broke away from there because they didn't get along with them after the passing away of Gailer's father, Eric Majola.[48]

Sinuka also maintained that, 'It seemed as if Spring Rose didn't want to participate. They didn't get along well with the officers of the PE Board, from the way I saw it.'[49] Thozamile Botha traced these disputes and rivalries back to 1963, when both St Cyprian's and Spring Rose withdrew from the PEARB, driven out by dissatisfactions over perceived mishandling of matches. They accused the PEARB administrators of biases towards certain clubs. After breaking away from the PEARB, St Cyprian's and Spring Rose played in separate tournaments.

In 1963, St Cyprian's mooted the idea of forming a KwaZakhele rugby union with Spring Rose. At that time, St Cyprian's was the strongest club in KwaZakhele, but still it had neither the resources nor the experience to bring that idea to fruition. Whites, under Singaphi, who had remained at the helm of the PEARB administrative leadership during their breakaway, had gained administrative experience in running the board, and this in turn explains Singaphi's proficiency when it came to the PEARB's constitutional matters.

By 1971, Qeqe's Spring Rose was in a much stronger position when it came to resources and experience to consolidate and bring to fruition the idea of forming a breakaway KwaZakhele rugby union.[50] Botha explained:

> Back to 1963, there is a school of thought which believes that when Spring Rose and St. Cyprian's pulled out of the [PEARB], the latter club already had the idea of a KwaZakhele rugby union, but did not have the ability and the resources to implement it. The KwaZakhele rugby clubs believed that they were strong enough to form a sub-union and that St Cyprian's was capable of leading such [a] sub-union. The death of Eric Majola and the [PEARB's] decision not to heed to the request of Spring Rose to postpone the fixtures on the weekend of his funeral, worked right into the hands of St Cyprian's plan to form the KwaZakhele rugby union ... Then Spring Rose, angered by these decisions, garnered the support of other clubs including St Cyprian's to pull out of the [PEARB].[51]

In 1971, a playtime squabble raged between Whites and Vultures, a second-division rugby club. Whites allegedly won the match by cheating. Songongo, the one who is said to have cheated as the Whites linesman in that game, claimed that a Whites defeat would not have gone 'down well with the people. By "the people", I don't mean supporters of Union, but the rugby public.'[52] Relating how he apparently cheated, Songongo animatedly recalled:

> We played against Vultures. I was the linesman ... The match ended. No score. Sides were changed. I cheated there. The wing player got out ... I got out. I looked that way, I scored. We defeated Vultures. So, I nearly died. The supporters of Vultures chased after me. But I

> ran, my friend! I ran like that! But as I ran, I knew that I didn't care. I didn't care, we beat them, that's it. I didn't care.[53]

At the start of the 1971 rugby season, when Spring Rose faced Whites in a derby, its players refused to take to the field in protest against soft points apparently due to them from the previous season in a match against St Cyprian's. This resulted in the cancellation of the derby.

The majority of black rugby clubs had not yet, at the time, adopted a multiracial sports ideology. It was only from 1972, when Kwaru affiliated to the non-racial SARU, that a non-racial sports ideology began to gain considerable traction among Qeqe and his associates.

Before then, proponents of non-racial sports, including Qeqe, all participated in racially segregated, state-sponsored rugby. However, Qeqe and his associates at the time might have been amenable to the growing tide of non-racial sports liberation ideology. Qeqe had been conscientised at a formative age,[54] and Harold Wilson recalled his and Qeqe's conscious socialisation when it came to non-racial sports in Port Elizabeth during the 1950s. Both teaching primary school at the time, they would meet to play cricket on Sundays. Wilson was administrator of the PE Lads club, while Qeqe was in the administration of Spring Rose. Wilson recalled:

> So I met Dan Qeqe on a Sunday afternoon. He was a teacher. I was a teacher. As youngsters, we had just started playing. He was a hooker. I was flank at number eight … We regarded Sunday as a practice [day]. And then we played against one of the black teams … All those teams, all the black teams, Easterns, all of them, we used to play them … And so we talked to each other, and that is how it is our vision to have a uniformed, united organisation in which our people can participate in.[55]

According to Mveleli Ncula, there were long, drawn-out machinations, meetings and schemes aimed at bringing non-racial sports to Port Elizabeth long before Majola's death. He explained:

> In fact, the funeral of Majola was a camouflage … because already, people like Bhuti Silas Nkanunu and Mr Den [Dennis] Siwisa were

> always meeting with the members of the Western Cape Rugby, which was a Coloured union. And those guys were already under the umbrella of SACOS. As you remember, SACOS, the cry was that you can't play normal rugby in an abnormal society. So the guys in the Western Cape were already imbued with that spirit. And they decided now to spread it to other parts. And Eastern Cape was regarded as the home of black rugby, as you know. And therefore it was natural to be targeted, you know, to participate under SACOS. Dan Qeqe, Den Siwisa, and Silas Nkanunu were already attending these meetings. The Majola funeral then gave them an opportunity now to spread the gospel of non-racialism. That's when it started.[56]

Botha, in turn, affirmed, 'While the argument that the reasons for Kwaru's breakaway from the PEARB was not in pursuit of the non-racialism philosophy may be valid, it cannot be denied that some of its leaders were involved in progressive political activities.'[57] These political motivations were not, however, discernible at the time.

This is an important point to make, because there is a temptation to draw causal non-racial versus multiracial ideological links to conflicts between the PEARB and Kwaru. Before Kwaru was formed, there were no apparent dissatisfactions with the ideology and stances of SAARB and multiracial sports. With the politicisation of sport from 1956, it became easier to draw bifurcations between pro- and anti-apartheid sports bodies. State-created sports bodies, with their establishment in 1935 by Prime Minister JB Hertzog,[58] became apartheid ideologue bodies, and so PEARB and its administrators, such as Singaphi and Dwesi, readily became demonised.

This understanding of which sports body and which sports administrator was pro- and anti-apartheid is not quite as clear-cut, however, despite the fact that it has gone down in history in a linear, parallel fashion. In Port Elizabeth, there existed a degree of incestuousness in the associations between Qeqe, Singaphi, Dwesi, Mdyesha, David Mbane and others. In the 1960s and 1970s, Qeqe, Singaphi, Dwesi and Mbane were all members of the Port Elizabeth Joint Bantu Advisory Board[59] – and this serves to deconstruct the notion in Kwaru's populist oral history that there were acute, innate political differences among these individuals.

It is an impression that has falsely claimed that there were two political camps right from the beginning. Even when non-racial sports gained traction, and Qeqe fully campaigned on its behalf, the incestuousness among individuals in state collaborationist bodies remained – right up until the late 1970s. They were all members of the PEARB and SAARB. Rather, it was Mono Badela, Silas Nkanunu and Dennis Siwisa who came directly from anti-apartheid and non-racial sports liberation organisations and traditions.

Many sports administrators who became non-racial ideologues, including Qeqe and David Mbane, served in the same local state collaborationist bodies, such as the native advisory boards, as Singaphi, Dwesi, Mdyesha and Tanana. In fact, Qeqe, Singaphi, Dwesi and Mbane all sat on the same PEARB, and constituted part of the deliberations on the Bantu Registration and Labour Bureau, rent collections, home evictions, welfare and recreation, poor relief rations, the Ferguson Road Youth Club, the National War Memorial Hall Youth Club, the New Brighton Oval Stadium, the KwaFord Stadium and the Wolfson Stadium, as well as on the dissensions within the PEARB.[60]

So, while the PEARB readily became a pro-apartheid sports body post-1956, black rugby administrators tended to occupy somewhat ambivalent positions, despite their avowed non-racial sports liberation ideology. There was thus a murkiness of ideological loyalties. Non-racial sports bodies uneasily accommodated administrators who professed non-racial sports liberation ideology, yet carried responsibilities in local state collaborationist bodies.

Even their commitments to multiracial sports ideology cannot be understood in a linear, parallel way. Ideological lines were foggy at times, and racial compartmentalisation of multiracial and non-racial sports was not always clear in one continuum of time. For instance, Mdyesha, veteran sports administrator in SAARB, had long warned against the racially discriminative manner in which sports fields and sports amenities were used to favour one racial group over another.

Mdyesha pointed this out to the Cape Town Municipality, which was seen to act in favour of coloured rugby clubs, offering them privileged access to stadiums, in contrast to African rugby clubs. Sometime in the 1960s, he wrote to the Department of Bantu Administration of Cape

Town protesting against the provision of sports amenities in favour of the then predominantly coloured SARU. He warned that 'SARU is allowed to make use of our grounds when we and our Union are not allowed to use grounds belonging to Coloureds will ultimately lead to trouble of a very serious nature'.[61]

It is clear, then, that it was the politics built into the commotion behind the birth of Kwaru that gave it an overarching and abiding political impression.[62] The skirmish took on a political hue because of the attention that it received from both the local and national cabinets. It was Kwaru's affiliation to SARU, an affiliate of SACOS, already a well-known critical opponent of multiracial sports, that made Kwaru's birth political.

The commotion even came to the attention of the Port Elizabeth Joint Bantu Advisory Board. With Qeqe, Singaphi, Dwesi and Ximiya attending the 1971 meeting of the board as elected members, and Reverends Molefe and Jolobe as nominated members, along with AT Yeko,[63] the meeting noted:

> A number of rugby clubs were dissatisfied with the election results of the Port Elizabeth African Rugby Board. As a result of this, nine rugby clubs broke away from the P.E.A.R.B and formed their own union called the KwaZakhele African Rugby Union (K.W.A.R.U.).
>
> This has had repercussions at the national level, resulting in a split in the executive of the S.A.A.R.B. The Joint Bantu Advisory Board's aid was sought to settle the differences between the two local rugby unions and to form a properly representative Port Elizabeth African Rugby Board.
>
> The Advisory Board decided that the constitution of the P.E.A.R.B. was in urgent need of revision. A new constitution is accordingly in the process of being drawn up. It is hoped that the new constitution will be accepted by both unions and so be the instrument of reconciliation.[64]

Acknowledging these imperfections in his assessment of the institutional history of the University of Fort Hare, Daniel Massey asserted that, 'Years removed from the events they are discussing, interviewees are of course susceptible to romanticising the past, or to placing it in a context to fit with their current beliefs.'[65]

The need for comprehensive oral historical accounts of Kwaru's history is remedial in the face of a large gap created by its undocumented history, and it is these gaps that have created spaces for embellishment. In its paranoia concerning political activism, the apartheid government shut down much of the documentary processes of Kwaru's activities. This clampdown was similarly applied to other non-racial sports activities elsewhere in South Africa.[66] Taking photographs of the play and scores of Kwaru and other non-racial sporting bodies was not allowed, and certainly not encouraged.[67] As Ray Mali explained:

> And unfortunately, very little written material is found, because when the apartheid government came into being, when they see a cricket scorebook with these names, *ja*, *zizinto zeANC ezi. Baph' aba bantu*? (yes, these are ANC activities. Where are these people?) People had to be rounded up because they appear in the cricket scorebook, hence you don't have a lot of records. You don't have pictures.[68]

Mpumelelo 'Sbhidla' Majola, also a former Spring Rose and Kwaru player, added that:

> One of the major issues Kwaru faced, why you don't get the history of Kwaru, of non-racialism in sport, was that the recording of matters concerning Kwaru was not allowed. Reporters were not allowed, nothing was allowed, do you understand? So, even in the field, no one was allowed to take photographs ... There were no recordings permitted. There was nothing permitted. But it was clear that Kwaru was being used by political organisations, do you get what I'm talking about? It was used by the ANC, it was used by the PAC. All the political organisations used Kwaru.[69]

Kwaru's leadership was to be dominated by Badela for the next six years, with Qeqe in the background. Nkanunu and Siwisa were also not in the Kwaru executive committee. Nonetheless, Qeqe played a significant role, and built his base during this time. He had grown into a popular figure in rugby and non-racial sporting circles, well regarded for his hard work ethic, sense of commitment, strict financial discipline, and empathy for impoverished sportsmen.

Songongo, however, ascribed Qeqe's absence from Kwaru's first executive committee to his reputation for instigating club break-ups, splits and breakaways – a reputation that had doggedly followed him and his associates in Spring Rose. 'If Qeqe and his associates had emerged in the leadership at that time, from Spring Rose, it was not going to garner support.'[70]

Qeqe's life and times are thus unavoidably a social history of the struggles of the people of Port Elizabeth. The man and his historical context should be holistically understood if one is to offer up a well-measured social and institutional history of Kwaru and Port Elizabeth. As Nick Salvatore put it, 'The value of understanding a particular life in its broad social context is precisely this: it examines the process of historical change through an individual who, like other humans, grapples simultaneously with complex forces both public and private.'[71]

His role in the birth of Kwaru reflected long-held traditions, patterns and a culture of rapturous beginnings – and endings – of rugby clubs. These had begun to spring up in the last quarter of the nineteenth century, and he rode them, a move that led inadvertently to the birth of Kwaru. By their hands, they created a vehicle in Kwaru that forged new political traditions of political activism, moving forward the collective political and social aspirations of the people of Port Elizabeth.

6

'UP KWARU!'

On 3 April 1981, the 37-year-old senior lecturer in Theology at the University of Fort Hare in Alice, Reverend Makhenkesi Arnold Stofile, addressed the Victoria East Rugby Union (VERU).[1] Drilling zeal into them as VERU's outgoing president, he said, 'I have enough confidence in our players that if they exert themselves to the full and do not suffer from inferiority complexes, then we should be equal match even to Kwaru, Tygerberg, etc.'[2]

In the 10 years since its formation, Kwaru had changed the face of rugby in South Africa. As Ray Mali attested, it was:

> … something that changed the face of rugby in the whole Eastern Cape, and in the whole of South Africa … It was something that reshaped the whole set-up of rugby, and it moved on to places like Graaff-Reinet. We had Central Karoo. Down here we had SEDRU – South Eastern District Rugby Union. We had the Border guys here.[3]

Kwaru arrived on the black rugby scene with a powerful and characteristic playing prowess that went on to beat many of SARU's much older affiliates. As Stofile confirmed in his 1981 address, Kwaru's SA Cup-winning streak was something VERU ought to emulate. With Kwaru assuming the position of a leading beacon in non-racial sports, it inspired a significant following of rugby unions, pushing newer rugby unions to join non-racial sports liberation bodies. VERU thus came into existence significantly moulded by Kwaru.

In 1973, Stofile and his associates established VERU, a union driven by a highly capable political force in the form of GN Stofile, MD Jobodwana, R Currie, R Cebisa, Mthobi Tyamzashe, Smuts Ngonyama, M Mana, GX Ponono, Ngconde Balfour and S Sintu.[4] So committed to non-racial sports liberation was VERU, Booley pointed out, that it 'saw sport not only as recreation but also as a base to continue the struggle against apartheid. At the same time the union openly referred to sport as an institution of non-racialism'.[5]

While Kwaru stumbled into non-racial sports, VERU purposely rooted itself in it. Growing from four to 25 rugby clubs, it affiliated to SARU in 1980, playing in the Rhodes Cup Tournament that same year.[6] Underlining this commitment in the same address, Stofile reminded VERU that it was formed 'not because of any accident of history, but because we wanted to foster the ideal of normal sport, non-racial sport. Those who were in the first two years of the Union's existence will remember the resistance met against the effort.'[7]

The 1972–74 swarm of Port Elizabeth-based students at the University of Fort Hare significantly influenced the non-racial direction of rugby at the university[8] – a move directly inspired by the formation and nascent political struggles of Kwaru in Port Elizabeth. And so Kwaru became not only a role model when it came to rugby skills, but a widely influential, political symbol of black pride.

In the 1970s, non-racial rugby and non-racial sports in general spread widely, and this was particularly felt in the Eastern Cape. Non-racial rugby had become so pervasive that '[even] in the rural areas like Tshatshu, Qalashe, people were driven to play non-racial sports, because that's all they knew that was coming up even in their areas, it was non-racial rugby.'[9]

For the first time in the history of Port Elizabeth's black communities, a rugby union became a political and cultural sensation all rolled into a commanding playing force. Emblematic of emerging black consciousness, its rhinoceros 'with that horn'[10] insignia was appropriated as 'Up Kwaru! It was a 'Black Power' salute subverted in sport, in a packed stadium named after a living black man at the height of apartheid. So, 'when you raise that fist, even if there is a police informer in the midst there, we are just saying, "Up Kwaru." That is a "Black Power" salute for some of us.'[11]

It was no coincidence that Kwaru embodied the spirit of black consciousness at such a time, in a Port Elizabeth historically highly responsive to anti-apartheid political mobilisation. Judge Somyalo reflected on how it was no coincidence either that Kwaru soon appropriated black pride. This was the political mood of the time in which Kwaru came into being. He argued that Kwaru filled the void, following the ban of the ANC and the PAC of Azania. And it particularly filled that space at a time that was ideologically dominated by Black Consciousness and the activities of the Black Consciousness Movement (BCM).[12]

Kwaru's message of non-racial sports liberation spread far and wide fast. Judge Lex Mpati, then a Grahamstown-based rugby player in the fold of SEDRU, and later a SARU administrator, remembered a Kwaru that was fast attracting attention when he visited Langa Township in Cape Town in 1971. It was a sensation that soon assumed a political tone, and attracted the attendant clampdown:

> That's what I heard, in '71, and came, after Eastners, later on, I started hearing about this KwaZakhele Rugby Union playing rugby and commented on in Xhosa radio, when they played their games. And Kwaru got, got publicised, as it were, because there was commentary on their games. I don't know, it stopped later on because the powers that be must have realised that, hey, here's something happening. We don't agree with this team that's playing in the non-racial fold, and being publicised and getting time on air. And the commentary on Kwaru stopped.[13]

In just a few years, Kwaru had quickly metamorphosed into 'The 'Mighty Kwaru … beating every team they played against.'[14] It won the SA Cup in 1975, 1976 and 1979.[15] And central in moulding Kwaru's playing prowess was Dan Qeqe and his doggedly Herculean training regimen. His was a highly unpopular routine, with its own peculiar balance between physical fitness, ball and rugby-playing skills.

Nonetheless, it was Qeqe's trademark training style that turned the Kwaru team into a sensation. Animatedly recalling a match between Kwaru and the 'Blues', the University of Fort Hare Rugby Football Club team, hosted in Alice in the mid-1970s, Tyamzashe painted the following scene of Kwaru's showmanship:

> I was at Fort Hare, and Fort Hare, the Blues, their rugby team, wanted a match with Kwaru. I remember we played the curtain-raisers in Alice, at the Davidson Stadium. It was an evening game. Kwaru was not there. Hey! Where is this Kwaru? Hey! We just saw a convoy of cars. Poo! Poo! The stadium went wild. These guys came out of these cars, already in their kits. Remember everyone says that they'll be late. From the cars, into the field. I'm talking about household names. You know when a big man is playing another, they don't use their stars. I'm talking about Themba Ludwaba. I'm talking about … yho!
>
> I just say, these guys! I mean, I never knew rugby and forward play until I was associated with that thinking. They had this thing called 'the Rolling Maul'. When it's a few yards from the scoring line, the chances are that they are going to score, because they move like this thing [gesticulating a wave with hands]. It's called the 'Rolling Maul' … They're just rolling … What I'm trying to say is, I started to say, we can beat white guys with this kind of rugby that they're playing.[16]

Ngconde Balfour reminisced with similar energy about that match: 'Kwaru and Fort Hare. Bro' Stof was running here on the line. Bro' Stof was a bulky person. He ran on the line when we were leading Kwaru.'[17] And, after the match, Balfour recalled how Qeqe, using his old tried-and-tested pilfering ways of recruiting players from outside Port Elizabeth, failed against Stofile's determination:

> After the match, we met with Oom Dan. Oom Dan tried his best to get some of us to go to PE. And Bro' Stof said, when I told him that Oom Dan said, 'Ngconde, can I see you?' Bro' Stof said, 'He is not going anywhere … This is the captain of VERU, you can't do that … He's teaching here, and we want him to stay here, here in Alice.'

> ... And we told Bro' Stof, not knowing anything, thinking that we were going to get paid. There was no money at that time. And he said, 'No, no, no, no, you are not going to get paid, Ngconde.'[18]

Although not on the Kwaru executive committee,[19] Qeqe shaped Kwaru's rugby-playing character. Many remembered his punishing training methods, often placing a premium on physical fitness over 'fancy' rugby skills taught by the then coach, Mohammed Agherdien.[20] Arghedien had a preoccupation with 'skills, ball control, this rugby that New Zealand plays – keep the ball; four men, four hands; you know, how to bump into another player, turn and give a ball out, do you understand?'[21] A stickler when it came to his belief that '99 per cent fitness, and other things, like skills, are in that one per cent,'[22] Mpumelelo 'Sbhidla' Majola recalled Qeqe's gruelling training methods:

> Baas Dan, his thing was one: 'My children, I see what Arghedien is doing to you. It's shit, my friend! But then, my children, first run around the field.' And then you are going to run and run and run. When he sees that you are about to get exhausted, frog jump then was standard, it was his favourite. One, two, one, two. You would frog jump then.[23]

And then, when the team was completely exhausted, Qeqe would throw in impromptu races from Veeplaas to the New Brighton Beach and back – a combined distance of 22–26 kilometres. On these additional races, Majola pointed out, 'No one dare says he is tired. You do what Baas Dan says. He was that kind of person.'[24] Nonetheless, they 'were not panting at all. We were used to it. It was part of the menu. We knew it.'[25] Respectful and yet loathing Qeqe's presence on the field, Archie Mkele recalled of his gladiatorial training style:

> In Kwaru he was assisting with the coaching, you know, and he was strict, DDQ. You know when he was training, we could feel it. It was hard. It was unlike the other guys ... Yho! *Isele* [the frog], frog jump, he used to like it. By the time we finished playing, we would be finished, my friend. With DDQ, we were not happy when he's around. We knew it was gonna be hard training.[26]

And, with Agherdien's training in 'fancy' rugby skills concluded, '[Qeqe] would again time us as we were leaving, when we were done. If he fancied to take us for training again, he would do it. No one would complain. "You are going to shit, my friend!" he would say.'[27] And matching Qeqe's keenness for hard, extreme training was his commitment to Kwaru's team cohesion. Valence Watson, a former Kwaru player from the Wallabies Rugby Football Club, remembered:

> He was always there for training. He didn't have to be there. He was there before anybody else. And in winter when it was very cold, my wife would make sandwiches for the players, for after practice. And Dan would make sure that 'Ma'am', Mrs Qeqe, would make a pot of soup. So the players would come off the field, would go to the Qeqe home, and they would feed the players.[28]

Qeqe also made personal financial commitments to Kwaru players. When the concept of sponsorship was alien to black rugby clubs, individual black entrepreneurs in Port Elizabeth's townships often found themselves roped in to offer financial aid to specific clubs. So it became customary for each club to informally adopt a local businessman as its sponsor. Songongo recalled Qeqe's financial sacrifices:

> He used to sacrifice a lot for Spring Rose, because at that time, club money was embezzled. He used to sacrifice a lot, to the extent of buying jerseys from his own pocket, and use his own lorries to ferry us. We used lorries then as players. He was a generous person. For instance, if you struggled financially, a poor person, he would take you aside and buy you rugby shoes, buy everything for you … And there were not a lot of people who had money at that time, do you understand?[29]

Few other players had either the ability or the inclination to make such financial sacrifices. Ray Mali, then a regular waged worker, was one of those few players. Recalling his own financial sacrifice to his club, he stated:

> My club, Orientals, the Blues, didn't have the kit because the

> stronger faction in our club took it. I had to give up my monthly salary at the bottle store in 1971, to buy a set of jerseys at Croft Magill, a sports shop in town, to kit those 18 players who were going to play … I had to give it up to buy these, because I was asked by the club. And my family understood. We had to do it. That was in 1971, in order to make it possible for my club to be part of that.[30]

Qeqe's commitment to Kwaru also often found expression in the encouragement he offered players. Songongo recalled that, 'He would go past you, and watch you and encourage you. There was one thing he always drilled in you at that time I was in Spring Rose: keep away from drinks. Keep away from drinks.'[31] Ncula also remembered Qeqe for his teetotal ways, although he was slightly less rigid at triumphant times following a well-executed administrative task by his players:

> No, he didn't drink. He was a teetotaller … But one thing he was good at, again, I mean we were still young, we were still drinking at that time. He'll say, '*Hayi* [No], guys, you've done good work,' and take money out of his own pocket, not from the Kwaru money, and say, 'Go and buy yourself stuff.'[32]

One innovation Qeqe used to make sure that alcohol abuse did not get in the way of fitness and performance before a game was a strategy known as *kulukuthu*. *Kulukuthu* is not a verb in its own right, but an isiXhosa sound-associative word assuming the place of an adjective or verb sometimes. It is a sounded mimic of a thudding, a sudden and rushed hurling of a throng of people in an enclosed space. Ncula explained that this practice entailed gathering all the players in a small hall at the back of Qeqe's place the Friday night before the game. It was also a practice that certain rugby clubs in East London put up their players in community halls the night before games.[33] There, Qeqe and his wife accommodated them for the night, with all their meals and other assortments prepared, so that they woke fresh and ready the following day. After the game, they gathered at Qeqe's house again.[34]

However, Qeqe's teetotal, disciplinarian ways seldom bore fruit on the home front. Frustrated, he grappled with this with his own out-of-wedlock son, Michael. Unfortunately, of all his children, Michael bore a striking resemblance to Qeqe in every physical aspect and dimension. It was this likeness that unfortunately tumbled out in public as the spitting image of a drunken Dan Qeqe. Mpumelelo 'Sbhidla' Majola recalled how this tragi-comedy had played itself out once in Cape Town, when everyone who had seen Mike thought that he was a drunk Qeqe.[35]

Alan Zinn also emphasised this aspect of discipline, pointing out that, 'There's a social aspect to the whole sport thing, the whole discipline of it, because you can't be having drugs and alcohol, and you want to play.'[36] This determination to ensure discipline often spilled over off the field. Songongo recalled his personal experience in this regard:

> Like, the senior officials of rugby clubs … they would go and check on you without you knowing that they were checking on you. They would ask if Thami was at home, do you understand? Maybe it's about nine, past nine, you're supposed to be home … A car would just park outside there, 'Is Thami available?' 'No, he's not here.' They're going to ask about your whereabouts tomorrow. 'When did you come back home last night?' Do you understand? Baas Dan was a disciplinarian in that way.[37]

The social aspect also related to administrative skills development. This often included the character development of players, who found these valuable in their career and work-skills development. Said Zinn:

> You're learning skills. And then when they think you're good enough, they say … you can be our club rep to the union, mmh? Then you go to the union meetings. Then you have to report back. Then from the union, maybe you're gonna go even higher, to the SA, to the SA meetings. So there was a whole lot of training and development going on, naturally, from the bottom.[38]

Ncula referred to this as a 'passing the baton' to the next generation. He maintained that Qeqe was 'very good at that, because he said let us give an opportunity to younger people … He did the same thing with Kwaru as well. When he saw that there were youngsters like myself and others, and like Feya [Sobikwa] there, then he withdrew a bit.'[39]

Gerald Majola affirmed his own training in sports administration and development from Qeqe in the same way. He pointed out that this was often necessary back then due to a lack of administrative staff. And so players had to dabble in the administration of their rugby clubs and Kwaru, while still contending with the rigours of training and playing, as young as they were. This went a long way in their training on constitutional interpretation and the intricacies of the procedures of meetings.[40]

Numerous leading administrators in post-apartheid South African sport came under Dan Qeqe's training. These included Danny Jordaan, Alistair Coetzee, Silas Nkanunu and Ray Mali. 'All these people came from the same [hands] … We were all, at one stage, all of us were heading the sports of the country,'[41] Gerald Majola pointed out.

The immersion of a young black player in a rugby club often meant profound social mobility opportunities. Impoverished young men from the townships and informal settlements achieved upward mobility through rugby, certainly much more swiftly than what they would have hoped to achieve through the traditional school–college–work route. A spectacular rags-to-well-to-do story coming out of Kwaru and Spring Rose is that of Lucky 'Coach' Mange. By the age of 64, Mange had been involved in rugby for five decades, having started his rugby career when he joined Spring Rose in his teens in 1969.[42] Within two months of joining Spring Rose, he had moved up to its senior side. From there, he was selected to play for SARU.[43] Narrating how he started out in rugby, Mange reminisced:

> Yes, Vuba. Then I used to carry his bag, and I used to watch the Rose players. And, hey, I was beaten as punishment at home for coming home late after spending time with Spring Rose players. But I knew that I loved rugby … You see, in the past, we used to even marvel at the players getting dressed about to go home. I used to watch them, because in the past we used to impersonate everything they did. Even the way they walked, their styles, the way they were, we used to impersonate them … Then I joined them.[44]

Other players who also joined rugby clubs were inspired by older black players, and watching them changed their perceptions of professional black rugby. Many black players from rural and farm areas were initially exposed to rugby that was played bare-chested. It was called *kalgat* rugby, the rural form of rugby played 'without jerseys as youngsters,'[45] recollected Archie Mkele. Ngcaphe recalled that:

> I arrived here in Port Elizabeth in 1967, coming here from the farms, from that side of Greenbushes … I remember watching rugby, [the] first few matches, that I watched here … I watched Bhomza Nkohla … To be quite honest, it was the first time I watched grown men playing rugby. At the farms at that time, rugby was played by boys. Secondly, it was the first time I saw people playing rugby wearing jerseys, because when we played rugby, we played half-naked.[46]

Mange, whose family was from eMaplangeni, an informal settlement in New Brighton, has only two years of high school education. It was only by way of socialisation through rugby that he came to realise how different his own youth had been compared to those of middle-class youth from better areas in the townships. As he put it, 'I was shocked when I saw that Khaya [Majola][47] had a bedroom. Yhu! These chaps! Then when I started working, all this motivated me that I should hurry up in getting well settled.'[48]

Mange looked with fresh eyes on his home environment when he started working because he saw how his rugby skills made him a valuable member of the team. As he expressed it, '[It] became clear that I was important, they even pick me up with cars.'[49] The impact of playing club rugby thus reoriented his perceptions of family and his responsibilities, bolstering his determination to aim for a much higher standard of living. 'Now, I saw quite early that, hey, these people, I don't want them to see my personal environment … Then, when I started working, I realised that, no *maan*, I didn't know that a person should take care of his house and family. I just lived. And an environment has an influence, you see?'[50] Elevated to playing for Kwaru meant that he flew with the team to different locations for matches. That in itself inflated his self-worth and status.

Some of the transformations in the attitudes of young black rugby players were conveyed through role-modelling. Mpumelelo 'Sbhidla' Majola related how the professional and social demeanour of some Kwaru administrators left a profound impression on his perception of what an upstanding member of society should look like:

> [We] are able to run families from playing there in Spring Rose. You see, Mr Siwisa, when they attend functions and matches with their wives, and the wife of Bro' Stof and their children, and the wife of Toto [Tsotsobe] ... Remember that it is families who attended those functions and matches, those families ... You look at these gentlemen, the way they are so dignified.[51]

Kwaru's effectiveness enchanted Port Elizabeth's townships. Rugby was enormously popular – way more so than soccer. For instance, in a Kwaru–Natal rugby match played in 1973, gate collection passed R8 000, inclusive of Kwaru's donation of R500 to the *Evening Post* School Fund. The match had gone on, 'despite gale-force winds and driving rain on Saturday' and 'Kwaru still kept up a festive air at the Zwide Stadium where the drum majorettes of Newell High School entertained the crowd before the big game'.[52] Mrs Nozuko 'Girlie' Pikoli, who was then a young lady managing her father's general dealership in Veeplaas, remembered how intensely popular rugby was:

> So when these teams would be playing at Dan Qeqe, I'm telling you, nothing happens, even taverns they don't work. There's no one. Nobody gets drunk. Soccer, there's no soccer to play on that day. You know, people are sitting there with their radios, [those] who can't go to the stadium. And the radio, you can hear from anywhere.[53]

Similarly, Gerald Majola remembered:

> Kwaru, when Kwaru played, even going to town, on Saturday, people by eleven o' clock, they are rushing to be at the Dan Qeqe Stadium because they would not get a seat ... That's why, I think, even the consciousness, the political consciousness in PE was that strong, because it was easy to drive it through sport, because the

> main thing then was rugby. Rugby had a pull. Football of *eBhayi* [Port Elizabeth] was not as, as, it's bigger now than rugby. But it was not even half of what rugby was when Kwaru was still at its height.[54]

A further indication of the popularity of rugby was the overcrowding at the stadium, and how that had become a constant feature. In 1978, overcrowding caused a riot. 'A press report and inconvenience caused by overcrowding were the main factors creating the tense atmosphere in which rioting occurred at a rugby match in Port Elizabeth on Saturday, a leading sports administrator said last night.'[55] The press went on to quote Qeqe, 'What added to the tension was the inconvenience of sitting in a crowded stadium virtually all day. There are about 2000 seats and more than 20 000 attended.'[56]

A major cause of the riot was a mistake made by a referee. Reverend SM Arends cautioned how that mistake was excessively up-scaled by fans. Then the chairman of the Port Elizabeth Coloured Management Committee, he commented, 'But I feel people must accept that a referee can make a mistake, and that a rugby match is a not a matter of life and death.'[57] In another press report on another riot, Qeqe tried to calm down the fans, promising them a better game in the following Kwaru–Eastern Province (EP) match. Fans had nonetheless shouted, 'We shall not come, we shall not watch until we get a better team.'[58]

As much as Qeqe was central in moulding Kwaru into a formidable playing force, his role in forging its iconic political status between 1971 and 1977 was overshadowed by Sipho Arthur Mono Badela. Popularly known as Mono Badela, he was a rotund fellow, built close to the ground. Many considered him charismatic, intellectual and politically astute. 'Mono had ability,'[59] Watson said of him. Watson further characterised Badela as 'by no means a dictator'.[60] 'He was a democrat to the extreme. That was Badela. He always wanted to encourage the other people.'[61] Some of these traits emerged against a background that included well-grounded credentials in political journalism.

Badela was Kwaru's publicist, strategist and unwitting hype-maker, and became synonymous with the construction of the struggle-iconic Kwaru image.

One crucial event led by Badela that catapulted Kwaru to public notoriety was the recruitment of the Watson brothers into Kwaru in 1976–77. A Kwaru executive board meeting had decided to encourage the Watson brothers to join different Kwaru-affiliated rugby clubs. Thus, Cheeky joined Spring Rose, Valance went to Wallabies, Gavin joined St Cyprian's, and Ronnie became a member of Park Rovers.[62]

'Mono Badela came to our shops and heard Christian music playing. And he asked, "Are we Christian?" and we said, "Yes." He said, then why don't you come and help and do some coaching in the townships, which we then did. And in doing that, it happened to be the Kwaru players.'[63] Valance Watson thus described the first recruitment intervention he had with Badela.

Kwaru's public image thus loomed larger and larger, particularly after its first game involving the Watson brothers and other white players from Grahamstown. Following that game – regarded by Danie Craven as having 'reflected badly on the country'[64] – Alan Paton telephoned Badela, registering that he was 'disappointed to learn from the Press at the weekend that they were being harassed by police and others to abandon their stand'.[65] Qeqe played an actively supportive role,[66] but it was Badela who took leadership in these campaigns and activities.

Watson described the rationale behind their involvement in township rugby, and the impact this had on Kwaru:

> I think, in my view, the most important thing was not the rugby. The most important thing was the liberation. And if rugby can go to a degree to help that process, then so be it. We did have a voice. We were able to touch the world. I mean, this was a worldwide thing. I mean, all over the world, the Kwaru non-racial sports struggle was making the media.[67]

Born and bred in Port Elizabeth, Badela credited his political conscientisation to his mother. 'I got this talent and ability to go through the struggle, I sucked it from her,'[68] he said and, further narrating his route to political conscientisation, reminisced that:

> While I was here in Port Elizabeth, I saw political movements. I watched everything during the bus boycotts. I was new in this political struggle. I started these right from the beginning. It

> originated in 1957 ... That time I was still wearing short pants. That was the first time I had a clash with the police. We were arrested by the police.[69]

He went to Newell High School, and then proceeded to the University of Fort Hare. Although he had aspired to be a lawyer, he started out working as a recreation officer, opening Patapata, a youth club in New Brighton.[70] It was particularly through his journalism, practised at the *Evening Post*, that he created space for the hype that would centre on Kwaru. Affirming this role, Ngcaphe maintained, 'It's easy to publicise, to market this thing, and Badela is a journalist for the *Evening Post*. So, we were in the newspapers all the time.'[71]

His political journalism skills were honed during his years at the coalface of reporting apartheid's conflicts. Professor Guy Berger, former head of department of Journalism and Media Studies at Rhodes University, wrote in tribute to Badela in November 2002, 'How does a young white South African become a journalism professor, getting there via political imprisonment, time in exile and a job in the alternative press? The answer is: the influence of Mono Badela.'[72]

Berger credited Badela's journalism with putting major South African trade unions, the Port Elizabeth Black Civic Organisation (PEBCO) and the Congress of South African Students (COSAS), on the national political map.[73] He wrote that, 'That quality was evident in Badela's bylines that came to national prominence on this paper's predecessor, the *Sunday World*, banned in 1977. His articles caught my eye as a young student at the time because they brought inspiring news of the otherwise unreported heroic struggles.'[74]

Also paying tribute to Badela, Chris Barron remembered him for covering 'some of the most brutal violence of the apartheid era in the Eastern Cape during the 1970s and 1980s'.[75] Consequently, he was subject to a number of bannings and constant police harassment throughout the 1970s and 1980s. In June 1978, a meeting of the Writers' Association of South Africa (WASA) in Port Elizabeth, of which he was part, was banned as a breach of the Riotous Assemblies Act.[76] In the same year, 'three white and three black policemen in two cars visited Mr Badela's home in New Brighton shortly before midday',[77] and confiscated WASA publications.

In 1979, Badela was 'suspended from future meetings'[78] of the Port Elizabeth Community Council, along with B Mtomboti, the *Eastern Province Herald* reporter; Jimmy Matyu, Johannesburg representative of the *Evening Post*; and Dennis Siwisa, a *Daily Dispatch* representative. The council 'considered reports from various newspapers, the content of which was not to its satisfaction'.[79]

Badela fell victim to 'abduction, attempted murder, and severe ill-treatment'.[80] During the 1985 State of Emergency, 140 people were killed in political violence in Port Elizabeth,[81] the city – according to Tom Lodge and Mark Swilling – leading the death toll.[82] Secret police files revealed that 113 people were detained in Port Elizabeth and its environs during the 1985 State of Emergency.[83] As recorded in those files of 12 April 1985, there were '8 black people dead in 70 incidents'.[84]

On 5 June 1985, Mono Badela was, according to a police file, a '[victim] ... stabbed on the head (multiple wounds)'.[85] This came about as a result of his abduction and the severe, ill treatment he suffered at the hands of the Azanian People's Organisation (AZAPO) during a series of conflicts between the UDF and the 'Third Force' that had infiltrated AZAPO.[86] Commensurate with the seriousness of political insurgency in the area, police declared Port Elizabeth 'Prio 1 area' in 1985[87] – an indication of police prioritisation of the implementation of 'stabilisation and normalisation' measures in the area.[88]

Firmly in the leadership grip of Badela, the charismatic 'true blue ANC man',[89] Kwaru thrived between 1971 and 1975, despite state onslaught. In September 1971, the New Brighton and Fort Beaufort cricket clubs received permission to continue with their fund-raising mini-tournament on a municipal field, initially withdrawn because of Kwaru's participation.[90] This was driven by the collapsed membership of the two cricket clubs and Kwaru, the leadership of which were essentially the same people. Both cricket clubs were by then within the non-racial sports fold, and because the playing fields were under the PEARB's control and management, they were compelled to play on open fields. The withdrawal of the permission had come directly from Koch. As the press report outlined, 'The letter from Mr Koch said that the cricket board should take note that in view of the dissension in rugby circles, no clubs which have broken away from the PEARB should participate in any proposed match.'[91]

Badela's Kwaru executive committee wanted Solly Rubin, then mayor of Port Elizabeth, to intervene.[92] Patronage over the use of playing fields dispensed by local authorities had created divisions between the two dominant sports ideologies, with Mdyesha's prophecy to Cape Town's municipal authorities back in the 1940s that the racially motivated patronage over playing fields would 'ultimately lead to trouble of a very serious nature'[93] finally coming to pass. The seriousness of his prophecy also assumed a dangerously political hue, with Kwaru intentionally riding these political conflicts. At times, it did so out of sheer frustration, seeking not only to catapult itself into a non-racial sports liberation agency, but also to mainstream its involvement in anti-apartheid struggles. Kwaru then progressively became an anti-apartheid struggle platform.

In 1974, Kwaru stood its ground against fermented media reports that it was leaving SARU. These reports came immediately after the alleged dissatisfaction of some Kwaru players at SARU's decision to shelve the awarding of the SA Cup in 1974,[94] following a squabble between Kwaru and the Western Province. Boldly affirming Kwaru's non-racial stance, Badela pointed out that Kwaru's decision to remain in SARU was irrevocable. He insisted that:

> We joined Saru in 1972 because we were attracted by their policy of integrated rugby and the selection of national teams on merit. We joined Saru because we fell in love with the belief that sport knows no colour or race, a belief that has led to the loss of our playing fields and rightful facilities. There is something more important to us than sport and that is our human dignity and pride as human beings. This is our belief and not – I repeat – to win trophies.[95]

Mpati particularly singled out Kwaru's commitment to non-racialism as its most enduring historical feature. Observing this commitment from the gallery as a SARU administrator, he maintained that Kwaru 'stomached' all the state onslaught brought on by its commitment to non-racial rugby.[96] Thus, between 1971 and 1975, Badela's Kwaru leadership steadfastly held on to non-racialism against state onslaught.

The state's relentless attack expressed itself in the withdrawal of permission for Kwaru to play on municipal grounds. Then, in 1974, the Bantu Affairs Administration Board took away Kwaru's permission to play at the Zwide Stadium, Koch again exerting pressure on Kwaru to return to the fold of the PEARB. Unfaltering in its commitment to non-racialism, Kwaru was, however, 'prepared to play matches in the open veld, as in the past, rather than be intimidated into joining the National Bantu Rugby Board'.[97]

The attacks on Kwaru had thus become harsh and more dictatorial. As reported, 'Kwaru received a directive through the office of the Cape Midlands Bantu Affairs Administration Board, that because of Kwaru's continued affiliation to the non-racial South African Rugby Union, Kwaru might be deprived of playing facilities in the Port Elizabeth townships.'[98] The Bantu Affairs Administration Board continued to deny Kwaru access to the Zwide Stadium, with Koch attempting to upgrade the matter to cabinet level, determined to force Kwaru's hand and accept the directive of the local state. As reported, 'Kwaru was given permission to attend talks with the officials in Pretoria on condition that the delegation did not discuss the directive but advised Pretoria how Kwaru would effect its affiliation with the National Bantu Rugby Board.'[99]

It was to be a back and forth of attacks and counter-attacks. Kwaru lost many of these in tough litigation. This suppression on playing fields, however, snowballed into long-term consequences unforeseen by either Kwaru or the local state: the building of the Dan Qeqe Stadium. The black people's stadium that was to emerge from all of this became a powerful, black, political and social symbol and movement never before seen in Port Elizabeth or, in fact, elsewhere in South Africa. The building of the Dan Qeqe Stadium, however, planted the seed of cracks, eventually leading to the first implosion in Kwaru. And it was that melee that propelled Dan Qeqe. He rose to become a formidable force not only in the non-racial sports liberation struggles, but also in the political and social struggles of Port Elizabeth.

Perhaps the roles he carved out for himself and the history that has been carved out for him on the building of the Dan Qeqe Stadium came with some Machiavellian machinations.

7

BUILDING *e*DAN QEQE

By 1975, local state onslaught on Kwaru's playing-field rights was continuing unabated. Under pressure from Dr Craven and the South African government, the Cape Midlands Bantu Affairs Administration Board disallowed Kwaru from using the Zwide Stadium.[1] The decision was relayed in a letter by Louis Koch, chief director of the Cape Midlands Bantu Affairs Administration Board.

This punitive action came out of a 'deep rift'[2] in 'non-white rugby groups', triggered by Kwaru's refusal to nominate its members to the Leopards, who were set to play against the British Lions. Ray Mali asserted that, '[The Leopards] were part of the set-up that made sure that they would toe the line.'[3]

The entire set-up of the British Lions rugby tour of 1974–75 was orchestrated by Sipho McDonald Tanana, who managed to persuade the administrators to host it at his home turf of Mdantsane.[4] From Mdantsane, East London, he admitted that he took advantage of divisions in Port Elizabeth's black rugby circles, considering the anomaly that was the conflict in the city. In his observation, 'It was only in PE …'[5] that this conflict had developed between non-racial, multinational and the local state. He had then convinced the Minister of Bantu Affairs and Administration that the match should be played in Mdantsane. And so, in 1975, Kwaru found itself grasping at straws, in need of a playing field.

There was some urgency: Kwaru was in a bind, with an obligation to host SARU's premier SA Cup final match of 1975. But it had no stadium to host the match for the SA Cup it so coveted. Admitting to this urgency, Silas Nkanunu remembered, 'Yes, the Dan Qeqe Stadium, you see, we were denied facilities, Kwaru, by the local authority under the administration of Koch … We had an SA Cup final. I think us, Kwaru, played against Tygerberg … And no ground to play.'[6]

Kwaru's split from the PEARB meant that the most talented players were taken from the PEARB. With Kwaru and its cream players having moved to the non-racial fold, this had left a void in the Leopards. Nyondo distinctly remembered the sequence of events behind the British Lions tour that eventually led to the withdrawal of permission for Kwaru to use Zwide Stadium:

> And what had happened is that in 1974, pending the arrival of the British Lions, what they had wanted was that they approached Kwaru, to say that there are a few players that they would want to see. In fact, [the] South African Rugby Association wanted a few of the stars from Kwaru to play for the Leopards team. And of course, quite understandably, that was chucked out. And then the might of the state was used via Louis Koch to say, close the Zwide Stadium for Kwaru, that they must not be allowed to play at the Zwide Stadium. Then that left Kwaru with a major problem: where are we going to play our fixtures?[7]

Wilson also maintained that SARU refused to contribute to the consolidation of a 'native team' in Leopards, which contradicted their ethos of non-racialism, both in spirit and in practice. Consequently, the Cape Midlands Bantu Affairs Administration Board took away the use of all the fields Kwaru played on in Port Elizabeth. And so Kwaru was left without a playing field,[8] and resorted to playing on school grounds. For Easterns, that was KwaZakhele High School, while Spring Rose played at Newell High School. But this arrangement still left a long list of other Kwaru-affiliated clubs who had no playing fields.[9]

There was thus an urgency to find a field for Kwaru to host the SA Cup final match of 1975. What followed next was an opening of the floodgates of theories on how Dan Qeqe and his associates identified and appropriated the land on which the Dan Qeqe Stadium was built. It is a minefield of theories, the veracity of each hanging on a skilful interpretation, a balance between documented history and oral histories. The truth thus lies in the merger between documentation and orality, because as standalones they fail to offer a comprehensive understanding of how the stadium came to be. That sense of inconclusiveness is a reflection of how the past shaped the present, and allows us to better understand how the present Dan Qeqe Stadium has become so dysfunctional.

Saddled with a rather bizarre ownership structure, the current state of the Dan Qeqe Stadium is testimony to how the land was appropriated. The dilapidated stadium has no identifiable property deed. The land belongs to no one. The infrastructure belongs to and is managed by Kwaru, now an ordinary, single rugby club, no longer an amalgamation of clubs. Gerald Majola also admitted to how the historical acquisition of the stadium has led to its current state. He reasoned:

> So, even if you ask the municipality to look for the ownership deed of the land, they will never find it in their archives. They do not have records of that piece of land. They got that piece of land through the BAB [Bantu Administration Board]. And that land was occupied by Chinese people and other people, there at Veeplaas, but I can't get the whole story.[10]

In court papers filed in 1982, there was an attempt to officially locate the ownership of the land and the stadium. The attorney for the plaintiff (Kwaru), a Mr Kroon, attempted to address the matter. He stated that, 'The Dan Qeqe Stadium is the property, it is situate[d] on a property owned by the East Cape Administration Board, but the KwaZakhele Rugby Union built up that stadium. Who is the occupier of the stadium? – The KwaZakhele Rugby Union.'[11]

But the East Cape Administration Board (ECAB) had ceased to exist, and so this tenuous grip on the understanding of the ownership of the land and the stadium has filtered through to the present. The Nelson Mandela Bay Metropolitan Municipality (NMBMM) has neither an ownership nor a management claim on the land and the stadium, effectively hindering the municipality from maintaining and improving the stadium.

Even Dan Qeqe's own account is implausible, riddled with contradictions. In documentation, Qeqe offered a highly sanitised, transparent, legalistic and above-board narrative. He admitted that, 'Meanwhile, we had discovered that an open space in Veeplaas was earmarked for future sports development and I headed a delegation which saw Mr Koch. He agreed to our developing and using it.'[12]

Harold Wilson offered a quasi-conspiratorial narrative. He explained that there was an intense non-racial union meeting that had deliberated on the matter. A faction in the meeting swayed towards taking over the locked stadium by force – a faction with which he had sided. However, the other faction, wary of a bloody confrontation with the local state, was not prepared to take the risk. Eventually, the latter won the debate. Wilson recounted:

> So, I had to tell Dan, 'Dan, this is the situation. I'm sorry, my friend, I haven't got the manpower to support you now at this stage.' So, he said, 'Harold, tell me whether I'm right to what I'm going to do.' So I said to him, what? He said, 'I made contingency plans, knowing what the Department of Bantu Affairs can do. I am going to take two fields, open fields, at Veeplaas, opposite the house of Dan.'[13] Dan, he was one of the first locks of the 1950 Bantu team. He was a businessman.[14]

Ncula also expressed surprise at how Qeqe had identified the piece of land. 'Then, people like Dan [Qeqe], Silas [Nkanunu] and Siwisa [Dennis] decided that, 'Hey, guys, let's try and secure an open field, where we can go and play.'... Then I don't know how it happened that Baas Dan, you know, Dan Qeqe ... how he got a piece of land at Veeplaas,'[15] Ncula pointed out.

The land had been an open field used by local cricket clubs and African Bombers, Kwaru's second-league rugby club. Nkanunu pointed out that much of the property in Veeplaas was, in part, privately owned, registered to residents.[16] The Native Affairs Commission back in the 1950s leased some land in Veeplaas from a Port Elizabeth-based businessman of Indian descent, who had used it for commercial purposes. The Port Elizabeth City Council had then set up offices on the land for the registration of native pass documents.[17] So, a significant proportion of Veeplaas land belonged to or was leased as commercial property to Indians and other non-white groups, jostling for position with privately owned residential land.

Gerald Majola went on to assert that Qeqe, Lamani, Ximiya and other associates on the Native Advisory Board might have used their intimate knowledge of the inner workings of the board to identify land in the townships with vague ownership. Majola reasoned that:

> … they had to beat the system to do certain things, because that's what they knew, [that] Koch couldn't do anything. As much as that information came from the BAB, that land was cordoned off. Both the BAB and the municipality, both of them did not own that piece of land for whatever reason. I don't know why.[18]

Nozuko 'Girlie' Pikoli, whose father was a member of the New Brighton Native Advisory Board following his recruitment by Qeqe, witnessed the intelligence gathering his father and Qeqe practised with *izibonda*, the headmen of the board notorious for their corruption and loyalty to the township superintendent.[19] *Izibonda*, however, are far less renowned and chronicled for their double-agency roles. Pikoli maintained that, in her observations from the mid-1960s onwards, *izibonda* often ferried intelligence to Qeqe, her father and their associates. This afforded them leverage over what Koch and the local state had planned for the townships. She remembered:

> But some of them, you know, would give a lot of information. I know that lots of them, lots of them would come to my father. So he gets this information. That Koch used to come home, obviously thinking that he's trying to bring these ones under [his influence]. Meanwhile, already the headmen and what not, had already given him wind that this is how things are going, you see?[20]

The plausibility of these two theories may be rendered more believable by Qeqe's penchant for secretiveness. Affirming this trait in him,

Phumla said, 'Baas Dan was never open. Whatever he did, he did it alone … He wouldn't tell anyone. We also didn't know of the things he was up to. Most of the things he did, we heard about them when we were adults.'[21] Qeqe's granddaughter, Sinazo Vabaza, also confirmed that 'he was quite good at shutting his own mouth'.[22] Qeqe's long-time friend, Mrs Jumartha Milase Majola, also admitted that Qeqe was highly selective with whom he shared information. She pointed out that '…Baas Dan, these things, political matters, he didn't talk to us about everything'.[23]

There is virtually nothing in the public domain recording the initial identification of the piece of land on which the Dan Qeqe Stadium was built. Rather, the stadium appeared in the public media for the first time when the open field was being prepared ahead of the building of the stadium. However, a more plausible theory was put forward by Nyondo and Ngcaphe, one that is more believable simply because, straddling the two theories, it is a corroborative account.

Nyondo's version – verified by Ngcaphe's – resonates to some degree with Wilson's, who maintained that Qeqe had confided in him about his contingency plan to take two open fields in Veeplaas. And Qeqe might well have approached Wilson with his plan, considering Nyondo's explanation. Nyondo explained how Kwaru, following a litigation loss against the municipality on the withdrawal of the Zwide Stadium, had deliberated on workable options in a mass meeting. In that 1975 Kwaru mass meeting, Nyondo recalled:

> What do we do? The mood was very, very much angry … because that was tantamount to trying to put a stop to the existence of Kwaru, so to speak. So, what happened? At that time, I was living in Veeplaas … And we were getting to the bus stop closer to Zwide, walking through an open field where African Bombers Rugby Club used to be training, in an open field, in the place where it is now the Dan Qeqe Stadium.
>
> In that meeting at Ah! Nobantu Hall, among many proposals that were flying this end and that, I proposed, I'm talking about myself now as Amon Nyondo, I proposed what I thought was a solution. I said, 'Colleagues, let us not go into a confrontation with anybody. Let us go and play in that field where African Bombers is

> practising. That's the field which is empty and open at the moment. Let's go and play there.' The mass meeting of Kwaru adopted that.
>
> Qeqe was there in that meeting. He approached me, and said this is a good idea. He took it up and that is where Kwaru started to play their fixtures. And that is where the field got fenced in, and that is where Qeqe's activism came to the fore above every other person in Port Elizabeth, insofar as the issue of Kwaru is concerned … For some reason, it came out, that in fact that field was actually a private ownership of some kind.[24]

The ingenuity of Nyondo's idea was in convincing Kwaru not to litigate, again, against the Port Elizabeth City Council. Ngcaphe explained that after Kwaru's use of the Zwide Stadium had been withdrawn, Kwaru's leadership had taken the matter to the High Court, and lost the case. On the heels of that loss, Ngcaphe explained:

> [Now] Qeqe called us, calling us to Ah! Nobantu in New Brighton … Now on that day, we were debating on the matter of the appeal against the High Court decision regarding the taking away of the field from Kwaru. Now, a person who was not known in Port Elizabeth stood to talk. Actually, he didn't just stand up, he wrote a letter advising Kwaru against the idea of appealing, saying that we are going to lose the appeal. Then this person advised that we should take this field now known as the Dan Qeqe [Stadium], and that we should develop it. And he advanced the reasons there as to why this is possible. Then it was said that the person who had written that letter should stand up and come to the front.
>
> It was then revealed that this person was Amon Nyondo. Then he was urged to come to the front. I remember quite correctly him saying no, I'm comfortable here where I am at the back. He talks from the back, advising Kwaru to develop that field. Now, that field was developed. In that, Qeqe was very instrumental. There was no Dan Qeqe Stadium then. It was just a plain field … where African Bombers played.[25]

And so it was through Qeqe's extraordinary efforts in turning that piece of land into a stadium that it was named after him. Songongo also pointed out that Qeqe 'could organise labour to do something ... because that field is not Dan Qeqe [Stadium] for nothing, he built it himself ... He was that type of person, who could ask people to do something, and then the people would listen to him.'[26]

Underlying all these theories is the notion of a forceful appropriation of the land in the presence of local state onslaught. The local state perceived Qeqe and Kwaru as agents acting as proxies for the interests of the black people of Port Elizabeth. Moki Cekisani, a former Kwaru player and former detainee of the Black People's Convention, a former activist in the PAC of Azania, and a long-time associate of Qeqe, confirmed this. Cekisani underscored this notion of forceful appropriation, maintaining that:

> When we got the field, we decided that it must be a respectable field. Dan Qeqe funded all that. When we did that, we tried to apply the same system which is holding, managing our land. And they refused to give us permission. Then we said we're going to force ourselves into playing onto that field, because it's our land. That's Dan Qeqe who was in the lead.[27]

It was the compelling charisma that Qeqe leveraged to garner help in building 'the people's stadium'. He had accumulated considerable capital by means of his charismatic pull among the people through his selfless efforts in education advancement and civic matters in New Brighton and KwaZakhele townships. It is this reputation that engendered his strong connection with communities.

In a press caption dated 1975, Dan Qeqe is seen raking the open field along with a score of ordinary men. They worked the ground with spades and forks. Looking down and smiling, as if conscious of the picture being taken, he seems at ease working with others. Wearing a cotton jersey and loose-fitting, almost baggy, cotton smart-casual trousers, he seems to enjoy working with the crew.

The press article reported, 'Workmen have started transforming a barren piece of land in Veeplaas into a makeshift rugby stadium, venue of the SA Cup final between Kwaru and Tygerberg of Cape Town next Saturday.'[28] The article went on, 'The picture was taken at the weekend when Mr DD QEQE (foreground), a prominent New Brighton businessman, Bantu Advisory Board member and sports administrator, with a team of workmen were busy preparing the field.'[29]

Ngcaphe remembered how he found Qeqe, a wealthy businessman well integrated with ordinary men performing menial labour on that open field:

> I was curious about this stadium that was being built with corrugated metal sheets, with hammering going on, with this and that. I remember coming to the township and standing there, and I saw these grown men. I realised at that time that Qeqe, that this man was very humble. Qeqe was a high profile and prominent businessperson, a wealthy man. But when I got there, he was eating dumplings, seated down with the other men on a break at that time. They were eating dumplings with meat and all that, those people who were hammering, building the stadium with corrugated metal sheets, you know? So I saw then that this guy is humble.[30]

It was this picture of a wealthy Qeqe blending in with ordinariness that Mkhuseli Jack, later a prominent community activist in PEBCO and the Port Elizabeth Youth Congress (PEYCO) in the 1980s, painted. Then a teenager who had just arrived in Port Elizabeth from a farming area just outside Port Elizabeth, he recalled that in 1975:

> … round about March of that year, when the rugby season started, myself and some few boys, we were told that they're gonna start the Dan Qeqe Stadium, and they want boys to go and plant grass there. They asked volunteers to go. I volunteered, because we were told that this was a non-racial rugby association that was fighting for this and that. Although I wasn't strong in understanding that stuff, I was just willing to go and work, and work on that field … And then Dan Qeqe actually came there, all to find out that he was the main person leading this thing, this non-racial rugby which I didn't understand at the time. But we worked, and worked and worked. It was hot.[31]

Some civil society organisations that supported non-racial sports and

Kwaru, such as the South African Organisation for Desegregation, continued to exert pressure on the local state to re-offer the use of municipal stadia to Kwaru. A press article stated that, 'The Government and the Port Elizabeth municipality have been criticized for their continued attempts to frustrate the ambitions of the non-racial South African Rugby Union and Kwaru by the South African Organisation for Desegregation headed by Ramah Bhana.'[32]

Bhana saw it as unnecessary that thousands of rand should be spent on preparing a 'stretch of deserted land' to erect a stadium seating 20 000 spectators.[33] He went on to caution the local state and the national government to 'take considerable notice of the growing impatience of the Black South Africans and would advise that they rethink on the question of interference'.[34] Nonetheless, Qeqe and the community continued with their efforts to prepare the ground, putting up a temporary fence and erecting stands to seat, for the final SA Cup match, some 3 000 spectators.[35] Qeqe was assured that the makeshift stadium would be ready the following Saturday to host the SA Cup final match.[36]

Qeqe's first port of call for labour recruitment was his relatives. His nephew, McKenzie Sloti, remembered that he recruited all his immediate and extended family, and also used his own two trucks, and his own spades, rakes and other implements to load and deliver soil. 'There were humps there and holes, and we would load and deliver soil with his trucks, fill up and level those places … We worked there as a family, and roped in members of other clubs, volunteers,'[37] Sloti recalled. Mpumelelo 'Sbhidla' Majola also weighed in on how the exercise of turning the open field into a stadium was courtesy of the labour of Qeqe's extended family and that of the community. He pointed out that, 'That chap [Dan Qeqe] took his own trucks, and he took all of us there, with Thozi, Vusumzi, even Pikoli, Sizwe Kondile, all of us were taken, even Lucky [Mange] here.'[38]

Mrs Majola recalled that, in the evenings, Qeqe had to use his cars to light up the field. 'They had to go and plant grass in the darkness. Baas Dan had to take his own cars to light up the field. Mrs Qeqe and I had to go and cook, cooking for the people who were planting the grass at the Dan Qeqe Stadium,'[39] Mrs Majola recalled. Thozamile Botha also confirmed that Qeqe 'used his own trucks to bring sand and bricks and what you call, to build and fence off that piece of ground'.[40]

Big companies lent Qeqe a motor grader and water sprinklers to help in levelling the open field's hard ground,[41] but what was never revealed in the media was how Qeqe schemed, bribed and fought his way through various challenges, militating against the building project. Phumla maintained that much of the equipment used to level and prepare the ground was serially 'stolen' from the municipal depot. Qeqe bribed municipal workers to gain access to the tractors after work, take them to the open field and use them at night, and return them the following morning before they opened. She admitted that:

> He wanted those tractors at night, after hours, which is [why] they stole them. We didn't sleep, because they did all of those things at night ... He bribed those people, the ones who dug the ground ... He wanted those equipment that dug the ground ... Caterpillars ... They were stealing them. Remember, they were meant to have slept there. They were not meant to work until the following morning. They closed at four. They went and talked with those people who worked with the Caterpillars ... The mayor didn't know.[42]

Also not revealed to the public was how Qeqe personally contended with the local state's sabotage attempts. His fearlessness and authoritarian character helped immensely in the face of these obstacles. Gerald Majola recounted:

> No, he used to say that, 'Fuck, this is not happening, that's it.' ... When he says, 'This shit stops here,' he says it, and he means it ... He doesn't care if there's a chap as big as a bridge, however big he is, he would head straight for him, and he would throw himself at that person.[43]

Vusi Pikoli, too, affirmed this stubbornness in Qeqe, relaying that, 'When he was heated up, he dared everybody, especially *amabhulu* (boers). He said, "No, this is our country, man. We're going to build a stadium. Here, we're going to play here."'[44] In one epic confrontation that Phumla affirmed as an open secret, her father physically squared up with Koch. At the time, Koch was Qeqe's supervisor in the Port Elizabeth Joint Bantu Advisory Board. The confrontation was over the continuation of the building project following Corobrik's sponsorship of bricks and labour. Ford had also come on board as a sponsor.

Ncula recalled that on that day, Koch had tried to stop workers lent by Corobrik to lay bricks and cement on the open field. At 7.30 that morning, when Qeqe, Ncula and Feya Sobikwa went to check on progress on the field, they found that the Corobrik workers had not started working. On enquiry, they were informed that BAB officials, sent on Koch's orders, had instructed them to stop. Ncula recounted:

> Hey, Dan Qeqe, he was cross, very, very cross. So he got into his car, and off we rush to Koch. And fortunately Koch was in the office. It was roundabout quarter to eight, I remember. And one thing, Baas Dan, he was a very, very brave man. You know, he was not scared of anything. He just walked into Koch's office. And then Koch was saying, 'Hey, Baas Dan, what's going on?' Then Dan said, 'What's the shit you've done there at the stadium?' You know, it was, they nearly came to blows, and Feya Sobikwa had to stop them. And he forced Koch to talk to one of his officials to get those guys to continue to work. So, they just put around the bricks.[45]

Phumla insisted that they came to blows: 'No one talks about that. But my father related the story to us as it was … He slapped him. He said, there's nothing he's going to do to me. I am going to build that stadium. He had his foul language.'[46] Qeqe's aggressive behaviour synchronised well with his bulldozing personality. His granddaughter, Sinazo Vabaza, described Qeqe as:

> [An] ox. My father bulldozed wherever he entered. He had a command and you had no option but to listen, and do as he instructed. He was not a talker. He was an instructor. The truth was the truth to my father, regardless of how it might be received by the other person. He liked to swear, 'Shit, shit, my friend,' regardless of who you are.[47]

Badela's Kwaru executive committee had given Qeqe a 'blank cheque'[48] to buy materials to construct the stadium. In effect, this meant Qeqe had the organisation's mandate to buy, organise resources and build, using his own discretion. For accounting and auditing purposes, Qeqe was responsible for furnishing the executive committee with receipts. Using networks he had long cultivated as a businessman and community builder, he bought significant amounts of corrugated-iron sheets and other materials from scrapyards and other informal businesses. Often, these establishments did not, or were unable to, offer receipts. Also, he used a great deal of his own money and resources in the building project. It is important to note this, because it foregrounds the basis of the conflict that ensued two years later in 1977, leading to the first implosion of Kwaru.

It was in recognition of Qeqe's efforts that the stadium was named after him in 1975. On the day of the Kwaru–Tygerberg SA Cup final match, a gate taking of R11 578 was recorded.[49] Elated, the president of SARU, Abdul Abbas, confirmed that that year's SA Cup final had yielded far better takings than the previous year's takings of R5 000 at Adcock Stadium in Port Elizabeth.[50]

Abbas said, 'Record takings have eclipsed all our previous gate takings of finals so far.'[51] He then officially named the stadium the Dan Qeqe Stadium, and jabbed a defiant finger at the Kwaru crowd: 'I want you to adopt that name and leave it to the authorities to remove it even if by forcing us to play in the streets.'[52] The article recorded that, 'Mr Qeqe, a member of the Port Elizabeth Joint Bantu Advisory Board and a leading sports administrator, was in charge of the building operation that made it possible for more than 6000 spectators to be seated on Saturday.'[53]

Nyondo recalled that post-match moment when the stadium was named Dan Qeqe Stadium:

> So, they went on to that house with the takings of the people that were paying into the stadium, to count them that evening, for that successful SA Cup final. Abdul Abbas, who was the President of SARU, was there, because they would normally converge after a game in a given house. So they converged in David Mbane's house … And then, because of the work done by Qeqe in the field, and

> the fact that Kwaru had made that much money on that day, Abdul said this stadium must be called Dan Qeqe Stadium. That's how it got its name.[54]

Ngcaphe remembered the naming this way:

> Now, Kwaru didn't take the decision that the stadium should be named after Qeqe. It was never a Kwaru decision … Now, there was a Kwaru party there in the evening on that day. Abbas, the President of SARU, he announced that the field was Dan Qeqe Stadium. That's how the field was called the Dan Qeqe Stadium, and there was no one who challenged that. It became the Dan Qeqe Stadium from then on.[55]

FOR TYAMZASHE, THE ERECTION of the Dan Qeqe Stadium was a long-awaited and much-needed symbol of the much-touted black pride. He pointed out that, 'To me that stadium was so important to have because … he was telling us something through his activities, that actually you don't need to have everything before you do things. Look at me, I'm doing it. I'm building a stadium.'[56]

In this way, it came to the ownership of the people, effectively becoming a 'people's stadium'. Tyamzashe further described it thus:

> Remember now, once that stadium was built, that was the people's stadium, the trigger of this thing. And then, he managed to create a huge monster for, let's say, those who are anti the whole emancipation of blacks, because they say, 'Argh! Blacks will talk and not do something.' All of a sudden, there's a place we go to and play on Saturdays. We are going to the stadium. And we go in numbers.[57]

The naming of a stadium after a living black man, well profiled for his non-racial and anti-apartheid activities, at the height of apartheid, morphed a simple, open field into a site of political and cultural black resistance, pride and symbolism. Essentially, the Dan Qeqe Stadium and Kwaru breathed life into resistance, with Kwaru taking on political clout that extended way beyond rugby as a sporting code.

Vusi Pikoli maintained that the Dan Qeqe Stadium stood for

people's resistance against apartheid. Ncula also agreed that the Dan Qeqe Stadium became a 'people's stadium'.[58] Phumla observed that, particularly in the 1980s, in the face of recurring unrest and consumer boycotts, the Security Branch pleaded with Qeqe to stop or at least maintain some measure of control over the political and civic activities taking place at the stadium. To that, Qeqe, however, argued that the stadium was not his, but that of the people, and as such he had no control over many of the activities that took place there.[59]

The stadium also became a launch pad for underground political meetings. Valence Watson, who was then an underground ANC operative in Port Elizabeth, bore witness to this. He reflected that the Dan Qeqe Stadium 'became a rallying point for everybody. We could then talk politics, under the cover of being at a rugby match or at a club meeting.'[60] Mpumelelo 'Sbhidla' Majola understood this to be a substitute for banned black political movements and structures. He affirmed: 'All these organisations, where did they meet? They met at the Dan Qeqe Stadium. Once they played rugby there, political meetings were taking place on the side, you see?'[61] Mange described the stadium's political role in a more colourful way:

> They did it the mafia way. The mafia, *mos*, you see in the films, they are dancing there … and then you occasionally see that here's a certain meeting, and drugs are moving there … They are moving prostitution there, you see? A certain movement is happening there … That's how things were kept by these chaps, Siwisa and the others.[62]

Kwaru came to the rescue of some of the bullied non-racial sports codes whose functioning had effectively been truncated. Kwaru, Qeqe and the Dan Qeqe Stadium literally facilitated the ferrying of banned and pursued political activists into exile. They provided the space and resources for clandestine political meetings. So, the history of Kwaru, of Qeqe, is a history of black communities of Port Elizabeth. It is a history of how Kwaru and Qeqe helped shape the history and making of Port Elizabeth, as much as the inherited institutions and forces of apartheid shaped the city.

At the Dan Qeqe Stadium, discussions often broached allied subjects on non-sexism, one-man-one-vote, trade unionism, PEBCO, Motor Assembly and Component Workers' Union of South Africa (MACWUSA), and the Congress of South African Trade Unions (COSATU). Kwaru meetings and the stadium were also covers for the launching point for underground ANC cadres to skip the country into exile. Watson recalled one such occasion:

> For instance, in fact, Sonwabo Mbekazi, the way they skipped the country, Nojoko was a player, playing for Wallabies, which was part of Kwaru. So a group, about 11 of them, got a kombi from a chap called Balintulo in Uitenhage, and said, we're hiring a kombi to go to a club meeting in Port Elizabeth in Walmer, which they then did. On the way there, they said, now we're not going to a club meeting. We're going to Ficksburg. And the driver had no choice. So, under the cover of going to a club meeting, they skipped through Ficksburg, and on to Lesotho to the ANC. So, it was a cover.[63]

Following the erection of the Dan Qeqe Stadium, the local state reversed its decision to not make the Zwide Stadium and Isaac Wolfson Stadium available for Kwaru's use. A press article in 1977 reported:

> The ban on the Kwazakhele Rugby Union (Kwaru) using two of the biggest rugby stadiums in the Port Elizabeth African townships has been lifted. This was confirmed yesterday by the chief director of the Cape Midlands Bantu Affairs Administration Board, Mr Louis Koch, and the president of Kwaru, Mr Mono Badela.[64]

Kwaru, however, turned down the offer. This was swiftly followed by an avalanche of acts of sabotage and a string of legal actions against the existence of the Dan Qeqe Stadium. One such action was cutting off the stadium's water services. This was a result of long, drawn-out litigation between the ECAB and Kwaru in the 1980s over a disputed water bill. In 1985, this had peaked as an acute crisis, when only one tap was available to service 50 000 mourners who had gathered at the stadium for a funeral of 15 victims of political unrest.[65]

At the stadium on the day of the funeral, '[there] were long queues of thirsty mourners formed at the tap. Marshals from the UDF helped by bringing water in plastic containers to the bereaved families seated inside the fenced-off playing area.'[66] Mrs Majola, head of the Girl Guides in New Brighton, recalled the role she played that day:

> I requested children to deliver water there, so that the Congress meetings would not get disturbed because of the non-availability of water. Children had to carry buckets, going amongst crowds of people in the stadium. People kept on raising their hands as a show of who needed water, so that people could get water, helped by the Girl Guides with water there.[67]

It was reported that 'Mr Dan Qeqe, treasurer of the Kwazakhele Rugby Union (Kwaru), owners of the stadium, said the stadium had had a water service problem since a dispute two years ago between Kwaru and the then Port Elizabeth Community Council, which went to court'.[68] According to Qeqe, the Council had cut off the water supply because Kwaru had failed to pay its bill amounting to R6 500.[69] Qeqe further claimed that the matter had been settled out of court, and Kwaru had not been billed since then.

In the same year, the black Port Elizabeth local state, whose name had again evolved into Kayamnandi Town Council under the mayor, Thamsanqa Linda, also cut off the water to the Dan Qeqe Stadium. This time, the cut-off disrupted a religious gathering of thousands of members and supporters of the Inter-denominational Ministers Association of South Africa (IDAMASA).[70]

As with the previous water cut-off, Qeqe maintained that Kwaru had again not received a water bill since the settlement of the previous dispute. In fact, Kwaru's records reflected a financially healthy organisation. After spending more than R14 000 on improvements to the Dan Qeqe Stadium, Kwaru showed a building society fixed deposit of R10 944.50 and a balance of R2 291.52.[71] Kwaru was commended: 'The union must be one of the few in the South African Rugby Union that can boast takings of up to R900 from its normal club fixtures, and a maximum of R7 852 from an interprovincial match.'[72]

Qeqe argued that the ECAB had been supplying water unconditionally since they had been preparing for the SA Cup final match in 1975.[73] However, the secretary of the ECAB, Mr DJ Bezuidenhout, maintained that the water cut-off to the Dan Qeqe Stadium had not been influenced by Kwaru's non-racial stance. Instead, Bezuidenhout pointed out, 'We are not victimising them. We have been supplying Kwaru with water for some time now and at this stage we feel we have to legalise matters.'[74]

Qeqe railed against the mayor and the local state in general, stating that, 'If unjust and popular actions by government appendages like the Kayamnandi Town Council are allowed to exist, people cannot be blamed for taking every step to drum up anti-South African feeling.'[75] He also pointed out that the levy for sports and infrastructure services of R1 per New Brighton resident offset any services charges at the Dan Qeqe Stadium.

On his planned trip to New Zealand to campaign against the planned tour of the All Blacks to South Africa, Qeqe intended to raise concerns about the social injustices meted out to black people's sports facilities and infrastructure. His ultimatum was that his planned protest in New Zealand would be avoided if Dr Gerrit Viljoen, then Minister of Cooperation, Development and Education, accepted an invitation to travel to Port Elizabeth to intervene in the matter.

And so it was that history-making fell uninvited into the laps of Qeqe, Kwaru and the Dan Qeqe Stadium. No matter how inadvertent, the Dan Qeqe Stadium became a home to many political, cultural and social movements of Port Elizabeth throughout the 1970s into the early 1990s. It became a natural venue for mass funerals – an outlet for political lamenting, political conscientisation, and strategic planning in the 1980s, the stadium embracing many major civil unrest meetings and consumer boycotts of the period.

*e*Dan Qeqe in isiXhosa means 'at Dan Qeqe's'. There is perhaps in it a natural removal of 'stadium', replacing it with '*e*', an African invocation of 'home'. No one in the black townships of Port Elizabeth refers to the Dan Qeqe Stadium as a 'stadium', but rather as '*e*Dan Qeqe'. This is an overt embracing of Dan Qeqe Stadium as a home for the people of Port Elizabeth – a homely embracing of the people's history of Port Elizabeth which played out on the stage of *e*Dan Qeqe.

8

THE FIRST IMPLOSION (1977) ...

'*Makubhekwe eCentenary ... makubhekwe eCentenary. Kukho into egqats' ibunzi.*' – 'Let us head to Centenary [Hall] ... let us head to Centenary. There is a burning issue we need to address.'[1] Ngcaphe recalled Ronnie Madinda's[2] loud announcement at the Dan Qeqe Stadium in June 1977. The rather formal, and perhaps lazy isiXhosa-to-English translation, 'There is a burning issue we need to address', rests there. It does not wield the intensity of true urgency. It does not relay the bone marrow of it all. *Kukho into egqats' ibunzi*, literally, directly translated, means, 'There is something severely sunburning the forehead.' Focus is on the sharpness of the sunburn, a sensation brought by the nearness of the sun's rays to the forehead – the intensity of urgency.

The call turned into a hall putsch, with the Badela Kwaru executive committee summarily ousted by means of instant, populist hall democracy. 'Kwaru players have been thrown into the sea of confusion by a black wave of circumstances.'[3] Perhaps not dramatically enough, Benjamin T Skosana described the tone of the hall putsch of 8 June 1977. In his letter to the editor of the *Evening Post*, he blatantly labelled the incident a 'coup', the first documented reference to the unseating of Mono Badela's Kwaru presidency and his executive committee as a coup. Such was the organisational conduct of Kwaru by the late 1970s: uproarious affairs reflected and followed in the press, a true image of

Kwaru's embeddedness in Port Elizabeth's black communities, a 'union of the people for the people'.[4] The statement of Mr M Nduvane, master of ceremonies at the 8 June 1977 meeting at Centenary Hall, perfectly mirrored Kwaru's magnanimous status.

There may be a temptation to regard the incident as just another community sports organisation contending with its own chaos. It was not. Kwaru, Qeqe and his associates had moulded an unparalleled historic and historical force. Kwaru had become a bold political energy upsetting the sports–political status quo. Consequently, it attracted the attention of the Security Branch,[5] the ire of the cabinet, the irritation of the president of SARB, Danie Craven, and the bewildered attention of the international community.

People's custodianship of Kwaru found expression in public emotion, effectively shaping its organisational conduct. 'When Kwaru was under siege … like the threat from the Bantu Affairs Administration Board (BAAB); threat from this, threat from the security police … they would call a mass meeting. And that is what actually led to the coup against them.'[6] Nyondo explained the public emotion that developed around Kwaru. Ngcaphe, described it thus, 'Kwaru matters were handled emotionally, because people were emotional. When people returned from the stadium, they sounded out hooters in queues, Po! Po! Po! People followed Kwaru in that manner. There were no strong principles of accountability. It was just emotions.'[7]

These emotions often clouded and flouted Kwaru's constitutional principles and organisational regulations. Eventually, they became a flaw strategically used in ousting Badela and his executive committee. It was a weakness, developed during Badela's administration, to protect it from outside threats, and eventually used to oust it. Nyondo explained this weakness: '[When] there is an issue threatening Kwaru, they would call a mass meeting of Kwaru. And then, mass meetings mean all the followers of Kwaru go there. That was Badela's leadership weak point. They had all the good intentions.'[8]

When Ronnie Madinda loudly announced the urgency of a Kwaru meeting in June 1977, tabulated grievances against the Badela Kwaru executive committee were:[9]

1. The handling of finances and presentation of financial statements;

2. Selection of teams;
3. Inadequate facilities for the players;
4. Dissatisfaction over advance sales of tickets and the accounting surrounding these; and
5. Lack of proper entrance gates for the public who complained of being injured at the one narrow gate to the Dan Qeqe Stadium.

At Centenary Hall, Mr Ayanda W Mjekula, a member of the Easterns, delivered a 30-minute address. Outlining the grievances against the Badela executive committee,[10] he said, 'You have misdirected your energies after taking office on a gentleman's agreement. Because you have failed to supply us with properly audited financial statements, we emphatically do not want you to administer the finances of this organisation any longer.'[11] This was followed by a vote of no confidence, proposed by Mjekula. Shouting down muffled pro-Badela voices in what was fast becoming a meeting edging towards chaos and violence, Mjekula howled above the frenzied din, 'We ask you please to resign. The people have decided to supplant you with officials of substance, people who will provide the clubs with a proper constitution.'[12]

A heckling of vitriolic remarks weighed against Badela's executive committee: 'We don't need any explanations' and 'Just resign and leave the books behind.'[13] Mr Wilkinson M Maku, an executive committee member, said in a pacifying tone, 'Give us a chance. We are going to resign.'[14] Recalling the agitation and aggression that nearly turned violent, Ngcaphe remarked:

> Badela and his associates then went in and sat on the stage as the leadership of Kwaru. It was decided then that they should resign. Hey, the meeting became ugly now. The meeting was rowdy. They were saying that they must resign ... They said, 'Voetsek.' This word 'voetsek' came out at that time. They said, 'Voetsek.' Yhoo![15]

On how the meeting came close to a violent clash, Ngcaphe continued, 'Now Phakamile Lubambo and his associates, members of the Saints [St Cyprian's Rugby Football Club] went on to the stage, because it was clear now that a fight was going to break out. Other people were armed with axes and all these kinds of things.'[16] Ngcaphe had tried to argue in the meeting that the Badela executive be given a chance to respond. Recalling seeing Qeqe, wearing a long jacket, quietly leaning into the wall at the back, he tried to reason with the crowd. He pointed out that not giving Badela and his executive committee members a chance to answer was akin to detention without trial. He, however, was 'shot down by Ncula'.[17] And, out of deference, because Ncula was older than him, he had withdrawn and sat down.

Nduvane then summed up the grievances: dissatisfaction with Kwaru's financial statements, and the unsatisfactory treatment of players and members by the Badela Kwaru executive committee.[18] The hall putsch of the 11-man Badela executive committee was noted as historically disruptive to 'The KwaZakhele Rugby Union, regarded by many as the most successful African provincial rugby body in the Republic and SA Cup winners in 1975 and 1976', [19] the 'envy of rugby unions'.[20] In other corners, the coup was viewed as a 'mystery' driven by 'dissident Kwaru members'.[21]

Kwaru's constitution was thus upstaged and subverted through the invocation of the spirit of populist hall democracy. 'This is the union of the people for the people,'[22] Nduvane had yelled. However, as per Kwaru's constitution, the organisation's management was vested in the 15 affiliated rugby clubs and its executive committee, and 'not in the executive appointed by men from the street'.[23] Reiterating this constitutional procedure, David Mbane correctly argued that '[no] union or organisation is run by its supporters'.[24] Thozamile Botha also correctly pointed out that, '[notwithstanding] the claims of maladministration the leadership of Kwaru made up against the PEARB, it had its own share of internal challenges and actions indicative of an organization determined to flout its own constitution.'[25]

Badela indicated that a vote of no confidence would have to be passed by a majority vote of the representatives of the 15 rugby clubs serving as delegates in Kwaru's management.[26] And so, defiantly, Badela firmly stated, 'I am still the president and my executive is still in power.'[27] He had then laid out the correct constitutional procedure for effecting a vote of no confidence: only 30 delegates – two from each of the 15 rugby clubs represented in Kwaru management – 'had any say in the appointment of an executive'.[28] Badela's crying foul against populist hall democracy, a beastly entity he had created and nurtured, had, however, become unwieldy in his hands.

But the hall putsch was not a sudden puncture. It had been slow, a grumbling brew, plotted and schemed by both anti- and pro-Badela groups, the former essentially acting as a proxy for Qeqe and his associates. As the coup clouds gathered, Somyalo recalled driving to see Badela at his house on Limba Road in New Brighton. After reading an article in *Imvo Zabantsundu* on the squabbles in the Kwaru leadership, Somyalo felt that he could offer advice to his old, fellow alumnus from Fort Hare. For the sake of maintaining stability within Kwaru, as he recalled, he advised Badela to promptly convene elections.

Badela had baulked, his bet secured on the votes of the delegates of the second-division teams he had been mobilising for support, his hopes for a stay at incumbency resting on teams such as the Butcher Birds, African Bombers and Boiling Sea on his side. They had votes equal to those of the first-division teams, like the Union (Whites), Spring Rose, Easterns, St Cyprian's, Blues, Orientals and Wallabies. But the election did not take place. '[They] went to Centenary, and the voting didn't take place, *mos*.'[29] Somyalo had been surprised. 'I tried to warn that, hey, man, just put your house in order. Bam! It happened. Yes, it happened.'[30]

One of the challenges leading to the ousting of Badela's executive committee concerned grievances about the selection of teams. Silas Nkanunu asserted that 'the selection of the teams was problematic',[31] affecting in particular a number of star players from the Easterns and the St Cyprian's rugby clubs. Some of these challenges were bitterly litigated. Somyalo recalled: 'There were cases that were brought to court. Ncula was the match secretary ... in one of the cases concerning the teams. There were disputes about teams, and they went to court about these ... These were such matters that kept on seeping in, that kept on seeping in.'[32]

A major grievance, and one that perhaps stands out the most, was the mismanagement of Kwaru's finances. This was brought to light by suspicions regarding the siphoning of gate takings by some members of the executive committee. With Kwaru games attracting huge numbers of spectators and fans beyond the seating capacity of the Dan Qeqe Stadium, managing gate takings became a porous affair. Badela's treasurer, Mr M Grawana, was considered in some quarters 'a mischievous chap',[33] an allusion to the alleged mismanagement of gate takings. However, it is difficult, in hindsight, to verify such allegations from oral historical accounts. Nonetheless, elsewhere, Grawana was regarded as semi-literate, and therefore financially illiterate and unskilled in handling Kwaru's finances. Of Grawana, Ngcaphe recalled:

> I think this matter of the statements not financially audited, it summarises this thing, because Ronnie Madinda was saying; I remember the treasurer was Grawana. He said that Grawana does not even know the difference between a balance sheet [and] all those related things. Now Grawana was a truck driver ... He was not an educated man, really. I think then that the statements were not financially audited, maybe was the truth. I'm not sure.[34]

Then, conceding conditional defeat, Badela noted: 'The decision to resign does not mean that we recognise those who believe that they are in power now.'[35] Adding a 'however', he and his executive committee remarked that '[the] executive of Kwaru, in view of the dissensions caused by the so-called action committee, have decided in the interest of rugby, of harmony within the union and the avoidance of splits in clubs, to resign'.[36]

Behind the scenes, Badela did not, however, really concede defeat. Instead, he attempted to salvage his presidency by approaching SARU for intervention and advice, and his next move was to challenge the matter for reversal in the Port Elizabeth High Court. The SARU executive committee thus travelled to Port Elizabeth to meet with Badela and his executive committee. Meeting at the Holiday Inn, SARU criticised Badela for wanting to use 'establishment', 'racist' court institutions to intervene in non-racial sports–political matters. SARU insisted on not taking non-racial matters to racial courts, in adherence to the puritanical Double Standards Policy.[37] They eventually convinced Badela and his executive committee to drop the matter altogether, assuring them that they would address the dispute themselves.

This, in turn, unleashed a series of vindictive spin-off effects. Qeqe's Action Committee, which took over from Badela, used Badela's attempt at legal action to ban him and his executive committee members from participating in Kwaru affairs. Ngcaphe recalled with precision: 'Badela and his associates used to sit there [pointing to David Mbane's Melisizwe Butchery], watching rugby from there. Kwaru [Action Committee] did not want Badela and his associates, which I think was another blunder that we did.'[38]

In a bitterly mocking tone, Baba Jali, one of the Kwaru selectors, wrote a letter to the editor of the *Evening Post* about Badela's relegation to the viewing spot at the top of Melisizwe Butchery:

> Through the *Evening Post* may I have the pleasure of inviting your reporter, Mr Mono Badela, to witness rugby matches at the Dan Qeqe Stadium's actual playing field. There is enough room to accommodate him rather than witnessing matches from a room at the top of the butchery right outside the stadium. I feel that this will give him a better view of what he was to report about.
>
> We, the Kwaru selectors, welcome criticisms that help build up the standard of rugby, but we find it not easy to tolerate a reporter who reports from hearsay or one that is using the Press to fight his personal wars.[39]

However, there was an absence of any documented evidence that Badela used the press, the *Evening Post* or any other newspaper, to fight the Kwaru Action Committee. What clearly emerged, though, was Badela's conciliatory attitude towards Kwaru and the Action Committee post his removal. Bar his attempt at overturning the Action Committee's decision in court, he made a reconciliatory overture. In a 1979 press report, it was stated that:

> The deposed members of Kwaru executive have no intention of withdrawing from the rugby scene. Former president of Kwaru, Mr Mono Badela, said they would continue maintaining ties with their clubs to help in the promotion of good relations among Kwaru affiliates.[40]

Watson, in fact, noted how Badela took his enforced exit with dignity. He remarked that, 'Mono Badela himself took it very well, I thought … Badela should have been retained, to a large degree, because he had done so much to be part of the building, and so had Dan.'[41]

The ousted Badela executive committee comprised: Arthur S Mono Badela (president), Wilkinson M Maku, Samuel L Nghona (general secretary), S Mgengo, R Dondashe, Thomas Sullo, M Grawana, A Peta and M Mvula.

An interim action committee was elected, with the following members:[42] Ayanda W Mjekula, M Qinga, T Lukwe, Ronnie Madinda, ET Tawana, M Nduvane, Moki Cekisani, Mveleli E Ncula and W Toba. This interim action committee, however, soon gave way to the first proposed Action Committee, made up of the following Kwaru members:[43] Dumile Kondile (president), Dennis Siwisa (vice-president), Dan Qeqe (treasurer), Silas Nkanunu (Easterns), Herbert Fischat (Wallabies), Mveleli Ncula (Easterns), M Gonya (Easterns), L Mgubela (Spring Rose) and Ronnie Madinda (Spring Rose).

One of Kwaru's coaches, attorney Dumile Kondile, was proposed to take over from Badela. The new Action Committee was initially designed to be a lawyer-led structure. 'And the buzzword, the buzzword was that we would be led by lawyers now. That's why Kondile was drawn in … So, Kondile, Nkanunu, they were lawyers,'[44] remarked Nyondo. Kondile, however, responded with a mixture of both diffidence and nervousness. His timidity then morphed into a polite rejection by a Kondile renowned for shying away from controversies[45] – 'a person who does not like to get himself in controversy'.[46] Surprised by, if not nervous about, his nomination to the Kwaru presidency, Kondile commented: 'This is news to me. I don't know anything about this new move. Until such time when I am officially informed as to how I came to be elected as president, I have nothing to say on the matter.'[47]

The leadership proposal of a Kwaru Action Committee was thus finalised. Silas Nkanunu was elected president of Kwaru, Dan Qeqe as treasurer, Dennis Siwisa as secretary and Mveleli Ncula as match secretary. Other committee members were Herbert Fischat, H Njenje (second-division match secretary), R Masoka (third-division match secretary), Ronnie Madinda (trustee) and M Nduvane (trustee).

Grievances relating to alleged mismanagement of funds did not end there, though. In fact, those who directly implicated Qeqe were incendiary forces in the machinations leading to the Badela coup. Accusations of Qeqe embezzling Kwaru funds originated with the Kwaru-sanctioned stadium-building project, and the allegation fed into the factional dynamics and conflicts leading up to the coup. It is a part of Kwaru's story that has never found its way into its documented history.

Perhaps Benjamin T Skosana, who was a Kwaru player, best described the factionalism behind the Badela coup in his letter to the Editor of the *Evening Post*:

> Not everybody who has been directly involved in this coup has the interest of sport at heart ... I do not think anybody would have said anything had the whole business been conducted constitutionally, if not in an orderly way. Hooliganism should in no way be encouraged in sport and the meeting, or rather gathering on Wednesday, June 8, was not praiseworthy ...
>
> It appears that we are destined for a surrogate power, an idea which I do not at all relish. There is a dangerously and disgracefully parochial clique in Kwaru who will always be a threat to the union's harmonious progress towards self-betterment. Most unfortunately some of these elements command the majority of the many conscientiously stupid and ignorant fans who have also proved to be the most vociferous.[48]

Initial tensions with Badela's executive committee began with its accounting measures over the construction of the Dan Qeqe Stadium, and its request that Qeqe produce receipts and other accounting documentation on how he had spent the money. Nyondo explained:

> For some reasons, that's what sparked off a major crisis ... Lungi Nghona ... who was the general secretary ... He and the others had asked Mr Qeqe for the financial report of how Kwaru's monies were used in the development of that stadium. Because you must remember, there were sponsorships for that ... Now, the executive of Kwaru and Qeqe crossed lines around that. The result is Qeqe then was very uncomfortable with the executive.[49]

Difficulties arose out of Qeqe's unorthodox means building the stadium. Many did not lend themselves openly and squarely to formal accounting measures, protocols and methodologies. He had approached scrapyards and second-hand construction depots, hustled for certain logistics, and used his own money, transport and fuel quite often. With lines between his and Kwaru's money and resources blurred, stringent and formal accounting measures could not keep up. 'It could have happened that his money and Kwaru's money became one.'[50] That is when rumours and allegations of Qeqe embezzling Kwaru funding emerged. And then the clashes began.

Some of Qeqe's discomfort with the Kwaru leadership allegedly stemmed from his dislike of Badela. Some in Kwaru, such as Thami Songongo, regarded Badela as untrustworthy. Allegedly grandstanding in various corners, Badela appeared to have vacillated on policy and political stances. He postulated one stance in one corner, and some other in another corner – the alleged variances depending on individual interpretations, and on the particular platform. Sipho Tanana also remembered Badela as unprincipled. 'Badela was a funny somebody,'[51] Tanana had started off. 'He was educated. He played centre at Fort Hare. But you would never actually be sure as to where he stands. That's Badela, to such an extent that Dan didn't have much confidence in Badela.'[52]

Offering a similar perception of Badela, Songongo believed that Badela's installation as the first president of Kwaru had been a well-calculated manoeuvre by Qeqe and his associates. Tarnished with a history of instigating rugby club break-ups and splits since the 1950s, Songongo believed that, 'If Qeqe and his associates had emerged in the leadership at that time, from Spring Rose, it was not going to garner support.'[53] He assessed that the scales of power within Kwaru had long been tipped in favour of Qeqe:

> He was not wise, *maan*, as if he was not educated, that man. They put in these people, 'Hey, let us do this and that this way.' When he was taken out, he had known for quite some time that he could be taken out anytime, because even when Kwaru met, they met at Qeqe's place when it was scheduled to play. Even when it had won, the team and the crew went to Qeqe's place afterwards.[54]

Eric 'Kokie' Majola (top), Dan Qeqe (seated); student teachers, early 1950s (Qeqe family, Port Elizabeth)

Dan Qeqe with the extended Mbolekwa family from East London, his wife's family, early 1980s (Qeqe family, Port Elizabeth)

Fort Beaufort Cricket Club Executive Members. This is where Dan Qeqe learnt his sports administration skills. Standing, left: Dan Qeqe, H. Madikane (standing, third from left), Ray Mali (standing, fifth from left), Wilfred Khovu (standing, sixth from left) and Silas Nkanunu (seated, fourth from left). These members were to play pivotal roles in Kwaru. (Qeqe family, Port Elizabeth)

From left to right: Judge Cecil 'Doc' Somyalo, Qeqe's friend, attorney and business partner from the mid-1950s; Silas Nkanunu; and Dan Qeqe, early 1990s (Judge Cecil 'Doc' Somyalo)

Insignia of the oldest black rugby club, Union Rugby Football Club (Whites), founded in Port Elizabeth in 1887 (Thembile Matomela)

Dan Qeqe, late 1980s (Evening Post / Tiso Blackstar Group, Port Elizabeth)

Dan Qeqe relaxing with his grandchildren, late 1980s (Qeqe family, Port Elizabeth)

The Eastern Province Rugby Football Club, 1947. Dan Qeqe's mentor in sports administration and in the New Brighton Native Advisory Board, A.Z. Lamani, is seated fifth from left. Qeqe's archnemesis in rugby administration and colleague in the New Brighton Native Advisory Board, Singaphi, is seated second from left. (Mrs Pinky Nkanunu)

Kwaru team, including Colin Snodgras (standing, fourth from left) and Cheeky Watson (squatting, fourth from left), whose inclusion of white players in 1976 greatly upset Danie Craven and the government

UNIVERSITY OF FORT HARE RUGBY FOOTBALL CLUB 1949

BACK ROW L TO R: 1.Mrwetyana 2.Qunta 3.Zondeki 4.Burgess 5.Mafanya 6.Lujabe 7.Koloba 8.Mayekiso 9.Manjezi and 10.Tonjeni
MIDDLE ROW L TO R: 1.Forgotten 2.Makhene 3.Siwisa 4.Mogale 5.Forgotten 6.Rhukwana FRONT ROW L TO R: 1. Van Vught 2.Yanta 3.Mpamba 4.Mzimba 5.Ndziba

Dennis Siwisa, who was a founder-member of Kwaru and Secretary in its Action Committee (1977–1989). He is seated third from left, as captain of the University of Fort Hare Rugby Football Club, 1949, when he was a university student. (Siwisa family, Port Elizabeth)

Eastern Rugby Football Club, 1978, an affiliate of Kwaru, and one of the earliest black rugby teams founded in Grahamstown in 1904 (Mrs Pinky Nkanunu)

The Eastern Province Bantu Rugby Union team that participated in the 1957 President Giants Tournament. Qeqe's Spring Rose Rugby Football Club did not contribute players to the team became it had yet another fight that year with the administration of the P.E. African Rugby Board (PEARB). (Barry Sinuka)

Wilson F. Ximiya, on the right, Dan Qeqe's mentor in sports administration, the New Brighton Native Advisory Board, and Ciskei's politics (Jumartha Milase Majola)

Dan Qeqe with his wife, Rose Nonyameko Qeqe, early 2000s (Qeqe family, Port Elizabeth)

Dan Qeqe receiving a prize posthumously from the Andrew Mlangeni Foundation and the Department of Sports and Culture (Qeqe family, Port Elizabeth)

TOP *Eastern Province Bantu Rugby Football team, 1958. Spring Rose sent its players, Dan Qeqe and Eric Majola, to participate in the provincial tournament. (Barry Sinuka)*

LEFT *Kwaru team, 1970s (Mrs Pinky Nkanunu)*

Mrs Rose Nonyameko Qeqe, centre; on the right, Mrs Jumartha Milase Majola (Jumartha Milase Majola)

Kwaru's team member at play, Zola Yeye, holding the ball, at play (Qeqe family, Port Elizabeth)

A number of former players, administrators, and former political activists alluded to Badela's alleged role as a police informant, and many claim that this is what strained his relationship with Qeqe and his associates.[55] The allegations – no matter how widespread they may be – come from oral historical accounts with no corroborating documentation, and their veracity becomes more difficult to determine when considered against Badela's own strong struggle credentials.

Professor Guy Berger's anecdote, ambiguous as it may seem, may foster such a 'police informant' suggestion when it comes to Badela's reputation, an account lending itself to open-ended interpretation. It is the type of account that may have fuelled Qeqe's discomfort with Badela. In an obituary tribute to Mono Badela, who had inspired him when it came to political journalism, Berger recalled:

> Even more impressive at that time was his confidence and complete lack of fear. It was no big deal for Badela to take us to a whites-only Wimpy Bar and turn a blind eye to the security police tailing him. The same cops showed a special interest in him when interrogating me a year later, yet they could never quite convict him in court.[56]

Some who were much closer to Qeqe ventured to suggest that, perhaps, it was precisely Badela's charisma and 'star' status that drove Qeqe to bulldoze Badela out of Kwaru's presidency. Wilson went on to suggest that, '[The] only thing that I can think of is, Dan and them feared what was happening … That Badela would become too powerful within the rugby fold of Kwaru and set-up and things like that.'[57]

Numerous admonitions were directed at Qeqe and his associates against the undemocratic removal of Badela and his executive committee members. And Wilson personally rebuked Qeqe for his role in the Badela coup. He recounted that:

> Man, to be honest with you, I know about it. I personally said it's unethical and wrong, to go to a public meeting and decide on the fate of an organisation, to whom the people who voted against hasn't any standing within that. And it was also unfair of Dan and them. I used to tell Dan, 'You made nonsense here. Don't do it.' Sometimes he doesn't like it.[58]

Watson argued that the financial grievances used to oust Badela were unsubstantiated:

> Let's be quite frank. That argument they were using for coup was nonsense, do you understand? If the argument was that, you may need now some people who will take it to the next level, that's a different story. But that wasn't the argument to use. No, no, no, no. So the argument of misdirection of funds and stuff like that, that was nonsense, and team selection, incorrect. That was all nonsense.[59]

A lingering and constant variable in Kwaru's existence was the issue of state intervention, as decisively divisive and disentangling as factionalism. In the Badela coup, Koch came to the support of Qeqe's Action Committee. In a press statement, it was reported that:

> Mr RV Mankahla said that although members did not know that Kwaru had a constitution, it had been handed to the Chief Director of the Cape Midlands Bantu Affairs Administration Board, Mr LC Koch. He said in the constitution there was a clause that when members wanted to change the executive committee, nobody could stop them.[60]

As it turns out, Koch's support for the removal of Badela, a political thorn in the side of the state, and his replacement by another less-thorny political rival, might have been a miscalculation on his part.

The interim Action Committee was set up to address the particular challenges that had led to the ousting of the Badela executive committee. As Botha also pointed out, 'It must be noted that the Committee of 10 was an interim structure intended to address a specific problem at a particular moment, it was not meant to replace the constitutional structures.'[61] The first implosion in Kwaru had sown the seeds of the second implosion. And the accompanying political atmosphere of the 1980s made Kwaru all the more a political and social force.

9

… AND THE SECOND IMPLOSION (1982)

A profound sense of sadness accompanies many conversations about the second implosion of Kwaru, a gnawing sorrow at witnessing the end of history with the nakedness of their eyes – in watching history inexorably coming to a crushing end. And the poignancy in it all is how they were part of it, and could do little about it. As polarising as the story of Kwaru's end may be – and it remains to this day a divisive conversation – it continues to be framed along Qeqe/Nyondo, Kwaru/Zwiru factional lines, as much as the first implosion was triggered by the conflict between Badela and Qeqe, and between the Kwaru executive committee and the Action Committee.

In many ways, the Action Committee became a junta, even its name bearing an uncanny resemblance to that of many provisional military committees that have seized power from elected governments. And, like many such committees, it lingered in power unelected. This was despite the Kwaru constitution providing for an annual general meeting to elect an executive committee and management. This democratic deficit practically turned the Action Committee into the *de facto* Kwaru executive committee, without assuming all the responsibilities of accounting.

Throughout the 1970s, Qeqe rode the wave of the success and

turbulence of Kwaru. Particularly following the unceremonious ousting of Mono Badela's Kwaru executive committee in June 1977, when Qeqe succeeded to its Action Committee (1977–1989), his name became synonymous with Kwaru leadership. In a Kwaru popularly regarded as being led by a triumvirate (Silas Nkanunu, Dan Qeqe and Dennis Siwisa), the public face of Kwaru's leadership was nonetheless Dan Qeqe, its treasurer.

The lack of democracy within Kwaru might be explained, perhaps, by two factors. Fristly, the political activities of its leadership and the general ambience of state infiltration played very heavily into fears of how open democratic practices might derail the vision of Kwaru. Secondly, Qeqe and his associates might have harboured anxieties about the prospects of the new generation of Kwaru leadership caving under the destabilising forces of the local state. This new generation was significantly influenced by the June 1976 Soweto uprising and the attendant open democracy movement.

The Kwaru leadership had established a formidable political profile. This had brought them much closer to the scrutiny of the Security Branch and the local state. The Kwaru Action Committee triumvirate leadership of Qeqe–Nkanunu–Siwisa held firmly to the reins, while contending with harsh imprisonments, detentions and banning orders. In 1977, Qeqe and Siwisa were arrested in the Biko murder clampdown protests. Qeqe was arrested and jailed for two months, while Siwisa faced a 10-month jail term. These, however, served to fortify Kwaru's anti-apartheid iconic stature.

And so Qeqe's profile as a political and community activist was cemented. En masse, the communities of New Brighton and other townships of Port Elizabeth campaigned for the release of Qeqe in 1977. Pamphlets were distributed in New Brighton calling for his immediate release.[1] Qeqe's political profile – and, conversely, that of Kwaru – was further entrenched in the activities of PEBCO. Qeqe was imprisoned along with Badela, Thozamile Botha and Phalo Tshume, and, after his release, he was subject to a three-year banning order. Again, this further enhanced Kwaru's iconic anti-apartheid struggle stature.

Nkanunu had consistently played a significant supportive political role, providing legal services for detained activists. He also facilitated the ferrying of activists into exile, and connecting them with their parents when they were in exile.[2] Dennis Siwisa, also a long-time PAC activist,[3] played an incendiary political role. He had galvanised high school students of KwaZakhele and New Brighton to protest against the imprisonment of the 474 students arrested at St Stephen's Hall in New Brighton. Standing next to the then mayor of the Ibhayi Town Council, Mvelo Norris Singaphi, he had prompted students to mould their own struggles in their own terms. Vusi Pikoli, who had attended the gathering, recalled that in doing so, he had paraphrased Frantz Fanon's call for students to fulfil or betray the call of their generation.[4]

Whether true or imagined, state infiltration of Kwaru had become destabilising. Generating widespread mistrust and factionalism, a searing witch-hunt for police informants within Kwaru had taken root. Some maintain that the culture of sniffing out police informants in Kwaru came with the Watson brothers after they joined Kwaru in 1976. However, Mpumelelo 'Sbhidla' Majola traced this culture back to the founding of Kwaru in 1971. He argued that even back then, an association with the label *impimpi*, an informant, was deeply shocking and damning to a character. It all came about following the PEARB–Kwaru conflict, when the latter broke away from the former and some elements from the PEARB became susceptible to recruitment as spies. As Majola put it, 'So, there were remnants from that past that joined Dan Qeqe at that time.'[5]

State infiltration had become commonplace in Port Elizabeth in the 1980s, leading to a series of open conflicts on township streets. Most particularly, the local Security Branch had widely infiltrated Port Elizabeth's AZAPO, instigating a series of bloody conflicts between it and the UDF[6] that played themselves out in the townships of New Brighton, and other townships of Port Elizabeth and neighbouring Uitenhage.[7]

Majola explained how this culture of a witch-hunt for police informants collided with other volatile political and social developments in the 1980s. The emergence of *amabutho* on the political landscape rendered the tensions in Kwaru even more complex.[8] *Amabutho*, a group of militant youth who had aligned themselves to Charterist ideology and UDF mobilisation, were particularly interested in the control of civil society organisations in the townships, their methods of mobilisation often centring on coercion and physical threats, creating a cult of paramilitary presence. Activities aimed at the hunting down of and sniffing out of alleged police informants in Kwaru might have been given a stronger momentum when *amabutho* arrived on the political landscape.

Valence Watson insisted, though, that Kwaru was infiltrated by state security structures in the 1980s. He maintained that, by virtue of its elevated stature in the anti-apartheid struggle, Kwaru attracted immense political interest that sought to disentangle it from within. He pointed out that Kwaru had thus come under intense strain with the Security Police infiltrating its structures. Attracting around 30 000 spectators to a game, the organisation became attractive to the state and the Security Branch. Watson pointed out: '[There's] no doubt, the Security Police played a huge role because the winner in this would be them … But don't be surprised that on the Kwaru side, there were people pushing issues too. Remember, when the Security Police see conflict, they would enter the conflict.'[9]

In the wake of the 1976 student uprising, some younger members carried this emancipatory political spirit into Kwaru. In June 1976, high school students in Soweto staged a protest against the planned introduction of Afrikaans as the medium of instruction for all subjects taught in local schools. Students felt that they barely understood Afrikaans, and that compelling them to study in Afrikaans would take too great a toll. Moreover, they felt that their teachers were not sufficiently proficient in Afrikaans, let alone trained to teach in the language. But, more than anything, what drove students to protest was their abiding abhorrence of Afrikaans, a language they regarded as that of the oppressor.

The Soweto students' protests had much greater political and historical significance, extending beyond the moment of June 16, 1976. It had a national multiplying effect, effectively transforming the broad narrative of political demands and agitation. The movement ventured much further, into strident advocacy campaigns for democratisation of civic society institutions; the removal of native advisory boards; the institution of democratic township councils; workers' rights; the role of youth in society; and other political demands. These calls became more vibrant in the mood set by the pervasive black consciousness ideology.

The lack of democratic practices in the Action Committee – particularly when it came to free and fair elections and electoral processes within Kwaru – was set on a collision course with the expectations of the new cohort of Kwaru members streaming out of this generation. Ncula explained how the emergence of this new generation, who were then attending Newell and Cowan high schools, 'bought into the spirit of liberation'.[10] Led by Amon Nyondo, they influenced their clubs – Winter Rose, Cruel Tigers and Young Collegians – to become affiliated to Kwaru. 'They were all very young. Then they decided that now, with the influence of Amon Nyondo and the Watsons, they would challenge for positions in the executive of Kwaru.'[11]

Majola, similar to Ncula, rationalised this democratic deficit as a protective measure – a defence against challenges from the sinister machinations of factionalism instigated by Nyondo and the Watson brothers. Majola explained:

> All I is know is that Mr Nyondo arrived. So there was a manoeuvre hatched by another faction of kicking Mr Qeqe and Mr Nkanunu out ... All I know is that they said that Mr Nyondo came to PE, and there was a move to make him president, and remove Nkanunu as president, because the friends of the Watsons were getting things right ... I think old Dennis [Siwisa] was there at that time. They were being kicked out of office, to be replaced by Nyondo and his associates.[12]

Amon Nyondo, who had just been deported to Port Elizabeth by the Ciskei government for his non-racial sports activities, recalled the dissatisfaction among players of various clubs with the absence of elections. Upon affiliating Young Collegians Rugby Football Club to Kwaru, Nyondo maintained that numerous rugby clubs had resolved not to play fixtures until a new Kwaru executive committee was elected. In the meetings of the Young Collegians in 1981, there were rumours doing the rounds that some Kwaru clubs had resolved not to participate in fixtures unless an AGM was convened. They wanted a new executive committee elected. 'This was the mood. That is what was going on,'[13] Nyondo emphasised.

The recollections of Qeqe supporters of how the culture of a democratic deficit was formed are framed in a jocular manner, with Qeqe's authoritarian style of governance relayed in banter. And in these recollections the subtext has been glorified: Qeqe was wary of the local state onslaught of Kwaru. This was his way of driving out unseen Koch-led, state-driven forces acting against the existence and interests of Kwaru. These often came in the form of police informants allegedly planted in Kwaru.

Ncula, who was then Kwaru's match secretary, relayed in length how Qeqe suppressed the call for elections in Kwaru elective meetings:

> So I remember one AGM, where for the position of President, there were five candidates. And then, for the position of Treasurer, there were five or six candidates. At this particular AGM, Qeqe stood up ... Then he said, 'Guys, most organisations, they always break up because of elections, where positions are contested.' And he said, 'Today we've got five candidates for the presidency. Silas Nkanunu has done good work for all the years now. Can any of these five stand up and say, what improvements they are going to bring about, or can they do better than Nkanunu? Can they stand up, one by one?' Hey, nobody stood up. Then Baas Dan said, 'Okay, guys, it looks like Nkanunu stays as the president.'
>
> Then [they] came now to my position. Then the treasurer and the secretary. Then he said, 'Ncula has always provided us with pictures and time, well done. Is there anybody who can do a better job than him?' Nobody stood up. So, he said, he remains. Then came to his position. And then he showed the bank balance. He used to, he'll show the bank account for all the people to view and all that. So, he said, 'Is there anybody contesting for these positions that can do better than these?' Then he said, 'Look, guys, we've got the three main officials. Then we'll leave you to contest and continue with your elections, for the deputy president.'[14]

Gerald Majola similarly recalled this sly manoeuvre of a 'benevolent dictator',[15] and how Qeqe extended this practice to non-racial cricket bodies. It was partly aimed at grooming younger administrators. Majola recalled:

> Yes. All of them came through his hands. Danny [Jordaan], he became our president of the United Cricket Club, elected. He was elected first as secretary. Baas Dan, every position he held, he was treasurer. He handled the money. He was the executive of the United [Cricket Club], elected. Baas Dan stood up and said, 'Silas [Nkanunu], you are going to be president.' This is an AGM. Everyone was there. 'Silas, you are going to be president. Danny, you are going to learn from Silas. Piti, meetings are going to be chaired by you.'
>
> Remember that we were not always there all the time. We were grown up. 'So, Danny, you're gonna understudy Silas, but meetings will be chaired by you.' Khaya was secretary, he was my older brother. Baas Dan was now busy electing, 'Is there any person who has a problem with what I'm saying?' Who was going to answer him? 'Is there anyone who has a problem?' No, there's no one. 'There's your executive, gentlemen.'[16]

Majola further explained Qeqe's personality that drove and informed his authoritarian governance of Kwaru affairs:

> Baas Dan is authoritarian ... you should not stand next to him, because he would hit you with his knobkerrie. If you're going to oppose him on a point that did not make sense, you had to stand far from him, so that you could run away, otherwise he would corner you there. So it worked for him, and it worked for a lot of things, because sometimes democracy doesn't work.[17]

Also commenting on Qeqe's authoritarian, and rather intimidating governance style, Archie Mkele, who had also defected to the splinter Zwiru Group in 1982, pointed out that:

> I used to hear that, and that in meetings, in Spring Rose meetings, even in the meetings, there was an issue about him. The guys would go to a meeting with the hope that they were going to attack him.

> Aha! In that meeting he would go there, quiet. He would take his knobkerrie and put it underneath, and then he will sit and listen. The guys would be scared. No one will attack [him] … Then the meeting will run, and the meeting will be over, and then everybody will go home. He had that element … He wanted to do things in his own way. Otherwise, he was a good man.[18]

Mthobi Tyamzashe seemed to rationalise this democracy deficit as the basis for Qeqe's leadership foresight. It was a far-sightedness that sought a utilitarian value. However, it was a process that necessarily forced a leader to forsake democratic principles and processes. Tyamzashe explained:

> The question is: under which circumstances are these? And there are those circumstances where you want to retain the thing … [No], the guys are not leaders for no reason. They're leaders because they get results, and results are things that you don't leave to chance, to make sure that you get the team that you want. He made sure of that … These guys do have, they lead from the front … They can't say, it will be up to you guys voting. No. They say, it is good for the country. This is good for Kwaru. Therefore, I must get this result.[19]

Qeqe-aligned forces villainised the Nyondo–Zwiru camp as disruptive. 'Well, I'm not surprised to hear that he's been villainised. I'm not surprised because it really, the split was ugly. That split was ugly,'[20] Judge Mpati remembered of the second implosion from when he was a SARU administrator. Recalling the pain of the split, Ngconde Balfour remarked that, 'The biggest thing that happened to Kwaru [was] when it broke down, and Zwiru developed/emerged. It was very painful – the team that they had built for a very long time, they'd built that team for a very long time.'[21]

The villainisation of Nyondo focused mainly on his personality – a 'go big or go home' kind of man, as recalled by Tyamzashe, his long-time colleague in non-racial sports administration in East London and the Border region.[22] He was acutely sharp, brave and courageous, with strategic leadership skills honed in his long, non-racial sports liberation activism. Wilson pointed out that in non-racial sports activist circles, his intellect matched only that of the SACOS stalwart, Ebrahim Patel.[23]

Amon Mbulaleki Nyondo, now a practising advocate in Port Elizabeth, was born at Scheepers' farm, approximately 80 kilometres from Port Elizabeth. He spent part of his childhood in the Brickfields area, a township located outside Swartkops in Port Elizabeth, accommodating both Africans and coloureds. By 1962, when he moved to Zwelitsha, outside King William's Town, he began a regular commute. During school terms, he lived in Zwelitsha, and spent his holidays in Brickfields with his brothers.[24]

He attended primary, secondary and high schools in Zwelitsha, and worked in between to fund his education. Intermittently, he worked as a gardener, at Swartkops Hotel and at Coca-Cola. After completing his matric, he held a Grade Two clerk position in the Ciskei government's Department of Education. Throughout his primary, high-school and university years at the University of Fort Hare, he played rugby and participated in sports administration in various capacities. In Zwelitsha, he was a second-division rugby player in a lock-forward position. Playing social rugby, he played against local teams such as the Radio Xhosa rugby team. In 1965, he was a member of the All Blacks, a local rugby club, participating in Zwelitsha's inter-zone rugby fixtures.

It was at Fort Hare that he came under the influence of non-racial sports liberation.[25] There, Stofile and others had been mobilising various sports clubs into VERU and SEDRU. At Fort Hare, the Fort Hare Rugby Football Club, the Fort Hare Ring-Tennis Club, the Volleyball Club of the University of Fort Hare, the Red Lions Rugby Football Club and the Victoria East Soccer Union came under non-racial sports influence. The constitutions of these unions were uniformly replete with decrees that stated that '[membership] shall not differentiate on the grounds of race, creed, sex or religion'.[26] On affiliation, their constitutions also determined that they shall affiliate to nearest non-racial provincial units, in turn affiliated to SARU and SACOS.[27]

And so it was that Nyondo also came under this influence, further pushing him into the administrative capacities of non-racial rugby after his expulsion from Fort Hare following a mass student protest in 1973.[28] By 1981, he and his associates in non-racial sports had attracted the ire of the Ciskei, leading to his deportation to Port Elizabeth.[29] Nyondo,

Albert Tyulu, Douglas Maku and Fundile Mabece were arrested by the Ciskei government 'because of our push for non-racialism, and because of Kwaru's push for non-racialism, and getting the whole country, so to speak, to see that there is a need for us, as Africans, not to be used by the South African Rugby Board of the whites'.[30]

In particular, their activism in 1981 was largely fuelled by a fear that, at the precipice of Ciskei's independence in 1981, their non-racial union, the King William's Town African District Union (KADRU), would be banned. By the time of his deportation to Port Elizabeth, Nyando was deputy president of the Border Rugby Union and, in 1980 as well as the following year, he was elected president of the same rugby union, and also of KADRU.[31]

Banishing Nyondo back to Port Elizabeth by way of deportation right at the time of Kwaru's low morale was fortuitous. It lit a keg, setting into motion a chain of events that led to the second implosion. In Port Elizabeth, after he joined the Young Collegians Rugby Football Club, the club became affiliated to Kwaru. This came about following a formal meeting at Qeqe's house, after they had been summoned by the triumvirate leadership of the Action Committee.

The Action Committee's insistent refusal to convene an AGM hinged on a remnant of the Badela coup: that, until the Badela executive committee had returned Kwaru property, AGMs would not be convened. This was also reflected in court documents filed by Nkanunu, president of the Action Committee, who pointed out:

> First of all, it was reaffirmed that the resolution will stand, namely that Mr Badela (who was the former president) and his executive committee members should return the union property, that includes financial records and statements of accounts, balls, etc. before a general election could be held.[32]

The Kwaru-filed court document further stated that, although normal general elections were convened between 1977 and 1982, annual general elections were not held for office bearers in the Kwaru executive committee to give account.[33] In court documents, Nkanunu, however, maintained that after the Badela coup, a Kwaru executive committee was elected in 1978. It was then that he was elected president.[34]

The chain of events leading to the ousting of the Action Committee was sparked by conflict over the awarding of a trophy and awards to a Kwaru club. Emphasising the emotional attachment to trophies and awards among African rugby unions, Nyondo pointed out that '[central] to all disputes of rugby unions of the Africans will always be a question of a gripe relating to trophies. Very central.'[35]

The Pilbro Cup, the premier trophy for inter-club fixtures in Kwaru, was a yearly highlight. It carried attendant club pride. In 1979, it was won by Fabs.[36] The following year, Easterns won, and in 1982, the Wallabies. The conflict centred on how the bias of the Action Committee toward certain clubs dictated the distribution of resources to the awards ceremonies of the Pilbro Cup. Complaints were that the Action Committee spent more on awards ceremonies held at certain clubs to which they had greater affinity. For the Easterns, with strong loyalties to the Action Committee leadership (Nkanunu and Siwisa were members of Easterns), a huge award and celebratory function was held in 1980. So special was the function that Archbishop Desmond Tutu was invited as a guest speaker.[37]

When the Wallabies won the Pilbro Cup in 1981, the Action Committee leadership claimed that it did not have the resources to host an awards ceremony for them. Nkanunu even allegedly approached the leadership of the Young Collegians to host a Wallabies awards ceremony within their own club function, which they had planned to convene at Daku Hall in New Brighton. This squabble and unease served only to further aggravate relations between clubs and the Action Committee leadership, adding to the brewing discontent over the absence of elections.

Then, in 1982, St Cyprian's petitioned Kwaru to convene an annual general meeting.[38] The Kwaru constitution allowed for a petition signed by a minimum of six clubs to call for the convening of an AGM. Initially, the St Cyprian-led petition managed to successfully galvanise a minimum number of six clubs, but this attempt faltered when two of the six – Park Rovers and St Cyprian's themselves – withdrew their participation and signatures from the petition.

The president of St Cyprian's, Feya Sobikwa, long considered

Qeqe's right-hand man in sports and business affairs, withdrew his club, as did Park Rovers Rugby Football Club. The latter's president, Mr S Sqwebu, who was employed by Qeqe at the Dan Qeqe Stadium, withdrew his club's support due to a conflict of interest. A court's Notice of Motion filed by Nkanunu reaffirmed that:

> In the meeting which took place on the 24th January 1982 … The President of ST CYPRIANS and PARK ROVERS Rugby Football Clubs, Messrs F SOBIKWA and S SQWEBU, respectively were present in the meeting. Both Presidents informed the meeting that they knew nothing about the petition purporting to come from their respective clubs … They both further pointed out that their respective clubs had not convened meetings since the close of the rugby season last year and that their respective club secretaries had not been instructed to draw the said petition. Because the number of signatures to the petition calling for the special General Meeting was accordingly reduced to that [of] four instead of six secretaries as required … the petition was not valid.[39]

Then the Wallabies wrote a letter to other clubs, inviting them to the Sisonke Hall to further deliberate on strategies to launch a second petition. Ngcaphe, along with Nyondo, dissuaded the Wallabies from using the Pilbro Cup discontent in approaching the second petition. They approached the general secretary of the Wallabies, Pazzie Allah, and persuaded him to consider a new strategy in order to mount a successful second petition. And the new strategy, they said, had to have nothing to do with the emotional cries concerning their discontent with the Pilbro Cup. Ngcaphe recalled:

> We agreed as Young Collegians that, let us go to Wallabies and influence them in that way … We do not support you to do things in an emotional way, complaining about trophies you have not been awarded … Drop this matter … Let us follow that petition of St Cyprian's and normalise things in Kwaru, so that we convene an annual general meeting, because its five years since we've had an annual general meeting.[40]

Echoing concern over the absence of elections, and why he and his brothers moved to Zwiru, Watson rationalised the move on a grander Freedom Charter ideological scale:

> There hadn't been elections for a number of years, I think ... But the ANC propaganda thing was going through Kwaru ranks ... Now we've got a Kwaru that says, no voting now. We're not going to have AGMs for a while. Guys were saying, but [on] the one hand, chaps, we are caucusing, discussing about elections ... But why now that we are not able to vote here in our organisation?[41]

The petition gained the support of 15 out of 20 clubs, and so they convened a meeting at Sisonke Hall on a Sunday afternoon. It was decided at that meeting to send a delegation of 15 people representing the 15 clubs that had signed the petition to Nkanunu's house to present the petition.

On not finding Nkanunu at his house, they left a handwritten note with his wife, Mrs Pinky Nkanunu. In it, they demanded that Nkanunu, in his capacity as president of Kwaru's Action Committee, hold an AGM within 21 days. And if he did not issue a notice for such a meeting within seven days, the note read, the petitioners would assume that the Action Committee had no intention of convening an AGM. In such an event, they would then move for a vote of no confidence in the Action Committee at their next meeting. When Nkanunu failed to respond to the petition, at their next meeting at Sisonke Hall the group moved for a vote of no confidence on the Action Committee. *In absentia* of the Action Committee, Nyondo was elected president of Kwaru, with a new executive committee that included Fanie James as general secretary and L Mhlambiso as treasurer.[42]

But Nkanunu responded that the appended signatures of Thomas Sullo and GM Mvula rendered the petition null and void. Sullo and Mvula were members of Badela's executive committee, and they had been banned from participating in Kwaru affairs. The Notice of Motion affirmed this, pointing out that, according to a resolution of a SARU-chaired meeting convened at Port Elizabeth's Holiday Inn in Port Elizabeth immediately following the Badela coup, the Badela executive committee had been charged with not having returned Kwaru property. Until they had returned the property, members of the old executive committee had thus been banned from participating in Kwaru affairs. The Nkanunu-lodged Notice of Motion read:

> I would respectfully further mention that two gentlemen namely GM MVULA and T SULLO who are signatories on behalf of BUTCHER BIRDS and WALLABIES Rugby Football Clubs which was outvoted in about 1977 when the present Applicant's Executive Committee was elected … In terms of that resolution[,] until that happened, the members of the old Executive Committee were banned from participating in any way in Applicant's administration including individual club activities. This condition has not been fulfilled as yet. I accordingly, respectfully contend that these two abovenamed gentlemen were not competent to sign a petition on behalf of the aforesaid clubs.[43]

Effectively then, two Kwaru executive committees came into existence, each according itself legitimacy as a Kwaru executive committee. As Ngcaphe affirmed, '[And] we knew that we had two executives, but in our understanding, they are not a legitimate executive. Also in their understanding, we are not a legitimate executive.'[44] In that melee, Nyondo's executive committee and group came to be called the 'Sisonke Group' on account of their meetings regularly convened at the Sisonke Hall.[45] '[There was] the executive of Nyondo, which was called the Sisonke Group, because we were meeting at Sisonke; and then Qeqe and Nkanunu who were meeting where they were meeting,'[46] Nyondo explained.

Ngconde Balfour intimated that personal issues were driving conflict in Kwaru, maintaining that, 'Amon Nyondo and associates, and other people, and Oom Dan, tried his best to heal the divisions, but it was about personal issues.'[47] Describing himself as a difficult person to contend with, Nyondo located his villainisation in the hostile attitude of the Kwaru triumvirate leadership towards him. In his own words, he pointed out:

> Because of my involvement in what was seen then as an uprising

> against Kwaru ... Because you must remember that the three men were very central in this entire situation, in terms of not willing to say, let's allow these clubs if they don't want us. Qeqe was number one; Nkanunu was number two; Dennis Siwisa, number three. Those were the three men who would not listen to anything. And in that order, the champion was Qeqe.[48]

He reasoned that behind Qeqe's insistence on not giving in to a new Kwaru leadership was his conviction that he was the only one capable of preserving Kwaru against the onslaught of Koch and the local state. Said Nyondo:

> [The] gist of the whole thing is that Qeqe regarded himself as the only person who can withstand the might of the Bantu Affairs Administration Board, and represented by that white man, Koch. He regarded himself as the only man ... He did not trust that I could be in a position to do that. He never believed that ... And that is why he was willing to oppose that tooth and nail.[49]

The Action Committee continued to run the affairs of Kwaru as a *de facto* executive committee. Constitutionally, there was no structure in place with the mandate and power to dissolve the Action Committee.[50] 'It was a very informal thing right through. That is how it happened. That was the leadership of Kwaru. Now, when you had that, and you must remember as well that when Kwaru wins on the field, nobody pays attention to these nitty gritties.'[51]

By 1980/81, the clamour for AGM elections to elect a new executive committee was gaining momentum. The Action Committee's counter-argument remained focused on the need for the return of Kwaru property before AGM elections could be allowed. And, as Nyondo argued, for the Action Committee that was 'then usable to have a non-representative leadership in place throughout'.[52] In response, the Badela group consistently pointed out that it had, in fact, returned Kwaru property.

A slew of litigations filed by the Action Committee's Nkanunu then ensued. It began with an interdict against Nyondo, Fanie James (general secretary) and L Mhlambiso (treasurer),[53] through the attorney Thole

Majodina, who had taken the case after Dumile Kondile had refused it.[54] With the Action Committee emerging triumphant in court, it was assured of a massive support base. 'More than 30 people, including club officials, players and supporters, yesterday pledged their support for the KwaZakele Rugby Union Executive Committee,'[55] the press reported. At the time, Qeqe's banning order from the 1977 Biko clampdown arrest had just been lifted. At that meeting, Qeqe was 'given a prolonged standing ovation',[56] before committing to the crowd that, 'I will never stop serving Kwaru. Your support gives me more encouragement.'[57]

Between litigations, SARU held a number of interventions between the Action Committee and the Sisonke Group. In Nyondo's summation, SARU's view was that 'these guys must sort themselves out'.[58] The Sisonke Group sorely sought affiliation to SARU. It was a search for a home, a need for recognition as a legitimate, non-racial union. It was as much a search for affiliation as that which Kwaru had desperately sought in 1971.

Judge Lex Mpati pointed out that SARU could not afford to have yet another splinter group. Already, there were four rugby unions in existence in the Port Elizabeth/Uitenhage area: Kwaru, the Bethelsdorp Rugby Board of Control (BERCOC), the Uitenhage Rugby Union, and the District Rugby Union. 'We can't afford to have a fifth. I mean, by doing that, we are actually encouraging the split, rather than saying, we are working towards the two uniting again.'[59]

This multiplicity found expression in chaotic fixtures. In one well-documented, muddled fixture one weekend in 1982, the 'Nkanunu Group'[60] fielded six clubs, while the Sisonke Group had 10 teams at the Dan Qeqe Stadium.[61] On the field that day, as Ngcaphe remarked, strangely, the players did not collide with each other. 'They ducked each other. You could see that these were not truly played matches, but it's just that, these two clubs are paying allegiance to Nyondo and his executive.'[62] In another court interdict the Action Committee filed against the Sisonke Group following this chaotic fixture, Nkanunu explained the hilarity of it all: 'Briefly, each time two teams took the field, two other teams from their side also took the field with a referee and two linesmen. So you would in effect then have 60 people – 60 players on the field, two referees and four linesmen.'[63]

It was in that game at the stadium that Nkanunu, sitting with Qeqe, suggested they capitulate to the Sisonke Group. He pleaded with Qeqe to recognise the legitimacy of its executive committee over theirs. During that day, Nkanunu said, 'Qeqe, these people don't want us. Let's give in.' And Qeqe said, 'No, we can't.'[64] Nyondo recalled part of the conversation they had.

Nyondo also pointed to a class issue that apparently hindered him in taking over the Kwaru presidency. At that time, he lived in a shack, and was an employee at a furniture shop. This, he believed, played a major role in generating hostile perceptions about him. '[How] would we have a leader for a club who is resident in the shacks? Who the hell is this guy? I'm telling you, those were the insults that were flown around,'[65] Nyondo recalled. And Ngcaphe remembered in detail how at one meeting Nyondo's personal background was the object of disdain: 'Do you think a President of Kwaru can come out of the shacks? ... Do you think that from those shacks a President of Kwaru can emerge?'[66] Ngcaphe remembered how Mdange, a pro-Qeqe Kwaru member, lobbied against Nyondo taking over the leadership of Kwaru.

And indeed, a rule *nisi* was issued against the Sisonke Group, ordering that they should not be:[67]

1. Organising, arranging or causing rugby matches to be played at the Dan Qeqe Stadium, Zwide, Port Elizabeth;
2. Disrupting or in any way interfering with rugby matches, organised and arranged by the Applicant at the said stadium under the auspices of the Applicant; and
3. Disrupting or in any way interfering with the management and conduct of the affairs of the Applicant.

However, that did not prevent the tragedy that occurred at the Dan Qeqe Stadium. It is a well-documented event described in the minutest detail in both oral and documented accounts. Amid a stampede, fights with knives, axes and other weapons ensued between players and followers of the two groups at the Dan Qeqe Stadium, resulting in four fatalities. Nyondo described in detail how the tragedy unfolded:

> [There] was then pandemonium, if one were to say. Numbers were swelling … The clubs came up, and every time they were arriving, we said, guys, don't get inside. And then there was then a mood that developed, a hostile mood that developed. And some of the guys, they were trying to peep through the cracks, to see what's happening inside there. They noticed that Dan Qeqe's breakdown truck was parked there, behind the stadium's grandstand. The guys were there, and they were moving around. They weren't there to play rugby, but they were there to occupy the field …
>
> More than one person died. I was told that there were four people that died on that day … They drove through, and, before they drove through, Mthana was stabbed just behind the neck by another person through the cracks.[68]

Violence in its most naked expression split the communities between the Action Committee and Sisonke Group formations. They sought each other out, attacking each other. Archie Mkele described one such gruesome community attack:

> The Spring Rose guys, I still remember, I was accused of being a ringleader of that split, myself and another guy, Benjamin Skosana …[69] We were the people that were influencing the clubs, the twelve clubs, and all that, you know. They used to go, they used to raid us, door to door …[70]

In an Action Committee court case filed against the Sisonke Group following the skirmish at the Dan Qeqe Stadium, an exasperated Judge Stewart remarked:

> I do not see that it can do the game of rugby any good to have two different groups as they are in this case, who are apparently unable to agree as to who will play tomorrow afternoon and who will not play … If indeed that happens, then those before me today will have to search their consciousness to find out whether they [is] not in fact responsible. The blood of their brothers [is] shed because of a game of rugby, they must answer to the Maker for that blood.[71]

These commotions took a heavy toll on Qeqe, grinding against his character, incrementally giving way to a darker side of him. The day after the stadium bloodshed, Ngcaphe noticed the following about Qeqe and some of his associates:

> Now, what was very hard about Qeqe that day, as much as I respect him; on that day four people died, the following day, they had a braai at the stadium. We were there by Johnson Road, sitting there nearby Vusani's. Then we saw them there, Qeqe was holding a brown parcel.[72]

The darker side of his character, a more uncouth and profane Qeqe, was a result of exasperation and exhaustion. It even found its way into his dealing with Kwaru's organisational matters. Of Qeqe Gerald Majola observed:

> It did damage him a lot ... he had developed a habit of swearing. He was not that old man loved by the people. And this, this, that's why I say this thing killed sport and the dignity ... So, even that honour you had for that person goes away. And that respect you had for him goes away. So, he lost a lot of that because of what happened.[73]

Following the stadium bloodshed, Nyondo decided that fights with the Action Committee were not worth the loss of lives, and so he decided to formally constitute the Sisonke Group into Zwiru, the Zwide Rugby Union.[74] The emergence of Zwiru took the 'cream' of rugby clubs and players from Kwaru – just as Kwaru had taken the best clubs and players from the PEARB in 1971.[75] Although VERU initially refused to play against them, Balfour attested to the strength of the new Zwiru. And yet, despite these acerbic commotions, he acquiesced to Qeqe's insistence on remaining on the non-racial rugby scene. He remembered that:

> When it broke down, some of us felt, we are not going to play against Zwiru. We want to play against Kwaru, but unfortunately, the players wanted to play with Zwiru, because they were not outsiders ... Oom Dan stayed through that. He stayed through that

> because, to him, what was important was not this side or that side. It was about non-racial rugby.[76]

And as much as Kwaru was embedded in the community, the reverberations of the second implosion ruptured New Brighton and other townships of Port Elizabeth. Gerald Majola observed:

> Financially, we were not attracting the crowd we used to attract, both Kwaru and Zwiru. There were factions, and people … remember there were a lot of other people who were not playing rugby, but those people used to come and enjoy. Now, they don't want to be associated either with Kwaru, or with Zwiru, because … there were even fights outside, raiding each other, because someone had been knocked down by a car at the stadium … So, now families were not talking to each other, people were not greeting each other. I remember coming back from Cape Town … I knew everyone. Your friends were my friends. But now, they were scared of paying me a visit, because hey, there was tension between the Spring Rose, and maybe the African Bombers, or whatever.[77]

Ironically, the second implosion thus 'killed Kwaru the same way Kwaru had killed the PE Board',[78] observed Songongo. And Qeqe had led the killing of the PE Board, as much as he was central to the self-immolation of Kwaru in the second implosion. Yet, who instigated what commotion that led to the downfall of Kwaru and the emergence of Zwiru can never be reduced to individualistic and simple understandings. The biography of Kwaru, from its birth to its death, is a social biography of Port Elizabeth – and Qeqe remains part of that social biography. Dan Qeqe played a leading role in the birth of Kwaru and the Dan Qeqe Stadium. It was a leading role, shaped equally by the social, political and cultural forces he inherited. To a significant measure, he had also swayed these forces to steer the direction in which Kwaru moved and the stadium functioned.

And yet, despite it all, it is incredible how an ordinary sports club became the epicentre of people's political and social struggles. Even more astonishing is how such an ordinary black rugby union stoked the ongoing fears of the Port Elizabeth local state and national cabinet

– fears that the sports–political white establishment was jostling with, in playing the imagination and aspirations of Port Elizabeth townships and black South Africans. This is a demonstration of how a seemingly insignificant feat in regional history, of regional personalities and regional movements, left footprints that helped shape South African history. They are historical markings that prove how regional personalities, movements and actions are as significant as national ones in steering South African politics and societies. Qeqe demonstrated how little Kwaru mastered the art of contending with the sustained sanctions of the local state, the harassment of the Security Branch and the abiding counter powers of cabinet, while listening to the winds of non-racial sports liberation, Charterist and black consciousness ideologies, and the destructive heresies of *amabutho*.

10

QEQE AND PORT ELIZABETH IN THE 1970S

The 1970s saw a prosperous Dan Qeqe at the height of his powers, and on a warpath against inherited injustices, as much as his own political contradictions. It was his busiest, most productive decade. It saw him winning, scheming, betraying, bulldozing, rebelling, withdrawing and being jailed. He 'was involved in a lot of things, a lot of things … I was amazed as to where he got all this energy for all these activities,'[1] Somyalo observed of him. In all these undertakings, he led. Mrs Majola also affirmed that Qeqe, 'In everything, he takes a lead.'[2] And wherever he went, wherever he was, trouble followed him.[3]

Qeqe continued to battle, however, with his contradictions. On the one hand, he was a firmly non-racial sports and anti-apartheid activist. He was even arrested during the Biko clampdown of unrest in September 1977. On the other hand, he served on the Port Elizabeth Joint Bantu Advisory Board, and campaigned for seats for his colleagues in the Ciskei General Assembly of 1973, canvassing on behalf of Wilson F Ximiya, Chief Lent Maqoma and Chief M Mabandla for Ciskei parliamentary seats. He was intimately involved in the formation of the Ciskei homeland government right from the early 1970s.[4] In that role he was a conservative counter-revolutionary, appropriating the role of an amaJingqi sub-ethnic group representative of the Victoria East Council area in Ciskei.

But, even more distinctive was that the 1970s saw Qeqe immersed in bold and innovative educational initiatives in the community. What stood out in these was his self-initiated project to upgrade secondary schools to high schools in the townships of New Brighton and KwaZakhele. Before, due to Newell High School being the only high school in New Brighton and KwaZakhele, the majority of black youth exited the schooling system on completing Form 3 (the current equivalent of Grade 10).

Traditionally, and in droves, they joined the unskilled and semi-skilled labour force in the fast-industrialising Port Elizabeth–Uitenhage industrial complex. Qeqe's school upgrading project markedly changed the trajectory of education in Port Elizabeth, and the number of black pupils who could go on to university and other institutions of higher learning significantly increased.

BY NOW, QEQE HAD strengthened his base. Physically, that base was represented by his petrol station and the hall space at the back of his house in the upmarket Thembalethu suburb of New Brighton. To Ambassador Phumelele 'Stone' Sizani, a former PEBCO and UDF publicity secretary,[5] Qeqe's garage and residence represented everything communal and political about black Port Elizabeth. For him, 'the gathering in front of his petrol station allowed me to listen without participating … I noted local and national politics, community matters, sports, discipline, business and cultural issues that had to do with the recent, current and future.'[6]

Tanana also asserted that Qeqe was 'hands-on'[7] when it came to most political, civic and sports matters in Port Elizabeth. And, not surprisingly, 'you'd find that most people met at Qeqe's. Even if you had a meeting, the group from East London and Port Elizabeth, if you want proper feedback on matters, you had to go to Qeqe's.'[8] Balfour also remembered his 'base' as not only a meeting place, but also overnight accommodation for non-racial sports liberation and political activists who had come from afar.[9] As Songongo had also noted, this was where Kwaru players gathered before and after a match, even during the Kwaru presidency of Badela.

The attraction of his base and his charm and empathy for the needs of the poor fed into each other. It was Qeqe's innate love for the people of his community that saw to it that he became a pillar of social welfare. In his butchery, he consistently wrote off the debts of customers who were unable to pay, often to the irritation of his wife. Ncula recalled that:

> And also the other thing that made people to love him was his sympathy for the poor. You know, Dan Qeqe, with his shop and butchery, there were people who would go and buy on account [credit], and so on. And they'd never come back and pay ... He never raided those people who didn't pay. He just writes them off. *Ja*, he just writes them off. And he was very sympathetic to the poor.[10]

It was also where he harboured political fugitives (Vusi Pikoli, Sizwe Kondile,[11] Thozamile Majola and Phakamile Ximiya) on their way to exile, hotly pursued by the Security Branch.[12] Phumla, oblivious to the fact that they had been deposited all that time right under her nose at the back of her home, was completely thrown when she pounced on them one night. She recalled:

> So, when I went to the back rooms, my father said, 'Phumla, go and put diesel into this car.' So, I know, we were not supposed to switch on the lights there, *mos*. There were restrictions ... There was a curfew on petrol ... When I was about to finish up on putting the diesel, they said, 'Hey, Phumla.' When I looked up, 'Yhuu! Here they are, these people who are being hunted!' They left [gesticulating with a good-bye wave].[13]

The 'base' was also leased out to some of New Brighton's sports clubs. One of them was a karate club where a teenager, Mkhuseli Jack, trained. For Jack, this was where Qeqe once memorably displayed his peace-making acumen. He remembered one particularly chaotic incident between his own karate *dojo* and another's. His *sensei*, a karate instructor, had written a letter of invitation to a fighting contest between their karate students. Jack's *sensei* had previously trained the instructor of the other karate *dojo*. However, apparently taking offence at the invitation, the invited *sensei* wanted the contest to be held immediately.

In haste, he rushed with all his karate students that evening to Jack's *sensei*'s *dojo* at the back of Qeqe's house, challenging them to a fight on the spot.

> There was blood all over the place. I mean, with our own karate suits into the streets in the middle of, I mean, late at night, the cars, and it was all white this side, running out. And Dan Qeqe, of course and his family and his wife and his children, all came out to try and stop a fight of karatekas. But anyway, Dan Qeqe, of course, never took sides on this fight. He was just of the view that, *aargh*, it should have been done properly. And then that was it.[14]

Qeqe's involvement in political activism was, however, shaped by the political ambience of 1970s Port Elizabeth, which was primarily influenced by two traditions: the post-1973 resurgence of the trade union movement and the Black Consciousness Movement. These traditions left an enduring political imprint, significantly shaping even new configurations of the movements going forward into the 1980s.[15] The dynamics of the Black Consciousness Movement birthed AZAPO nationally. In Port Elizabeth, however, it was infiltrated by apartheid state security structures, resulting in bloody localised AZAPO–UDF clashes in the mid-1980s.[16] The Black Consciousness Movement also influenced the birth and ideology of both PEBCO and PEYCO.[17]

Equally, counter-revolutionary movements aimed at constructing the government of the Ciskei homeland flourished in Port Elizabeth. Qeqe's involvement in Ciskeian politics in Port Elizabeth was motivated by past ethnic–national emotionalisms. He also felt an unbreakable tie to the amaJingqi in Chief Maqoma's territories.[18] It engendered in him a strong political commitment to black consciousness, inspired by Chief Maqoma's largely successful guerrilla warfare campaigns against British colonial incursions onto his lands in the nineteenth century.

Qeqe's ties to Ciskei politics were invoked in three ways. The first was the connection to his birthplace, ethnic ties and clan relations with Ciskei's President Lennox Sebe (1973–1990). Qeqe was related to Sebe as a Tshawe. However, this was a maternal clan relation, and not necessarily a close bloodline relation.[19] The second tie came through the close mentoring relations he had with Wilson F Ximiya, Chief Lent Maqoma, Chief M Mabandla and AZ Lamani whom he campaigned for when they stood for seats in the Victoria East Council area.[20] Lennox Sebe stood for a seat in the Zwelitsha area.[21]

Qeqe, Ximiya, Lamani, Maqoma and Mabandla had been approached to stand for elections as early as 1971. However, Qeqe had refused to go to parliament in Ciskei, opting instead to campaign on their behalf.[22] In this way, Qeqe could be said to have symbolically reprised his traditional family role in Port Elizabeth. This was the customary maternal family role of interlocutor–counsellor to chiefs coming to Port Elizabeth and Uitenhage to connect with their subjects.[23] Qeqe's family role was mediatory, linking Chief Maqoma to his 'subjects' living and working in Port Elizabeth, Grahamstown, Cradock and other nearby towns. Mali explained this connection:

> [The] majority of people based in PE, they come from that area – the Grahamstown area, Cradock, Fort Beaufort, King William's Town, villages around East London – that is the bulk of that voting power for Ciskeian politics. Now, most of them are resident outside of the borders of Ciskei, and a number of them are based in Cape Town. Now, that block vote comes from those urban areas.[24]

This affirms Peires' assertion that Ciskei was heavily urbanised and industrialised, with a population scattered across the nearby cities and towns. Unlike in the Transkei, however, these so-called 'subjects' had little respect for chiefs and tradition.[25]

Qeqe then went about in New Brighton, KwaZakhele, Zwide and other townships in Port Elizabeth campaigning under the slogan of *Khulula*, representing the party of Ximiya, Lamani, Maqoma and Mabandla.[26] Mali explained that the Sebe Group, operating under the Ciskei National Independence Party, were represented by the slogan, *Bopha*, which means 'tie together', figuratively getting people together. Chief Mabandla and his group were represented by the slogan, *Khulula*, which means 'open' or 'free up'.[27]

Qeqe's third tie was his political relationship with Sebe – an alleged commitment Sebe had made to Qeqe and his associates that he would relinquish power to Mandela and the ANC upon their release from prison and unbanning.[28] Although Sebe was known for dumping one strong man for another when his usefulness had expired,[29] there is no documented record of this agreement between Sebe, Qeqe and his associates. Nonetheless, Sebe's alleged reneging on such an agreement apparently disillusioned Qeqe to the extent that he ceased his involvement in Ciskeian politics.

However, other accounts claim that Qeqe was under substantial pressure from his colleagues in non-racial sports and anti-apartheid politics to disassociate himself from Ciskei's politics. The creation of the Ciskei homeland government was not only a counter-revolutionary position, but entailed painful human resettlements that did not sit well with the consciences of Qeqe's associates. Large groups of people were forcefully moved, mainly by the ECAB, from Eastern Cape cities and towns to the fledgling Ciskei. Between 1960 and 1982, the lives and livelihoods of more than 3.5 million black people were disrupted.[30] Consequently, between 1960 and 1983, the populations of the homelands rose from 39 to 53 per cent.[31]

By the late 1970s, the enterprise was in full swing, with both the ECAB and the Ciskei government on the pulling and pushing ends. In a piece of correspondence titled *Survey: Ciskeian Xhosa*, dated 5 July 1979, from Koch to Mr H du T Hefer, secretary of the Ciskei Commission based in Silverton, Pretoria, Koch enumerated in detail the ethnic–regional identities and gender of black people liable to be moved from Port Elizabeth to Ciskei. He tallied that out of 355 506 males, and 398 320 females, there were 546 238 Ciskeian Xhosa compared to 160 252 Transkeian Xhosa, and 47 336 who were deemed 'Other Xhosa'.[32]

Ncula maintained that this association with Ciskeian politics came close to tarnishing Qeqe's reputation.[33] Wilson claimed to have rebuked Qeqe, saying, 'When Lennox Sebe became president of Ciskei, Dan was there. It's only when Dan came to SARU that we said, 'Look, Dan, you can't be there. You can't be there on that side and still want to be with us and SACOS.''[34] Vusi Pikoli and his student–youth political associates had collectively expressed dismay at Qeqe, Ximiya and Lamani, suggesting that they were attracted by the perks that went with serving in the parliament and civil service of Ciskei. In fact, Ximiya went on to become Minister of Agriculture in Sebe's administration. Pikoli and his fellow activists were deeply dismayed that, after they had dissuaded them from participating in the Native Advisory Board, they were now 'graduating into homeland politics'.[35]

THE MID- TO LATE 1970s saw Qeqe upgrading secondary schools to high schools, forever transforming the education landscape of the black child in these two townships. Before then, school education only went up to the junior certificate level, the current equivalent of Grade 10. In recounting the history of New Brighton from 1903 to 1953, Gary Baines affirmed that, 'For most part of our period there was no secondary school in New Brighton either. The only secondary school which admitted African students was Patterson High School in Mount Road.'[36] The New Brighton Native Advisory Board's request for the establishment of a secondary school had been ignored for many years by the Port Elizabeth City Council. Consequently, this cumulatively contributed to the challenge of juvenile delinquency on the streets of New Brighton.[37]

In the 1970s, upon completing Form 3, it was mainly only a few middle-class pupils who followed the long-held tradition of enrolling at boarding schools in Ciskei and Transkei, particularly if they wanted to acquire a matric certificate and enrol for studies at institutions of higher learning. Pikoli and Sloti followed this tradition, attending the University of Fort Hare and Healdtown, respectively. Pikoli explained how the trend produced a ready labour force that fed into the labour needs of such manufacturing firms as Ford, General Motors, Dulux and Firestone.[38]

But by the mid-1970s, even that route to boarding schools in Ciskei and Transkei had generated its own set of challenges. Influenced by a long-held culture of political mobilisation and the recent black consciousness sway in Port Elizabeth, pupils from Port Elizabeth had cultivated an unacceptable anti-authority, rebellious reputation among school authorities in Ciskei and Transkei. As Qeqe put it, '[Many] of the children from this area have been refused admission to schools in the homelands because they are regarded as troublemakers.'[39]

Qeqe steadfastly believed that 'the only weapon to fight illiteracy and ignorance is education'.[40] In pursuit of this goal, he worked with colleagues on the advisory board, particularly with Reverend George B Molefe. In many ways, Molefe was Qeqe's predecessor in advocating for the betterment of educational opportunities for the black child in New Brighton, leaving a significant imprint in the town, with Molefe Primary School named after him. Reverend Molefe, along with another leading education and community activist, Reverend James James Ranisi Jolobe, trained in theology at the South African Native College. There, along with Africa Nzimande, they were popularly known as the 'indivisible trio'.[41] Their training at the college made an indelible impression on their outlook on public service. As noted, 'The privilege of tertiary education made a deep impression on both men. After their ordination they devoted their talents as teachers and their influence as ministers towards rectifying and raising the appalling standard of African education in South Africa.'[42]

In 1953, Reverend Molefe became the first African in the Presbyterian Church of South Africa to be elected as a moderator of the Presbytery, taking over from Reverend Jolobe as head of the Presbyterian Church of New Brighton.[43] They both became respected leaders in the town. In 1978, Molefe received an honorary degree for his outstanding service to the church and community.[44]

Reverend Molefe was a political and social conservative who put much faith in collaboration with white establishment institutions. He was significantly inspired by conservative African–American educational institutions, such as the Tuskegee Institute, from the time he was a student at the Union Theological Seminary in New York.[45]

Molefe had undeniably played a formative role in Qeqe's perception of community and public service. His was a political conservatism that might have been imparted to Qeqe too. However, Molefe's approach to community work was tightly bound to the church. Both he and Jolobe were faithful to state and church structures, implementing a firm liberal approach in addressing racial reconciliation.[46] This approach put them on a collision course with the ANC in New Brighton, however, subjecting them to vitriolic attacks.[47]

Qeqe took the mantle from Molefe, and at first they put their trust in the advisory board to commit to the educational upliftment of the black child in New Brighton. They were, however, bitterly disappointed. When their repeated requests were not heeded, both Qeqe and Molefe felt stifled.[48] A marked difference in *modus operandi* between Molefe and Qeqe was Molefe's rigid insistence on centralising church structures when it came to raising funds for this exercise. Nozuko Pikoli, who witnessed Molefe's work, recalled, 'You see, Molefe ... used to galvanise funds, especially from the church.'[49]

Qeqe's aim was to upgrade Cowan and KwaZakhele secondary schools into high schools, and to achieve this he broke ranks with Molefe's tradition. This was not due to any radical ideological shift, but because of the local state's refusal to assist in the schools' upgrading project, and the incapability of the parents to commit to funding. Other challenges communicated to Qeqe were apparently structural. Mpumelelo 'Sbhidla' Majola remembered that 'there was some regulation that in the townships one could not build a double-storey building. They said that the land in the township was not suitable for that. So, this is one of the things that led Cowan to not be upgraded into a high school.'[50]

By the mid- to late 1970s, Qeqe and his associates on the advisory board had grown discouraged by the half-measures and ill-willed attempts of the Cape Midlands Bantu Affairs Administration Board to commit to this project. In 1975, they openly chided the local state, pointing out that the education of African children in the Port Elizabeth townships was 'badly planned'.[51] They 'expressed concern at the slow rate of progress being made by the Cape Midlands Bantu Affairs Administration Board in building more schools and additional classrooms and they were also deeply concerned at the sudden change of policy in allocating new school buildings'.[52]

In 1973, Qeqe and Molefe condemned the less-than-adequate improvements made to a township school. Referring to the new building that had been added to Mzontsundu Junior Secondary School at KwaZakhele, Qeqe objected to the construction of cement floors, saying, 'We don't want this new school with cement floors because it will destroy the lives of our children.'[53]

Molefe further pointed out that he and his colleagues on the advisory board were disappointed at finding out that the new school building would only have 10 classrooms. No provision had been made for a principal's office, a science room or a homecraft room.[54] The local state's response, received via a letter from the Department of Community Development, informed them that 'the loan authority had precluded the building of specialist classrooms at the school'.[55]

Qeqe criticised the report given by the chairman of the Education Committee of the advisory board and the officials of the Department of Education, claiming that they had not delivered on what they had promised: the building of 102 additional classrooms before January 1976.[56] Qeqe was 'deeply disturbed' to learn from McNamee, the former New Brighton superintendent, that only one higher-primary school with 16 additional classrooms was scheduled to be built.[57] Also, he was concerned that six classrooms for Loyiso Secondary School and four for Inqubela Higher Primary School in New Brighton were to be added before school opened the following year in 1976.[58]

Qeqe had come to the realisation that the local state did not intend to upgrade the two secondary schools to high schools. Realising the futility of relying on the local state and the New Brighton community, Qeqe dug into his own pocket, donating R2 000 to the project, and requested that parents donate a similar amount.[59] He also reached out to a few black businessmen, such as Mr Jonas and Mr Khabani,[60] and Cowan Secondary School's principal, Frank Thonjeni. Mpumelelo 'Sbhidla' Majola recalled that Qeqe and the people he recruited to the project 'upgraded the school by force, very much against the wishes of the whites'.[61]

Teenage Mkhuseli Jack, when he moved to Port Elizabeth in 1975 and was looking for a school, found himself in an overflow intake of 300 to 400 pupils. This overflow, which was meant to be accommodated at Cowan, took their classes outdoors, in the absence of classrooms. Jack recalled:

> And Dan Qeqe, at the time, I noted him coming into the school … Nineteen seventy-five [1975], coming into Cowan High School with his pick-up bakkie or a bakkie, a truck. And he was busy, you know, transporting, cutting cement, bricks and wood, and so on. And he

> was busy extending two classes, so that they could accommodate the overflow of Cowan. We were new, this group I'm talking about. So, but then, he was wearing shorts, and came there himself [and] work and push and so on. This was really impressive.[62]

Sloti pointed out that Qeqe worked relentlessly, back and forth, his *modus operandi* to ensure that he upgraded Cowan and KwaZakhele secondary schools more or less at the same time:

> They started building one class at KwaZakhele High School, which became Form 4 the following year for the children who had passed Form 3. He moved on to Cowan, adding one class. He went back to KwaZakhele and added one class for Form 5. It was two, two, the classes they built at that time. Then those schools ended up being upgraded because of the classrooms they had built.[63]

By 1979, Qeqe's efforts had won the support of the Department of Education and the New Brighton community. Molefe, reporting on the progress of the project undertaken by a special committee headed by Qeqe, commented on the 'great enthusiasm' shown by parents.[64] By the beginning of 1980, the special committee had applied to the Department of Education for the recognition of matric offered by the two upgraded schools, Cowan and KwaZakhele.

In some of the rectifications of civic injustices that Qeqe initiated, he occasionally resorted to unorthodox, and rather forceful and even violent methods. This projected an image of a maverick defender of people's rights in New Brighton. He clearly demonstrated this in how he stopped *izibonda* or headmen from ejecting people from their houses for rental defaults. Gary Baines has written extensively about the endemic corruption of *izibonda* in house allocations and evictions between 1903 and 1953.[65] This carried on into the 1970s, when Qeqe was a member of the advisory board.

Housing eviction notices were issued by the Port Elizabeth Municipality in terms of the Housing Act No. 4 of 1966. Between 1970 and 1971 in New Brighton, 11 519 eviction notices were issued. Only 177 evictions were carried out, and of these, 160 were reinstated after payment of the outstanding rentals, with only 17 tenants permanently evicted.[66] In KwaZakhele, a township less well serviced than New Brighton, there were 27 170 eviction notices served. Only 1 per cent of these were carried out – a total of 284 evictions. A total of 199 were reinstated after payment of arrears, and only 85 families, out of a total population of 88 000 individuals, were permanently evicted.[67]

Qeqe addressed the corruption in his individual capacity, as he had done with the schools upgrading project. Unlike James Mpanza, who had turned social discontent on housing into a collective political campaign for Orlando, Soweto residents in the 1940s,[68] Qeqe addressed the matter on a case-by-case basis. Sloti explained that his uncle, Dan, had been deeply moved by the injustices of evictions on account of rent defaults. More painful was the harsh manner in which these were carried out, with *izibonda* throwing furniture out of the house, without any form of negotiations or alternative arrangements being made for housing.[69]

Mpumelelo 'Sbhidla' Majola recounted one particular incident involving a rather odd tenant in upmarket Thembalethu:

> For instance, one of our neighbours, Bhilayi, Mr Bhilayi, was thrown out of his house. Those houses are big, and people wanted to move into his house. Bhilayi was well known. He had his own particular lifestyle. In modern times, you can call him a criminal, you know? So, people looked down on him, and found it inappropriate and above his station that he lived there … I remember we were small then, and the headmen were called to throw him out of his house. They called Mr Qeqe … Baas Dan came over. The headmen left, running away. He literally chased them away, and he used his foul language … He would say, 'You are going to shit, my friend.' He would say, 'Go and shit. Come with your *boer*.' The headmen ran away. So, he was that kind of a person.[70]

The knobkerrie-wielding Qeqe was regarded as a brave man who feared no one.[71] In outlining this bravery, Judge Somyalo recalled how Qeqe came to his aid in securing a proper, comfortable house for his young family when he started practising as an attorney in the mid-1970s. Then, Somyalo lived in a two-roomed house at 207 Gqamlana

Street in New Brighton. 'There were houses, [but] you could not get a house. You could not extend a house ... You know, things were really, really, very tough.'[72] He detailed his housing-procurement difficulties, struggling with a ubiquitous and well-oiled bribery system. It was well managed by *izibonda* who were, in turn, overseen by a location superintendent pliant to corruption.

As Somyalo put it, 'Most of the municipal police, you had to bribe them. It was common. If you wanted to get any favours, you had to bribe ...'[73] Scoffing at bribery as inappropriate and repugnant, he rather negotiated for a house on Dora Street in New Brighton. The house he eventually found was quite comfortable for his family – a four-roomed home, with extensions and bathrooms. He concluded the deal with the proprietor of the block encompassing his house, without the involvement of local authorities. However, the landlord suddenly reneged on their agreement, and wanted to evict Somyalo and his family. He then approached Qeqe for help:

> I went to Dan Qeqe. I explained to him, 'Look, man, I've got this problem.' And he said, okay, he arranged that we go and see ... [There] was somebody above the superintendent ... Let's go and see that chap, McNamee. Indeed, we went there. We go there, and Dan gave that chap fireworks. I was there ... McNamee, he gave that chap fireworks. Not in a bad sense. He said, what are you? This is the person ... why are you? And then this chap phones Stomielautous, and said, bring this, bring this. My position was rectified there and then.[74]

Perhaps Qeqe's most selfless act was how he salvaged Mrs Majola's house. She and her late husband, Eric Majola, and the Qeqes had bought houses in Thembalethu at the same time in the mid-1960s. Mrs Majola maintained that towards the end of the 1970s, she was on the verge of paying off the balance of the mortgage. However, the municipality wanted to kick her and her family out of the house. And so Mrs Majola recalled how the enraged Qeqe intervened:

> Yes, they wanted my house ... I went with Baas Dan. I was working at Daku at that time. I used to work there at the municipality. I

> worked there for 22 full years here at the municipality. He said, 'Let's go and attend to this challenge with your house' ... We got there when they were on tea break ... He said, 'I came here on behalf of Jumartha to attend to this matter concerning her house.' He said, 'What is happening here?' He said, 'What is happening is also going to happen to my wife. I have paid my house to the full. And she hasn't fully paid up her house. No, it's 10 years,' and this and that. He said, 'Tell me what is her settlement balance? How much is left?' Baas Dan paid up the settlement balance that had remained.[75]

QEQE ADDRESSED PUBLIC discontent on township housing matters by means of a collective. In a quasi-formal manner, he had been elected by Thembalethu homeowners as their spokesperson in the mid-1960s,[76] and in late 1979, he intervened on behalf of 28 homeowners of six-roomed houses in Thembalethu who protested that service charges on their houses had 'shot up by as much as almost 50 per cent a month' at the beginning of April 1979.[77]

As per the agreement concluded between homeowners and the municipality, there were set monthly instalments of R16 for 30 years, but then service charges were increased from R7.67 to R14.11 per month, without consultation with the homeowners.[78] Up until March 1979, Thembalethu homeowners were paying R23.07 in monthly rentals. Of this amount, R16 was for the instalment on the house. The new rentals therefore had increased to R30.11 per month.

They also protested against the land ownership of their houses. The land was still owned by the Port Elizabeth Municipality, rather than by the homeowners themselves. Qeqe protested that, 'This is more disturbing when we hear rumours that the very land on which our homes are situated is still owned by the municipality. We are prepared to fight this to the bitter end.'[79] They urged the ECAB to refer all future petitioners from black residential areas in Port Elizabeth to the councillor of the ward concerned.

The row between Thembalethu homeowners and municipal authorities was deemed to likely end up in court,[80] and Qeqe reported that Thembalethu homeowners had employed the services of two attorneys to represent them in court against the ECAB. Qeqe maintained that the ECAB had no authority 'whatsoever' to increase service charges on their homes,[81] arguing that Thembalethu had been established as a homeownership scheme in 1964. In that scheme, homeowners had concluded a deed of sale with the local authority, and not with its subsidiary, the ECAB. He pointed out that, 'We are taking exception to this sort of thing. Our contracts are with the Administration Board.'[82] To Qeqe and his fellow homeowners, the ECAB's function was akin to that of an estate agent – collecting rent on behalf of the municipality.

At the beginning of May 1979, Thembalethu homeowners signed a petition demanding an explanation for this increase from the municipality. However, Mr Frank Ford, the regional manager of the Port Elizabeth Community Council, denied that there were increases in service charges. He argued that the service charges had remained unchanged since Thembalethu had been established in 1964.

In his capacity as sub-committee head on Public Transport and Traffic of the Port Elizabeth Joint Bantu Advisory Board, Qeqe pursued similar civic protests in 1974, opposing the application for increased bus fares by the Department of Transport's Local Road Transportation Board.[83] As per the planned increase, African bus commuters were to pay 43 per cent more on cash fares. On weekly bus tickets, this came to a 33.3 per cent increase. In a 20 working-day month, this translated into an increase of R2.40 in cash and R2.80 for weekly tickets, thus pushing the cash bus fare total to R4 a month, and the weekly ticket to R3.60.[84]

Qeqe argued that the proposed bus fare increases would have 'appalling' socio-economic impact on Africans if they were accepted and implemented. Africans were already hit hard by price increases in almost every commodity. They would shoulder a higher cost of living, and the 'price of everything is going up, but our pay packets are as thin as ever'.[85] His argument was supported by the chairman of the Coloured Management Committee, Mr Donald Cairncross. Qeqe called for a greater government subsidy for African commuters. He claimed that the municipality owed them at the least this form of help. However, a spokesman for the Midlands Chamber of Industries maintained that, although the increase was unfortunate, it was inevitable. The spokesman called on employers to take the increase into account when considering wage increases.[86]

It was these incremental let-downs that weighed on Qeqe, inexorably leading to his departure from the advisory board in 1977. There were other minor, but not insignificant, local apartheid repressive measures that might have added to his disillusionment with the advisory board. One such incident was the police locking up his daughter along with other children one night at the beginning of 1977. On that evening, five black school-going children were arrested by the police at Happy Valley, a beachfront entertainment area in Summerstrand. They were subsequently locked up in a police cell until 2 am the following morning.[87]

The children were charged with 'being in a White area after 9 pm'.[88] The police had arrested them and drove Mpumelelo and Nomvuyo Nyoka, Tammie Mbere, Xoliswa Speelman and Belinda Qeqe around Summerstrand in the back of a police van with an Alsatian in it, while they tracked other night-pass offenders.[89] Finally, after Dr PPS Nyoka, the father of two of the children, located them after conducting a long and frustrating search, they were released on a payment of R10 each in admission of guilt fine. Qeqe promptly escalated this to a case of racism, commenting that '[high]-handed acts like this by the police are harming race relations'.[90] He promised to take the matter to the next meeting of the advisory board.

Yet the immediate pressure facing the Native Advisory Board – and Qeqe – was the explosive public call for its dissolution. The black communities' call was effectively a call for radical change in local governance representation, and came in the wake of a highly charged, political ambience in Port Elizabeth and countrywide, particularly as it followed hot on the heels of the June 16, 1976 student unrest, which radicalised the political mobilisation of black societies. But the more immediate and direct influence was the Soweto Committee of Ten, led by Dr Nthato Motlana.

Following the June 1976 student uprising, a group of Soweto youth had approached Dr Motlana with the aim of drawing up arrangements that would allow Soweto to autonomously run their civic affairs following the demise of the Soweto Urban Bantu Council. As Dr Motlana expressed it in an interview he gave in 1979, 'We want to arrange our own affairs and not have someone from the West Rand

Administration [government agency] arrange for us.'[91] He felt that the Soweto Committee of Ten, in its sheer presence, made a statement to Afrikanerdom that Soweto residents would decide on their own future.[92]

And so, in the wake of the clampdown following the murder of Steve Biko, 1500 registered voters of New Brighton came together at the Centenary Hall to call for the dissolution of the Port Elizabeth Joint Bantu Advisory Board. Communities had been particularly provoked by the proposed introduction of new community councils – a new black local government configuration purportedly seeking to give black people direct governance of townships.

The meeting convened at New Brighton's Centenary Hall effectively decided to do away with 'the system of Bantu Advisory Boards', because they were 'not an effective mouthpiece of the residents'.[93] Furthermore, Qeqe and other advisory board members objected to the nomination process, labelling it a selection process rather than an election process, with the success of the nomination process hinging on the approval of the chief director and the superintendent. In 1976, Qeqe objected to the nomination process, pointing out that, 'When you are nominated you represent the views of the authorities and not those of the people. I will go back to the board if returned by the residents.'[94]

A press report stated, 'The long life of the Port Elizabeth Joint Bantu Advisory Board may come to an end today if its members heed the advice given to them by the township residents who have demanded its complete dissolution this week.'[95] Furthermore, it was reported that, 'The concept of the black community councils received a setback when tenants and residents of the Port Elizabeth African townships last night rejected the idea and called for a halt to the registration of voters to elect members of this body.'[96]

Leading the call was local businessman Mr AT Yeko.[97] Yeko was then mandated to accompany five members of the advisory board present at the meeting to report to Koch the decision of the New Brighton community. However, Koch was adamant that the advent of community councils was inevitable.[98] He argued that the meeting of New Brighton residents was not representative of the views of the majority of Port Elizabeth Africans. He added that, 'And I said this to a delegation from the meeting which included Mr Dan Qeqe and Mr AT Yeko.'[99]

The five members of the advisory board Yeko was to accompany to report to Koch were Dan Qeqe, Mr AS Mpondo, Mr WM Maku, Mr FT James and Mr TS Yoyo.[100] The BAAB had extended the life of the advisory board until January 1978, when elections were to be convened to elect members of the proposed new community councils.[101] At the advisory board's last meeting, its members had agreed by a majority vote that the community councils would be established with effect from 1 April 1978.

This view – the opposition to selection or nomination by the city council for membership on the advisory board, rather than election by the residents of New Brighton – was similarly expressed by fellow board members AZ Lamani and David Mbane.[102] Qeqe objected when he was informed in the press that all members of the advisory board were to be nominated by the Cape Midlands Bantu Affairs Administration Board. This would have also meant that his future in the advisory board lay in the hands of Koch. Qeqe eventually relinquished his seat on the advisory board by not attending three consecutive meetings without tendering an apology.[103]

Yeko and Qeqe subsequently established the Port Elizabeth African Townships Action Committee to fight for equal political rights of Africans.[104] To that effect, Koch labelled Qeqe a radical, saying that he had become prominent among the more radical elements in the townships.[105] However, elsewhere, Qeqe was considered a moderate.[106] Even his elder brother, America Qeqe, weighed in on the matter, publicly avowing his brother as a 'moderate'.

Writing in his capacity as a member of the Fort Beaufort Advisory Board, America – also a businessman – berated Koch for labelling his younger brother a radical. America reminded Koch of Qeqe's community and fund-raising efforts, which he had undertaken with him on the advisory board.[107] However, it is highly questionable whether America had written the letter himself, considering that all of Qeqe's 18 siblings were semi-literate.

At the beginning of the letter, America emphatically thanked 'all who worked for the release from detention of Mr Dan Qeqe, and particularly the Ciskeian government for interceding on his behalf, which led to his release after almost two months in detention'.[108] So, America might have had the letter written for him by a Ciskeian government official. The intention might have been to reflect an image of a nascent Ciskeian government not entirely averse to anti-apartheid activists.

THE 1977 BIKO CLAMPDOWN collided with protests against the setting up of the proposed community councils and the parallel establishment of the Port Elizabeth African Townships Action Committee. The net result of this confluence of events was a wide sweep of vicious arrests, with Qeqe and many other anti-apartheid activists and ordinary residents caught up in it all.

There were widespread calls for the release of Qeqe and Yeko, among them one from the Black Sash. In calling for their release, the Black Sash, from its statement signed by a Mrs P Melunsky, concluded that the two were imprisoned because they were 'opposed to the new community councils which BAAB is anxious to introduce'.[109] Melunsky surmised: 'Could their outspoken opposition to this new Government policy have been their reason for their detention?'[110] Melunsky further argued that the answer might lie in the *raison d'etre* behind the introduction of section 22 of the General Law Amendment Act. This was the legislation under which the sweeping arrests of the Biko clampdown were carried out. It was introduced, Minister Jimmy Kruger argued, to remove certain incendiary people from a scene of trouble, by arbitrarily detaining and prosecuting them.[111]

However, a more accurate understanding of Qeqe's arrest under the legislation hinges on Melunsky's last statement – the removal of rabble-rousing people from flammable scenes. Following the mass arrest of students from the St Stephen's church hall in New Brighton, Qeqe was arrested as he was about to give a witness statement at Algoa court while mobilising funds for the students' legal defence.

The 474 students – who had gathered to protest against the arrests of fellow students and to raise funds for their legal defence – were promptly arrested by the police, who also seized the money they had collected.[112] Qeqe's son, Mpumelelo, who was present at St Stephen's, remembered how he had escaped arrest in the nick of time.

He recollected, 'I was there, at St Stephen's. I heard the sounds of a police siren, and so I hurried and got out. So, by the time the police cordoned off the place, I had already gone out.'[113] Phumla observed the clinical viciousness of the police. 'That is when the Special Branch of the police came. Girls this side, they removed us, and everyone was arrested.'[114]

The net of the clampdown arrests widened. Police arrested other anti-apartheid activists and Qeqe's immediate and even extended family members, with the Security Branch pouncing on Qeqe's home at 3 am while he was in detention. They thoroughly searched his house for the next three hours, looking into 'every corner' of the house, including the adjacent recreation hall.[115] They then detained Mpumelelo and Qeqe's nephew, McKenzie Sloti, then a school teacher at KwaZakhele High School.[116] Mrs Majola recalled of that night in late 1977:

> Yes, '77, because I recall that time when he was in prison, and I slept here, at Mrs Qeqe's, keeping her company and giving her comfort over at her place. Her husband was imprisoned. One night, the police came, we were sleeping together. They came over to search her house. They searched her house, opening books. Mrs Qeqe and I just woke up and stayed up, and we made coffee for ourselves, and we let them do whatever they were doing.[117]

Soon thereafter, Ms Sizakele Leve, Qeqe's niece, was arrested at her workplace.[118] Mpumelelo remembered how the family arrests severely affected his father's health. 'When McKenzie and I were arrested, that's when he lost his mind. We were then detained at Baakens, at the Baakens Police Station … He was at Kabega … This frustrated him more. That's when his health deteriorated.'[119] The detention, though, did not have adverse effects on Qeqe's businesses. He was able to communicate to Mrs Qeqe instructions on running the businesses, and signed cheques during her prison visits.[120] During one prison visit, lasting for an hour and a half, 'several business matters requiring Mrs Qeqe's attention had been conveyed to him through the police'.[121]

Among those arrested over this time was Nosidima Pityana, Barney Pityana's wife, who had been detained in June of that year and then released the following month.[122] Dumile Kondile's law offices on Aggrey Road in New Brighton were raided, and the police confiscated some of his documents. A Mrs Gcina was also allegedly detained by the police, although there were no confirmations.[123] The secretary of Kwaru, Dennis Siwisa, was also detained for 10 months; his detention was extended on account of his political conscientisation of students at KwaZakhele High School, where he taught. His past political convictions dating back to the early 1960s provided additional motivation for his lengthier detention period.[124]

Qeqe's political activism, which saw him play a direct role in student politics, featured prominently in the trial of Saki Macozoma and his fellow student activists. He was then a student at KwaZakhele High School, and had been one of the leaders in the student uprisings of 1977. Following the arrests in 1977 of Saki Macozoma, Shepherd Ngakumbi and Mike Xego,[125] Qeqe became pivotal in providing financial assistance and logistical support to the incarcerated students and their parents.

The trial of these students, heard in the High Court in Grahamstown, proved to span a lengthy two years. Free of charge, Qeqe routinely put out his Frans, Ngwendu, Qeqe (FNQ) buses, transporting parents from Port Elizabeth to Grahamstown throughout the two-year period of the trial. His services even extended beyond the time of their conviction, and throughout the five years of their incarceration on Robben Island, he continued to ferry their parents from Port Elizabeth to Cape Town. At times, when he visited them in prison, he mediated between them and their parents on various matters. McKenzie Sloti remembered:

> He organised his bus under the company FNQ. There was a bus that came out every day, going to Grahamstown, taking parents of the detained schoolchildren, so that they would stay for a long time in Grahamstown. They stayed in Grahamstown for long periods because court officials kept on postponing the case. Parents moved from Port Elizabeth in the FNQ bus, organised by DDQ, for free, going to Grahamstown, until the case was through after they were sentenced for five years on Robben Island. He didn't leave it there. Even after they were arrested on Robben Island, he made plans and

> visited them now and then, also encouraging their parents. There were meetings held between him and parents ... Means were made for their parents to visit their children on Robben Island, that is, for those parents who wanted to visit their children. Even then, DDQ organised, mobilising parents whose children had been arrested at that time. There were a lot of things that DDQ did.[126]

Delivering a tribute to Qeqe at his funeral in 2005, the parent of one of the 1977 arrested students revealed Qeqe's selfless contribution, one of many that he kept to himself and took to the grave. Of this tribute, Phumla recalled that:

> There is a mother, Mrs Gongxeka, I was there *mos*, at KwaZakhele High School at that time. So what happened, her son was also there. She said she'll never forget. He transported them, and when they got there in Grahamstown, he bought them food. And then the case was postponed for tomorrow. He secured accommodation for them there. He made them food. And she will never forget. There were twenty-two, aah, nhe?[127]

The radicalisation of Qeqe's political activism is symbolised in the leading role he played in ferrying political fugitives into exile, among them Vusi Pikoli, Phakamile Ximiya, Thozamile Majola and Sizwe Kondile, sought by the Security Branch for the distribution of subversive literature.[128] Mrs Majola recalled that they, including her own son, Thozamile Majola, undertook their political work under her nose in the guise of participating at the Ivan Peter Youth Club that she headed. She recalled that, 'I didn't know that, here at the club, as they used to frequent there at the club, they were in the struggle. To me, they were just youth.'[129]

The Ivan Peter Youth Club was started in New Brighton in April 1970, initiated by John Kani, Mrs Jumartha Milase Majola and Mr Nyamie Pemba. In its founding papers, the club noted that the year of its founding 'marked a turning point in the history of New Brighton's social life'.[130] It focused on social group work in New Brighton and Zwide, purporting to be supporting the Bantu Affairs Administration Board's motive of lifting the moral standards of the youth and blotting out 'vulgarism', which the board viewed as threatening peaceful coexistence in black townships.[131]

Regarded as a 'small woman with a mighty heart',[132] Mrs Majola had put together a youth programme involving boxing, karate, judo, ballroom dancing, chess and choral singing.[133] In the activities of the Youth Week of 1977, Phakamile Ximiya – one of the youths with whom Vusi Pikoli had skipped the country into exile – participated as one of the judging officials in the table-tennis competition.[134]

Crosby 'Winky' Ximiya, who was one of the people who drove them into exile, admitted, 'Thozi Majola, all those guys I used to ferry them, and I'll go to exile, to Lesotho and Botswana. So now, the system picked up on me here. So I also got locked up.'[135] Qeqe orchestrated the entire process, working with his trusted and closest associate, Feya Sobikwa.[136] Pikoli remarked, 'Baas Dan is that type of person who would say something out of place, like, 'Hey, Feya, I've got a parcel for you to keep.' He's not asking you. He's not requesting you. Feya just had to do it. And those parcels are people. 'Just keep that parcel, Feya, until I tell you."[137]

Pikoli recounted extensively on how they skipped the country, and the central role Qeqe played in the process. Admitting to the centrality of Qeqe's role in it, Pikoli wrote:

> While the four of us were running around, senior members of our community stepped in. Knowing that we were in trouble they began making plans for us to get us out of town. These elders included Boet Sy[138] and the legendary sports administrator, struggle stalwart and father of Kwaru rugby Dan Qeqe, after whom the rugby stadium was named.[139]

Qeqe also intervened at times of operational malfunctions. Midway through the process, Pikoli and the group were delivered to Qeqe's youngest brother, Wridge, in King William's Town. However, Wridge had developed acute anxieties, afraid of information leakages to the South African and Ciskeian security officials that would jeopardise his long-term business and political interests there.[140] Pikoli recalled:

> We were supposed to calm down, stay here at the farm, work as farm labourers there, you see? But, hey, Wridge was shocked. He said, 'Hey boys!' ... We said, no, we were driven by Andrew, Danny's brother, the younger brother. We said, 'Andrew, Baas Dan's plan has failed, and Wridge now, we've got to do what we have to do. Drop us in Mdantsane.' ... He dropped us in Mdantsane, and that is how we left. And even then, Dan facilitated, because in East London, we got to Mike's place, a teacher. He organised transport to take us out. The last point that we left through was Matatiele. Again, Baas Dan and Silas Nkanunu were involved. We left via Dr Njongwe's house, who used to be the ANC chairperson.[141]

Tyamzashe attributed the historical impact of Qeqe on non-racial sports liberation to his overarching sense of practicality. He described him as 'practical. He was not just talking about, let's create these things ...'[142] This could, similarly, be regarded as Qeqe's approach when undertaking almost everything, from political activism to civic affairs. It also, perhaps, overshadowed the importance of ideology and political integrity – an aspect of his make-up that became his Achilles heel.

That he was no ideologue blindsided him. Even his allegiance to an eclectic mix of Charterist and black consciousness ideologies was not compass driving; they were not hardened and comprehensive political theories he committed to. This sense of practicality became his weakness. It lent him an enduring imprint of a political conservative and, surprisingly, counter-revolutionary.

However, Qeqe's place and how he homed himself politically in practical ways in Port Elizabeth's history are not harshly judged. Qeqe's historic and historical inputs far outweigh the negativities with which he wrestled. He fulfils his part in the history of Port Elizabeth with men and women, before him, who occupied similar momentary, dubious political stances, but are similarly not harshly judged.

This is perhaps an appreciation that people are not one-dimensional. Tyamzashe summed this up well, pointing out that, 'If you say that's not part of our history, but that's not true, because it is part ... So, you see, human beings are not so easy to read, that they are a continuous thing. Human beings have got many things.'[143] And so it was with shape-shifting Qeqe.

His attachment to practicality, meant that Qeqe avoided any rigid commitment to an ideology; he thus changed the face and the architecture of Port Elizabeth and significantly alleviated the inherited injustices blighting the people of the city. In these ways, he moved with the people's history of Port Elizabeth, drawing and outlining it, as much as it drew and outlined him.

In moving with that history, Qeqe sought to address the injustices of housing and homelessness, and the ravishes of capitalism on black consumers. He was determined to improve the education of the black child, defend hundreds of arrested students, and leave his mark in the broader civic affairs of Port Elizabeth. And so, in many ways, Qeqe shaped the people's history of the Port Elizabeth of the 1970s, as much as he submitted to its political and social influences that shaped his outlook and thinking in equal measure.

11

QEQE AND PORT ELIZABETH IN THE 1980S

By the late 1980s, Dan Qeqe had consolidated his wealth. His nickname, Baas Dan, had come to embody the grand position he held in Port Elizabeth. Well established in all areas of his life, he had become boss of all the pies in which he had his fingers. Despite his success, however, his unassuming demeanour belied his esteemed status. He came across as rather dour, often turning up in indistinct and well-worn, rolled-up, formal, long-sleeved shirts and cotton trousers – the unmistakable look of a middle-aged, seasoned door-to-door insurance salesman who never wore a wristwatch or roll-on deodorant or cologne.[1] Boisterous, he loudly announced his presence with his distinctively pitched, rolling voice.

And so Qeqe found himself in the 1980s a man of means in a tumultuous Port Elizabeth of rolling political insurrection. By the mid-1980s, Port Elizabeth was cited as the city that 'leads the township death toll'.[2] With the Eastern Cape boasting the longest tradition of anti-colonial and anti-apartheid resistance in South Africa, arrests and political conflicts spiked post the Defiance Campaign of 1952. Of the 8326 people arrested in South Africa in the wake of the Defiance Campaign, 71 per cent of the arrests were in the Eastern Cape.

Rory Riordan ascertained in 1988 that 'of the five black uprisings since 1948, three (the Defiance Campaign called by the ANC in 1952, and the two associated with UDF mobilisation in recent years) have centred on mobilisation and repression, if not on public leadership, in the Eastern Cape'.[3] Of these, Port Elizabeth alone accounted for 24 per cent.[4] In 1985 alone, 140 people were killed in Port Elizabeth.[5]

Covering the first State of Emergency in September 1985, the Detained Parent Support Committee (DPSC) reported that 64 per cent of South Africa's 2667 detainees were from the Eastern Cape. In the second State of Emergency, the DPSC noted that, out of an estimated 26 000 people detained throughout the country, the largest number, constituting 36 per cent, were from the Eastern Cape.[6] During that period, 20 youth congresses were convened in less than a year, the most prominent being the Cape Youth Congress, the PEYCO and the Soweto Youth Congress.[7]

Mass protests ignited the fires of defiance. 'It is the determination of the people to win their freedom. That is something about which military strength can do very little,'[8] remarked OR Tambo, the ANC president in exile. Commending the 'mighty struggles' that had broken out in the 1980s in Ladysmith, Hammersdale, Port Elizabeth and Port Shepstone,[9] Tambo continued to stress the importance of mass defiance campaigns. 'And I think that is simply because when once people reach a stage when they are defiant of death, and it doesn't matter how many of them are killed (we are even witnessing this in Zimbabwe), it doesn't matter at all. If they are determined to win their freedom, they will.'[10]

Driving those mass protests of the 1980s were abject mass poverty, mass loyalty to the Congress tradition of resistance and mobilisation, and unresponsiveness to the apartheid policy reforms.[11] In a 1986 Port Elizabeth survey, approximately 54.3 per cent of all black men between the ages of 16 and 65, and of all black women between the ages of 16 and 60, could not find employment. This amounted to 67 000 and 55 000 unemployed black men and women, respectively.

Of these, 25 per cent of black people who did actually have jobs were 'under-employed', working for R4 a day, or for a few days a week. Two out of every three work-seekers in the formal sector could not find employment.[12] Not unexpectedly, living conditions matched the spike in unemployment and under-employment. Approximately 45 per cent of black people's dwellings in the area were made up of shacks and informal dwellings.[13]

It was in these dire socio-economic conditions that what soon became the Port Elizabeth Black Civic Organisation (PEBCO) was conceptualised. Like many community-based organisations, PEBCO was mobilised as a result of local socio-economic dissatisfactions – a combination of high commodity prices, high public transport fares, low wages and landlessness.[14]

PEBCO emerged at the same time as other civic organisations began to mushroom in other cities, namely, the Joint Rent Action Committee, the Driefontein Residents' Committee, the Joint Commuters' Committee, the Cape Housing Action Committee, the Durban Housing Action Committee and the National Anti-South African Indian Council (SAIC) Committee. The founder-president of PEBCO, Thozamile Botha, explained that they started as a small group of community members. Calling themselves the Zwide Residents' Association, they protested against high water rates, high electricity tariffs and poor housing conditions.

But when they realised how pervasive these conditions were in other townships, even in coloured townships, they began to extend their reach geographically. It was then that they approached Qeqe, considering his experience in civic affairs. Botha explained:

> We started approaching people like Dan Qeqe, the lawyers, Ian Sogoni, to say, 'Look, we would like to form an association for New Brighton, Walmer, KwaZakhele, with the intention to create an umbrella body that represents Port Elizabeth on civic matters, so that people who want to have a platform to fight against the Bantu Administration Board and the community councils could use this vehicle, instead of being forced to get into puppet bodies.'[15]

He had become acquainted with Qeqe when he was completing his junior certificate at KwaZakhele High School. At that time, he had been a supporter of Spring Rose, and was close to the Majola family. Judge Somyalo was also involved in the conceptualisation of PEBCO, with Botha consulting him on the drawing up of its constitution. Initially, it was called PEBCA, the Port Elizabeth Black Civic Association. However, Botha changed it to PEBCO, insisting that it sounded better than PEBCA.[16]

The role Qeqe carved for himself in PEBCO was action-oriented. Jack recalled Qeqe's role in PEBCO:

> Dan Qeqe is an action man. He's a practical person. He was never, in my opinion, a man that stands in platforms, although he used to make a lot of speeches. But he wasn't those kinds of people who'd come up with long-researched academic speeches, and so on … He said what needs to be said, and dealt with it. [17]

Gerald Majola maintained, 'But he was not like Mr Fazzie, where he was going to stand in meetings and chair ANC meetings. I don't remember when it was said that Baas Dan had gone to attend an ANC meeting, anywhere.'[18] However, as much as PEBCO's tentacles extended, police arrests proved devastatingly far-reaching. The arrest of the PEBCO leadership in a 'police swoop'[19] was led by the divisional commander of the police in the Eastern Cape, Brigadier ESJ van Niekerk. They arrested the three PEBCO leaders: Thozamile Botha, its chairman; Mono Badela, who was also at that time chairman of WASA;[20] and Phalo Tshume, its secretary.[21] They were detained on 19 January 1980, under section 22 of the General Law Amendment Act, with the police said to be 'looking for a fourth member'.[22] The Act allowed for detention of up to 14 days for police questioning. At the initial arrest, Brigadier Van Rensburg also detained Botha (PEBCO's vice-president), Mr V Conjwa and Mr A Hole, while they were preparing for a meeting in a church hall.[23] They were then taken to the Walmer police station. In the fracas, a crowd that had gathered outside started to throw stones at the police vehicles. Missing them, they only hit and damaged a passing bus. The following day, the police arrested Badela at his home.[24]

Naturally, PEBCO attracted police security attention, largely because of the political activists with whom it worked. Botha admitted that some Kwaru administrators and players, such as Phalo Tshume, were also PEBCO members. 'Kwaru … sympathised with this, and the very same administrators of Kwaru were members of PEBCO.'[25]

A few of them who had just been released from Robben Island gravitated to PEBCO. In the 1980s, the 'mobilisation of counter-power' originated with black consciousness, ex-Robben Islanders, trade unions and student movements. And from among these activists emerged the five broad principles of political mobilisation and organisation: mass organisation, non-collaboration, non-racialism, democracy and participation, and class alliances.[26] Jeremy Seekings explained of PEBCO:

> PEBCO was mass-based, seeing itself as a representative of the 'community' as a whole. Whilst also emphasising action, it saw itself as much more than an 'action committee'. It also saw itself in more explicitly political terms, as a component of the emerging Charterist movement.[27]

Ardent Black Consciousness and strong ANC Charterist ideologies held sway in PEBCO. These had found expression in their meetings and dialogues.

Brigadier ESJ van Rensburg, Divisional Commander of the South African Police (SAP) in the Eastern Cape, said that, 'Police were looking for a fourth member.'[28] That man turned out to be Qeqe. The police declared that they had detained Qeqe for questioning because of an address he had given at a COSAS meeting concerning the establishment of a bookshop. 'The detention of Mr Dan Qeqe at his business in New Brighton yesterday brings to four the number of Port Elizabeth Black Civic Organisation (PEBCO) members being held by the Security Police.'[29] Like the others, Qeqe was also detained under section 22 of the General Law Amendment Act. And as he went into jail, the police released a Walmer PEBCO branch member, a Mr S Meke.[30]

Immediately following the lapse of the 14 days of detention under section 22 of the Act, the state saw fit to escalate the detention of the three, bringing their incarceration under the authority of the Terrorism Act. Further periods of detention were to be approved by a judge on application by the Commissioner of Police.[31] At the end of January 1980, it was reported that, 'A decision may be made today on the fate of the Port Elizabeth Black Civic Organisation leaders being held under section 22 of the General Law Amendment Act.'[32] A spokesman for the Security Police announced that police investigations were continuing, and that no decision had yet been made 'on any future action'.[33]

Soon after, Botha, Badela and Tshume were detained under section 6 of the Terrorism Act, 'a section that allows for indeterminate detention'.[34] Under the Terrorism Act, a person may be held in detention until the Commissioner of Police was satisfied he had adequately responded to interrogation. Only then would it be determined whether any further purpose would be served by keeping him in detention.

The Terrorism Act made provision for detainees to have visits from a magistrate and to make written submissions to the Minister of Justice in order to have reasons for the detention reviewed.[35] PEBCO protested against this. Its acting president, Mr Wilson Skosana, protested that, 'PEBCO's stand all along has been non-violence. I don't understand how detention under the terms of the Terrorism Act can be justified.'[36] Dr Alex Boraine, the Progressive Federal Party MP for Pinelands, also condemned the state's move against PEBCO.[37]

Black community and church leaders condemned the detention as 'unchristian, sinister and shocking'.[38] Mr Barney Paulos, chairman of the Uitenhage Black Civic Organisation (UBCO), protested that, 'The further detention of these men under section 6 shows how sinister are the South African laws. When first detained, they should have been charged and tried in court.'[39] Bishop John Murphy, the Roman Catholic Bishop of Port Elizabeth, argued, 'Presumably they spoke too clearly on their rights and demanded them, not only for themselves, but also for the voiceless who suffer because of discriminatory legislation.'[40]

Standing up for Botha, Reverend James Haya of the Holy Spirit Anglican Church in KwaZakhele, maintained that, 'Thozamile is a man of peace. He was open in his stand against violence and for peaceful co-existence.'[41] Reverend Welile Kani of St Augustine's Mission Church in Walmer raised concerns of detention interconnected with broader socio-economic welfare issues. Lamenting, he asked, 'Will it help at this time when things were coming right and Ford workers are going back?'[42]

PEBCO's executive committee subsequently met to galvanise efforts for donations to help families of the detained pay rent and buy food.[43]

Meanwhile, PEBCO continued to mobilise on matters concerning the planned removal of the Walmer location, and on grievances such as water tariffs and rents in Zwide.[44] Also, elections to replace the detained PEBCO office-bearers were convened. These particularly pertained to the detained members of PEBCO's New Brighton branch, Badela and Lizo Pityana.[45]

While Qeqe was incarcerated, Somyalo received a strange letter from Qeqe. He recalled:

> One time I got into the office and I found a parcel on my table. I didn't even know who had brought it. Do you see a toilet paper, a toilet roll? It was a letter written on it, with a pencil. I kept on rolling the paper as I read it. It was written by Dan while he was held at the police station at Walmer. He had given it to another chap. I later learnt that the chap was Dunster, who also played for Spring Rose, and who was a police officer. He did all of this secretly … I then read this letter. But then, there wasn't much except that he had relayed instructions on it to his wife about a few things.[46]

Phumla recalled her father's coping mechanism while in detention:

> I used to ask him, '[How] did you cope staying alone in that small place?' He'd say, 'You know, my child, I used …' He would step onto a bucket and look outside the window of the prison cell. And he'd see white children playing cricket. He said, I appreciated it, and shouted, 'Hey, howzit!'
>
> He said what he used to do to preoccupy his mind was to recall past events … He would then at some stage realise that even in the bush, when he went for his rite of passage to manhood … He said, 'I realised that, my goodness, even in the bush, what we did was to eat, get up, go and hunt, chasing after hares, and come back and relax.' He said, 'I realised that I should turn this situation around, re-imagine it and make it as if I have come to the bush for my rite of passage to manhood.'[47]

Wilson remembered how Qeqe had relayed his sustained loneliness in detention, and how he had coped with it. He recalled that, '[Do] you know what he told me? He said to me, 'Harold, it was so lonely, and the stress was such that I assumed the role of being an auctioneer. I auction this and all that.' He said that relieved his mind of his problems that he was facing in jail.'[48]

Qeqe was released 'only hours before the expiry of the 14-day detention period allowed by section 22 of the General Law Amendment Act'.[49] 'A man must be charged formally and immediately. For the family it is especially hard,'[50] Qeqe protested upon his release. In the same vein, he continued, 'Once one is detained one's situation often becomes misinterpreted. There is no court of law to prove one's innocence or guilt.'[51] And he went on to boldly pledge his continued support for PEBCO.[52] The PEBCO Three – Botha, Badela and Tshume – remained in detention under the Terrorism Act.

The PEBCO acting executive committee officially welcomed the release of Qeqe, with PEBCO Acting President Skosana declaring, 'We know Mr Qeqe has done a great deal for the community.'[53] Reverend Haya also commended Qeqe, saying that, as an outstanding social leader, he had occupied himself with the welfare of the people rather than politics.[54] Qeqe did not suffer any physical harm while in detention, nor was he subjected to any torture. Phumla confirmed this, saying, 'Maybe they tortured him with questions. These things they did to people, they never did to him.'[55]

With the PEBCO Three still in detention, the organisation began to show signs of strain, due mostly to external pressures exerted on the acting executive committee leadership. Signs of rupture were creeping in, as shown at a PEBCO rally in late January 1980 attended by more than 5000 people.[56] The rally made a strong and angry call for direct action to be taken for the release of PEBCO leaders from detention, with the PEBCO leadership committing to take such action upon the expiry of 14 days.[57] But then a speaker called for a vote of no confidence in the PEBCO acting executive committee leadership.

The PEBCO Three were finally released towards the end of February 1980. Upon their release, they were served with banning orders under sections 9 and 10 of the Internal Security Act No. 44 of 1950.[58] A similar banning order was issued for Qeqe for a period of three years.[59] The banning order 'prevented them from attending public meetings, may not be quoted, may not see more than one person at once and must be home by 6 pm and may not leave the house again until 6 am'.[60] A weekend curfew ran from 6 pm on Friday to 6 am on Monday.[61] The concern was that the banning order hindered the released detainees from obtaining gainful employment. Skosana condemned the banning order, declaring that the men should have been released unconditionally or charged in court. PEBCO felt obligated to start a fund to support the out-of-work men and their families.

Soon after his release from detention, Qeqe went to trial for breaching his banning order. He had allegedly travelled to Uitenhage to attend to a personal business matter. 'Mr Dan Qeqe, an executive member of the Port Elizabeth Black Civic Organisation, appeared briefly in the Port Elizabeth Magistrate's Court yesterday [on] a charge of contravening his restriction order,'[62] it was reported in the press. Elsewhere, it was reported that 'Member of PE Black Civic Organisation executive, Mr Dan Qeqe, made brief appearance in PE Magistrate's Court today on charge of contravening restriction order. Case postponed to April 3'.[63]

Phumla firmly denied that her father contravened his banning order. She argued that Dunster, the same policeman who had passed on Qeqe's toilet-paper-written letter to Somyalo, had lied to police authorities. Dunster claimed that he had seen Qeqe under cover of night in Uitenhage. 'That is when they lied about him … So Dunster, who was a police officer, went to the authorities saying that he had seen Baas Dan travelling to Uitenhage,'[64] Phumla went on.

Again, Somyalo, representing Qeqe in the case, explained the proceedings and outcomes of the trial:

> There was a security police who had claimed that he had seen him in Uitenhage in an evening, and yet he had never gone there … But the policeman, that one who had given evidence, floundered and floundered and floundered and floundered, to the effect that he was not found guilty.[65]

Sloti, who was living in Qeqe's house at the time, claimed that he had, indeed, been to Uitenhage. Moreover, Sloti maintained, Qeqe had serially contravened his banning order by visiting his farm in Greenbushes. 'But even so, now under the banning order, he would go out of town.'[66] He went on, 'During the banning, he would go to his farm, disguised and go to his farm, and come back.'[67] On the Uitenhage visit, Sloti recalled that:

> Oh, they took him again for interrogation. They had received information that he had been seen in Uitenhage, but they didn't have genuine evidence … But he had been to Uitenhage. They [police security branch] were right. But they didn't have substantive evidence for the court.[68]

Prompted by the claim that Qeqe might have, indeed, travelled to Uitenhage, Somyalo laughingly replied, 'I suppose we, as his lawyers, all we knew was that Dan didn't travel to Uitenhage.'[69] It was the secretive and scheming Qeqe who had triumphed.

Much of Qeqe's activism in Port Elizabeth in the 1980s focused on unfair electricity charges for township dwellers and the challenges of power generation. In the mid-1980s, in his capacity as chairman of the Iliso Lomzi Committee, Qeqe agitated against the ridiculously low electricity rebates for township residents.[70] As reported, 'Electricity accounts and the sale of State houses in the Port Elizabeth black townships have been sharply criticised, with electricity consumers complaining that the amount credited to their electricity accounts as State subsidy was far too low.'[71]

Electricity subsidy amounts were claimed to be as low as 70c at times, and sometimes stood at R4 and R6. They were allegedly 'not as impressive as earlier subsidies'.[72] Qeqe maintained that the Iliso Lomzi Committee had received several complaints from residents that their electricity accounts were no better than before the payment of the electricity subsidy. Qeqe announced that, 'We are arranging a mass meeting soon to discuss this because many people seem disappointed with the manner in which this subsidy thing is being worked out.'[73] Further, he declared that Iliso Lomzi was awaiting the outcome of a promised ministerial-level inquiry into high electricity rates and installation deposits charged.

Qeqe was regarded as a 'long-standing critic'[74] of unfair electricity charges by the ECAB. He was also regarded as the first person to raise the possibility that the electricity subsidy was not being paid to the ECAB's 8000 Port Elizabeth consumers, condemning the possibility that the rebate on the electricity bills of Port Elizabeth's African consumers would be less than that given to the white municipal electricity consumers. The Port Elizabeth city treasurer, Armandus Strydom, announced that a total of R234 000 would be credited to ECAB consumers in March 1984, and that the rebate would be 12.5 per cent.[75]

Livid, Qeqe denounced the rebate rate, pointing out that it was lower than the 13.5 per cent for white municipal consumers. He also highlighted the fact that white municipal consumers paid 0.049c per unit, while ECAB African consumers paid 0.065c per unit.[76] He asserted that the high electricity charges would reduce the entire township to bankruptcy.[77] Strydom, however, could not confirm the figures Qeqe had produced.

Qeqe then organised a mass township meeting to be convened on a Saturday evening at Centenary Hall to allow the community to deliberate on the issue. Strydom, on the other hand, claimed that, since the unit rate paid by ECAB African consumers was higher, the percentage rebate would be lower. He argued that the discrepancies in unit rate payments were based on the consumption reflected in the 1982/83 financial year.

Qeqe also intervened in civic complaints concerning power failures. In 1982, New Brighton experienced power outages three times. Qeqe had tried to intervene, contacting the Port Elizabeth Electricity Department, but to no avail.[78] Areas affected in New Brighton were the Thembalethu suburb, Dubula Street, and the lower areas of Connacher and Ferguson roads.[79] Mr Ivan Peter, the chief executive officer of the Port Elizabeth Community Council, pointed out that the matter had not been brought to his attention.[80]

At one point in the same year, New Brighton 'was plunged into darkness'[81] for two days. Qeqe condemned the municipality, denouncing that, 'We pay more than the city people for electricity and all we ask is that there is light when we turn on the switch. We are not paying for darkness.'[82] However, it was established that power failures were caused by an overload on the system. Another contributing factor was a fault in the high-tension cable on the municipality side of New Brighton, and the township's faulty transformer.[83]

In the midst of this melee, Qeqe's immediate family flourished, with a number of milestone celebrations. His daughter, Phumla, got married in 1984 in a fanfare wedding in New Brighton. 'It was a great social occasion when Phumla, the eldest daughter of the prominent sports administrator, Mr Dan Qeqe, and his wife, Nyamie, was married to Jerry, son of Mr and Mrs W Tshalala of Bloemfontein at St Patrick's Presbyterian Church in New Brighton,'[84] it was reported in the press. Indeed a huge social occasion, it attracted hundreds of invited guests as well as spectators from Port Elizabeth. 'Hundreds of people lined the streets to see the procession of cars as the bridal party drove to the War Memorial Hall in New Brighton where the wedding lunch was held.'[85]

The marriage was officiated by Reverend GR Phenya of St Patrick's Presbyterian Church, and assisted by Mr Frank Tonjeni. The wedding, marked by traditional Xhosa and Sotho wedding songs, was officially attended by 800 guests. The well-known stage and film actor, Winston Ntshona, was master of ceremonies, with guests travelling from Cape Town, Bloemfontein, Durban, East London, Umtata and Uitenhage. Members of the touring Boland rugby team were also among the greats. The speakers included Mr J Njenje, Mr B Mbolekwa, Mrs M Sali, Mr W Mokoena, Mrs E Thou, Silas Nkanunu and Mr T Gundwana.[86]

Qeqe was a committed family man. Mpumelelo reminisced, 'He loved his family. Family comes first to Baas Dan … although he knew that the people … are important to him, but then his family comes first.'[87] Mrs Majola remembered Qeqe as both responsible and committed, but with a rather unsentimental, austere and no-nonsense attitude worked into it. When it came to family outings, certain frills had to be planned and schemed around him without his knowledge. For instance, Mrs Majola recalled that:

> We want to go for Easter. Our children went to school in Durban … So, during Easter we travelled in Baas Dan's car to Durban. We didn't want him to drive us … He was going to take us straight. If we wanted to go to Kentucky Fried Chicken, he would drive us, and say, 'Here's Kentucky.' We, meanwhile, wanted to go shopping. We wanted MaCheapie.[88] We wanted to organise MaCheapie early …

> we went everywhere with MaCheapie. Baas Dan would take us to that designated place only … He didn't tolerate that nonsense … [He was] straightforward, but he was kind. [89]

He had been completely committed to his wife throughout her struggle with diabetes, first diagnosed in 1962.[90] Through surgical operations, leading to her leg amputation and being wheelchair-bound,[91] Qeqe consistently remained at her side. Although Mrs Majola claimed that Mrs Qeqe feared her husband, they had formed a very intimate and supportive relationship permeating all aspects of his life.

She had been a strong woman who knew all the details of Qeqe's businesses. As Mrs Majola attested, 'There was nothing she didn't know about, about his business, the business of her husband's because his business did not halt during all that time that Baas Dan was away.'[92] Even Qeqe admitted that she had made him a hero.[93] She also had a strong and decisive hand in the running of the affairs of the Spring Rose Rugby Football Club – a reflection of Qeqe's conviction when it came to empowering women early on. Mthobi Tyamzashe particularly remembered Mrs Qeqe's role in the administration of Spring Rose and Kwaru, responsible for writing and delivering letters. 'Now, that's the wife. We talked to the wife to get rugby going. So, to me, that was something else as well. We kind of broke stereotypes.'[94]

Qeqe's notion of commitment to family always entailed other families too, even beyond his extended family. He constantly adopted children and adults with various needs, housing them in his family compound. Gerald Majola remembered:

> Now, Mrs Qeqe never had the four kids that she had. Never. There were always more people at Baas Dan's. Baas Dan's house was like a hostel. It's a fact. You can see even now at the back of his house, there are rooms there. And out of the blue, he would look for a builder. 'Come, come, my friend.' 'What is he doing now?' 'No, oh, Milase, he is going to tell my mother …' 'So, Milase, I realised that so-and-so's child, I realised that he doesn't have accommodation, and I decided that it is better that he lives in my house.' They ended up living in his house, you know, with other people, and with families also. Baas Dan was the father of the people.[95]

In his personal life, his commitment to and passion for back-yard livestock farming proved to be a niggle for the Port Elizabeth municipality, an issue that was equally sensitive and contentious with township residents. It postponed resolutions on the matter in order to deliberate on a new approach, noting:

> This was a problem which had been troubling the Council for many years, but owing to the strong opposition from community leaders and owners of livestock which met all previous attempts to abolish stock the implementation of Council's resolutions regarding the prohibition of stock had been postponed for various reasons.[96]

From the mid-1980s, Qeqe insisted on farming pigs, cattle and chickens in the back yard of his garage in Thembalethu, his rural childhood passion for livestock farming having stayed with him right through to his old age. But it was particularly pig farming that serially put him on a collision course with the municipality, ending up in court. 'An application for the discharge of a well-known rugby administrator and civic leader, who appeared in the Commissioner's Court on a charge of keeping pigs and cattle in a proclaimed black area without a written permit was opposed by the State yesterday,'[97] it was reported in 1982.

The Port Elizabeth City Council had come up with a new approach for the maintenance of livestock in the townships. Residents, they instructed, were to dispose of their livestock once they were given sufficient notice to do so – a six-months grace period up to 30 June 1971.[98] Despite this new ruling, 50 per cent of the livestock still remained, and a further notice of disposal was given. After an audit of township livestock conducted on 17 August 1971, a total of 226 cattle, 129 goats and 26 sheep were impounded. The assistant director of Bantu Affairs and his senior staff were 'physically in command at every stage of this difficult and unpopular assignment'.[99]

Qeqe's dispute with the municipality began when, in March 1982, Mr GM Mhlanga, New Brighton's superintendent, found livestock in the back yard of Qeqe's petrol station. In court, Mhlanga maintained that the complaint did not come from the Thembalethu residents, but from inspectors from the Port Elizabeth Municipal Health

Department.[100] On 16 March of the same year, Mhlanga personally handed Qeqe a letter, requesting him to remove the animals before legal action was instituted against him. Mhlanga gave Qeqe another warning letter before 26 March. Mhlanga claimed in court that on 4 April and 3 May, he had visited Qeqe's premises again, and found that he had not yet removed the livestock.

Qeqe, represented by Nkanunu in court, argued that he had kept the livestock in his back yard since 1975. He also argued that the state had failed to prove that he had intended to violate municipal health regulations. AP Rossouw, representing the state, pointed out that Qeqe had been afforded enough time to get rid of the livestock, and had not done so.

However, Qeqe's daughter, Phumla, claimed that it was Thembalethu residents who had complained of a strong, repulsive odour from pig farming coming from Qeqe's yard. Relaying a significantly different sequential narrative of his dispute with the municipality, Phumla recalled:

> [He] had pigs, here in the garage. So, those pigs *mos*, it was stinky there. When you were in a taxi passing by that place, people in the taxi would say, 'Mmhm!' passing through Qeqe's. And then those people reported this to the municipality. People from the municipality came to take those pigs away, or whatever, from the garage. They came and reported the case to our house.[101]

Qeqe had chased them away with a knobkerrie, daring them to return with the same complaint.[102] As it turns out, Qeqe had a long-standing feud with Mhlanga in his capacity as New Brighton's superintendent, one that was exacerbated by the latter's eviction of residents who were late with rent payments or could not afford to pay at all. Mhlanga's actions went against the core of Qeqe's humanitarian belief in the welfare of the residents of New Brighton. As Sloti attested, 'All those houses at Ford[103] were under Mr Mhlanga. The problem was Mr Mhlanga, even a person who could not afford to pay rent there, Mr Mhlanga evicted him. He was responsible for the eviction process.'[104]

In 1989, Dan Qeqe turned 60 years old. By then he was truly a renaissance granddaddy of Port Elizabeth, the previous decade having witnessed an inexorable denouement of his energy output. Following the lifting of his banning order in 1983, he did not face another political incarceration, nor did any of his close associates in non-racial sports liberation and anti-apartheid political activism – Nkanunu, Siwisa, Sobikwa, or others. They had grown old and were perhaps significantly removed from the fiery coalface of direct political activism.

Qeqe had continued with non-racial sports liberation activities in the 1980s, participating in campaigns on the international boycotts of South African rugby and other sports codes tours.[105] It was not, however, activity that demanded as much exertion as Kwaru and other internal non-racial sports liberation activities had required of him in the 1970s and the first half of the 1980s. The Dan Qeqe of the 1980s had reached the pinnacle of his achievements. It was a decade that demanded of him the maturity, finesse and authority of his leadership. He had become a granddaddy who pulled strings, weighing in with the authority of his voice when needed.

The 1980s, however, had also been a decade of frustration, a bruising period. It had hewed a flustered Qeqe who had grown more impatient, abrasive and angry, and significantly removed from the old-world, gentlemanly charms he had been known for. Much of the Kwaru he had co-created had been pulled asunder. And the Dan Qeqe Stadium he had built had come into its own in the hands of the mass-based liberation struggles of Port Elizabeth.

Mass funerals and political rallies hosted at the Dan Qeqe Stadium had rattled the local Security Branch of the police. Visiting Qeqe at his home, they had often pleaded with him to stop holding these events. But he had thrown his hands up in the air, telling them that the Dan Qeqe Stadium, although it bore his name, had never been his creation, but rather that of the people of Port Elizabeth.[106] And as much as the political and people's fanciful moods had swayed Port Elizabeth, Qeqe had been swayed by them, shifting some in his own direction, becoming one with the social history of the people of Port Elizabeth.

12

QEQE RESTS: THE LEGACY

In 1997, Qeqe became the first black sports administrator in Port Elizabeth and the Eastern Cape to receive the President's Sports Award (Silver) for 1996–97.[1] Presented by President Nelson Mandela at a function held at the Presidential Guesthouse in Pretoria, he received his award alongside the Free State and Springbok cricket fast bowler, Allan Donald, who was presented with the Presidential gold medal. Other sports heroes awarded that evening were the cricketer Basil d'Oliveira, world motor-racing champion Jody Scheckter, boxing world titleholder Vic Toweel, and Comrades Marathon champion Bruce Fordyce.[2] These were 'sporting heroes of the past, whose feats had gone unacknowledged by the state'.[3]

'Receiving this recognition and being honoured by President Mandela makes me very proud,'[4] a beaming Qeqe commented. He went on, stating that, 'My efforts to introduce non-racialism in sport and allow political rallies to be held in the stadium resulted in my being detained by the security police. The Government was not happy with … non-racialism, which also received opposition from the white rugby establishment.'[5]

Dan Qeqe's nomination for the President's Sports Award (Silver) had not been an obvious one for the selectors in government – he had not been among those officially nominated initially – but had come straight from President Mandela. Mthobi Tyamzashe, director-general of the Department of Sport and Recreation and central to the nomination and award processes, recalled with precision:

> The one thing that embarrassed me … I was the DG of Sport, we had these things, 'Annual Presidential Sports Awards', where Mr Mandela would address sports people and all that. So, then there's this category of Lifetime Awards. And then he would ask, 'Can you suggest names for this?' We would suggest names. I remember one day, he says, 'I see your suggestions there – Dan Qeqe' … he added himself – Theo Mthembu, Dan Qeqe. He says, 'No, these people we used to hear about them in the Island.'[6] I was so embarrassed. I didn't even remember … Remember, I'm putting together the list as the Department of Sport. Then the list would go to him, through Netshitenzhe. To me, what was amazing is, he looks at the list, and he says, 'No, man, no, no. These are the people we've been hearing of.'[7]

That the reverberations of Qeqe's activism penetrated the walls of Robben Island is a reflection of how ostensibly lowly local and regional activist efforts are of great significance when it comes to the national imprint of social and political transformation.

Qeqe was 'no stranger to receiving awards'.[8] In 1995, Qeqe, then serving as a member of the Transitional Local Council (TLC) of Port Elizabeth on an ANC ticket, received the Sir Rufane Donkin Award.[9] He was honoured with the award along with Alison,[10] a rape survivor, and Peter Schwartz, an environmentalist renowned for the Save Our Beachfront campaign. The award was presented at the charter dinner of the Rotary Club of Port Elizabeth East. Each of the award winners received a plaque and a R1000 cash prize to be donated to a charity organisation of their own choice. Conceived in line with the Rotary Club's ethos of 'service above self', the award was given out for services performed beyond the call of duty. Attorney MW Randell, who had nominated Qeqe for the award, noted of him, 'His life has been characterised by a fervent will to achieve equality for those around him, necessarily having to take unpopular decisions which by their very nature attracted censure, pressure and even detention.'[11]

At the Sir Rufane Donkin Award dinner held at the Walmer

Bowling Club, Rotarian John McCready noted that Qeqe had been honoured for 'energetically devoting his efforts to community work for underprivileged and disadvantaged people and achieving equality for all'.[12] On choosing a charity to which to donate his R1000 cash prize, Qeqe opted for Mrs Jumartha Milase Majola's organisation, a woman recognised as 'a social worker who dedicates herself to elderly pensioners and helps aged ladies who knit and sew and sell their work because they cannot support themselves in a sufficient manner'.[13] Qeqe also appealed to Rotarians to support President Mandela in correcting social imbalances by 'uplifting the living conditions of underprivileged people'.[14]

In the haze of winning awards and receiving accolades, Qeqe continued in the 1990s to wage battles on behalf of black township entrepreneurs. As a township fuel distributor, he represented other black distributors in trying to secure fairer deals. Qeqe led the approach to the Cape Economic Development Forum (CEDF) and the Port Elizabeth/Uitenhage Taxi Owners' Forum (PEUTOF) to get better deals from the companies for which they distributed fuel.[15] This decision had been made at a meeting of township fuel distributors, attended by approximately 20 members who formed the Township Fuel Distributors Association. The meeting had elected three office-bearers: Richmond Vantyi (chairman), Fezile Sobikwa (secretary) and Dan Qeqe (treasurer).[16]

Qeqe pointed out that they wanted the CEDF co-ordinator, Valence Watson, and PEUTOF chairman, Government Zini, to help them. He expressed that they were 'quite unhappy about the oppressive attitude of the companies who are using us to help get their products to township traders'.[17] He further emphasised, 'We want them to investigate the issue of irregularities which were raised in October concerning the rates received on discriminatory lines.'[18] These 'discriminatory lines' had allegedly come from what he termed 'verbal secrecy'[19] between fuel companies and white clients. This had led to black distributors being paid lower rates than those paid to white companies that undertook similar deliveries.

One of the accolades Qeqe received in the 1990s – and one he had been particularly proud of – was his invitation to the inauguration of the United Cricket Board of South Africa. Attending the banquet dinner for that moment of unity among various sports bodies was the fulfilment of his long-cherished dream of non-racial sports liberation. He remarked, 'This is one of my happiest invitations, especially as a former provincial cricketer and a current administrator.'[20] In a triumphant tone, he further remarked that, 'Today, however, there is no longer Government and police harassment against players joining predominantly black sporting clubs.'[21] He had felt particularly proud that one of his cricket products, Khaya Majola, had been elected co-managing director of the United Cricket Board of South Africa.[22]

In 1995, Qeqe had also been tipped to serve on the executive committee of the Eastern Province Rugby Football Union for that year's season.[23] As then outgoing president, Trevor Jennings, had reported, they had planned to approach Qeqe to make himself available. He had been 'earmarked' for the position of chairman of the development and facilities.[24]

These accolades emerged as a result of the enormous influence Qeqe had garnered and had exerted over official sports and political authorities, many of them then occupying high-level and influential positions in official sports bodies and government, both provincially in the Eastern Cape, and nationally. Many had come out of his sports administration training, and he had worked with others as peers in non-racial sports bodies and in political and civic bodies. In exerting this influence, Qeqe had displayed in his characteristic bulldozing and somewhat aggressive manner. His granddaughter, Sinazo Vabaza, recalled:

> He was that type. I remember he had a conversation with one of the ministers. I am not going to be able to recall who it was. But it was sports-related. And he was swearing at him/her over the phone … He swore at him/her big time, that he/she was not fulfilling what he/she was meant to do, and he/she was a 'q' [reference to an 'arsehole' in isiXhosa]. 'This is a 'q' what you are doing. My friend, we didn't facilitate to put you in these positions for you to do these things.' He was that type of character, and as a result, he was respected by everybody for that, especially also by the white

> community because he could tell them off. He would tell them that, 'This is not it. It's not going to proceed that way. It is meant to be this way, and this way, and that way.'[25]

The awards and accolades Qeqe accumulated in the 1990s fell within a period of euphoria, a denouement of all manner of tensions and struggles. This was a period of transition to a new post-apartheid political dispensation. The change of times signified a period of folding up old vehicles and unfolding new ones entrusted to cater to people's pride, struggles and expectations. With the unbanning of the ANC, the PAC and other political parties, the transition period called for unity talks between apartheid state structures and the structures of the liberation movement. This necessitated the building of new post-apartheid structures, often coming out of bitterly hammered-out and complex negotiations.

At the end of the unity talks, the Dan Qeqe Stadium was, in 1992, officially handed over to 'the people of Port Elizabeth' by the United Cricket Board of South Africa. As reported, 'The Dan Qeqe Stadium was officially handed over by the United Cricket Board to the people of Port Elizabeth at a function in the stadium's new clubhouse yesterday.'[26] At the function, Qeqe pleaded, 'Let us play together, and let's not have fear for one another.'[27] Krish Mackerdhuj of the United Cricket Board, and formerly of SACOS, pointed out that sport was one way of putting an end to social apartheid. And in that process, establishment sport had a role to play in ensuring unity.[28]

But, in all respects, the Dan Qeqe Stadium had always been in the hands of the people of Port Elizabeth, from the time it had been spotted as a ground to be developed into a stadium. However, the lines of official ownership had remained blurred. In court papers surrounding the disputes and conflicts that had raged on, post 1982, between Qeqe's Kwaru and Nyondo's Sisonke Group, attempts were made at understanding the stadium's official ownership structure. Advocate Kroon, representing the plaintiff, Kwaru, had asserted that, 'The Dan Qeqe Stadium is the property, it is situate[d] on a property owned by the East Cape Administration Board, but the KwaZakhele Rugby Union built that stadium. Who is the occupier of the stadium?

– the KwaZakhele Rugby Union.'[29]

Official ownership versus the ownership of 'the people of Port Elizabeth', and how the matter was handled during the transition period in the 1990s, has led to multiple ownership claims over the Dan Qeqe Stadium. The stadium, the built infrastructure, now belongs to Kwaru, currently a single, local rugby club among many in Port Elizabeth. It is no longer a union of rugby clubs. However, the land on which the stadium is built remains with no official title deed.[30] In that state, the maintenance mandate of the Nelson Mandela Bay Metropolitan Municipality (NMBMM) has remained out of reach. The municipality has no legal responsibility to maintain or effect improvements to the stadium. Consequently, over the years, the Dan Qeqe Stadium has become increasingly misused and dilapidated. Gerald Majola, commenting on the current state of the stadium, its legacy and Dan Qeqe's contribution to the post-apartheid sports dispensation, noted:

> For even that matter of the stadium, it's a sin, to me, that the stadium is in that condition it is in, for his contribution in life. So I think it should, in fact, we should for the stadium to be [a heritage site], because PE has contributed so much to sport in this country than any other city, when it comes to black sport, including the ones that we see today, they come from here. Administrators, whatever you call it, at one stage, I was CEO of Cricket South Africa. Ncula was Deputy CEO of rugby. Silas Nkanunu was president of rugby. Ray Mali was president of Cricket South Africa … All these people come from the same, like Danny Jordaan in soccer. We were all, at one stage, all of us were heading the sports of the country.[31]

Unity talks also dissolved 'the mighty Kwaru'. The splinter group, Sisonke, which had formally constituted itself into Zwiru, had also been ravaged by infighting, leading to yet another splinter group in the late 1980s. It was the tradition of infighting and splitting that had given birth to Kwaru, and led to its demise. This tradition had continued within Zwiru, leading to further splitting. Thami Songongo, insightfully analysing this pattern, pointed out that, '[There's] a saying that goes like, "If you kill by the sword, you die by the sword." If you break away, they are also going to break away from you. You can see that even in churches. This group breaks away to form another, because even in that Zwiru, it experienced a split.'[32]

And so the transition period heralded new, untested vehicles of hope, disrupting old and trusted ones. It was a time of both birth and destruction. Perhaps the then president of SACOS, Ebrahim Patel, best summed up the spirit of the times when he noted that, 'South Africa is a country where you hope today and despair the very next day.'[33] In this, Patel further postulated, regarding the fears surrounding negotiations, that, 'There are two fundamental realities that must be addressed. The one is black anger. The other is white fear of non-racialism which to them, by implication, means that they will of necessity have to forego their monopoly of political power.'[34]

Perhaps Patel's analysis of 'white fear' requires breaking down. The state-sponsored, white-representing SARB insisted, for the most part, on particular continuities that would ensure its survival and vibrancy. Looming largest was their insistence on the continuation of South African rugby international tours. The then president of SARB, Dr Danie Craven, had made it blatantly clear that international rugby tours provided a financial lifeline to African rugby. Responding to Sam Ramsamy's pro-moratorium stance on international rugby tours in December 1990, he maintained:

> Incoming international tours generate money. If we don't have international tours, where must the money come from to continue with this programme? ... But how long must this moratorium continue, a moratorium which will damage the future of the game of rugby and sport in general? A moratorium which will deprive the 'lesser privileged' from opportunities, opportunities as far as upliftment as well as international contact are concerned.[35]

The ANC vociferously opposed international rugby tours. As far back as 1988, in preparation for the Harare Initiative, the ANC – along with the NSC and SACOS – had insisted on the boycott of South African international rugby tours and of other sporting bodies. Mendi Msimang, the ANC representative in London, writing to the International Rugby Board (IRB), maintained:

> As you know, the South African Rugby Board and the South African Rugby Union have taken the first steps to bring the entire rugby fraternity in our country under one non-racial controlling body. They have also agreed to work for the reorganisation of the sport so that it becomes truly non-racial.
>
> It is therefore clear that the SARB itself recognises the fact that up to now, it has not be a non-racial body. It is our view that the IRB should respect the judgement and not seek to perpetuate racism in rugby by approving the tour the press has spoken about.[36]

From Dr Craven's perspective, the programme steering the transformation of the rugby organisation into a non-racial entity needed to adhere to four goals: (1) Improvement of facilities; (2) Advancement of competition and tours; (3) Removal of apartheid restrictions; and (4) Unity among the white, African and coloured rugby bodies.[37] In his own and SARB's understanding, he firmly emphasised that, 'We have managed to unite the offshoots of the above organisation after years of toil and insults by some of our ministers of sport who must be held responsible for the fact that SARU is still not part of us and that SACOS and other bodies were created.'[38]

Indeed, the unity agreement reached by SARB and SARU in 1977 had been rejected by the Minister of Sport. The first forays into unity at the height of apartheid then collapsed. Even Patel acknowledged that, after this rejection, 'It was therefore clear that both the Board and SARU were victims of apartheid and that non-racial rugby was unacceptable to the South African government.'[39]

For SARU and other non-racial sports liberation bodies, the value of the Harare Initiative lay in opening up avenues to reach that non-racial sports dispensation. As Patel pointed out, on behalf of SARU, 'In this end SARU will always be party to any meeting where there is a sincere desire to diagnose and cure the ills of rugby – if rugby is to survive at all. That in effect was the essence of Harare.'[40] The joint statement issued by SARU, the SARB and the ANC in Harare in October 1988 read:

> The meeting came about because of a common desire on the part of all the participating organisations to ensure that rugby in South

Africa is organised according to non-racial principles. The meeting confirmed this position and argued that South African Rugby should come under one non-racial controlling body …

The leaders of the South African Rugby Board and the South African Rugby Union met with the ANC solely because of the belief that it can play a positive role to achieve the common objective shared by SARB and SARU. These leaders are ready at all times to meet and shall meet any other parties or groups that may also play such a role.[41]

Subsequently, it was agreed by SARB and SARU that in transforming this one, non-racial national controlling body, staggered steps ought to be taken. Firstly, both executive committees would report fully to their respective bodies, after which necessary committees would be appointed. Secondly, the committees would identify all expected problems, and refer the necessary proposals back to their respective bodies. Thirdly, SARU gave notice that all international rugby tours would be suspended until the completion of the amalgamation process. SARB, however, still had to finalise its position on this matter.[42]

But the lingering 'black fears' when it came to levelling imbalances between establishment and non-racial sports persisted beyond the Harare Initiative. In late 1990, the NSC insisted on focusing 'all immediate efforts on redressing the imbalances that the policy of apartheid has reinforced between advantaged and disadvantaged sport'.[43] In 1991, the NSC had the foresight to warn that the absorption of the disadvantaged non-racial sports into establishment sports would prove to be a flaw in the unification process. It stated that, 'The unification initiative of the NSC [is] intended for marriages between more or less equal partners otherwise they would be nothing more than absorption of alternative sports structures by establishment sports structures.'[44]

And so it was that the absorption of Qeqe's Kwaru into the establishment fold in the 1990s took place unwittingly – and yet with their eyes open at the same time. Emerging weak, bruised and exhausted from the infighting and splits of the 1980s, Kwaru was a pale, hollow shadow of its former glorious self. In addition, the rise of UDF-affiliated civic bodies and *amabutho* had usurped Kwaru's power.

Taking advantage of Kwaru's political and social standing, *amabutho* had coerced Kwaru – often recklessly and abrasively – into particular political agendas and directions. Kwaru had thus fallen victim to the same politically turbulent winds that had accompanied its birth in the early 1970s. Mpumelelo 'Sbhidla' Majola observed this trend in the mid- to late 1980s, noting that:

> At some point, Kwaru was called aside. There was this trend of calling us to meetings in corners, during the time of *amabutho*. Decisions were taken then ... The decisions that they took there, they took them for everybody, whether you were in school organisations or in Kwaru, telling us, you are going to meet ... They said you were going to meet, end of the story, whether you like it or not. You are going to meet there.[45]

The *amabutho* were a gang of crassly politicised youth in the townships, who tended to resort to mobilising consumer boycotts and stayaways based on violence. Their motives were thinly based on ANC ideologies, leaning more toward violent tactics such as tyre-burning blockades and 'necklacing', and forcing township residents who disregarded consumer boycotts to humiliatingly consume in public the products they had bought in town, such as cooking oil. For instance, in 1986, *amabutho* youths went door to door in New Brighton, destroying ID cards that had been issued to some residents by the Ibhayi Town Council.[46] Tom Lodge and Mark Swilling described *amabutho* thus:

> They have little knowledge of the intricacies of formal political organizations. Instead, they have fashioned their own military structure. Emerging independently from other township associations, the *Amabuthu* declare their allegiance to the African National Congress. For them, the ANC and its imprisoned leader, Nelson Mandela, are the liberators; but otherwise, their ideology is limited to a few basic slogans.[47]

Explaining how and why Kwaru had become destabilised by *amabutho*, Valence Watson argued:

> Well … my take is as follows: when Kwaru became this visible force, it became, of course … a vehicle for change. You could not any longer deny the fact that races have to play rugby together. And, of course, it went a long way putting a lot of pressure on the South African government and SA sport, because here was a group of people, they were playing together against the law. And, of course, because Kwaru became this very visible … for the movement against apartheid, amongst others, amongst PEBCO and MACWUSA, and eventually, as I said, in East London.[48]

But more destabilising for Qeqe's Kwaru and other long-established black rugby clubs of Port Elizabeth and other areas in the Eastern Cape was the uneasy balancing of the development needs of non-racial sports against the sustainability of white establishment sport. It was hammering for a reconciliation between non-racial and establishment sport with a centralised commitment to equity. And, unfortunately for Kwaru and other black rugby clubs, unity talks found them on their knees – weak, bruised and battered. What the NSC had forewarned had come to pass: the absorption of Kwaru into the mightier and better-resourced fold of establishment sport. With that, as many black rugby clubs and bodies dissolved, their legacies were snuffed out. Lamenting this loss, Ray Mali noted:

> You can't destroy something that was built in 1892, and say it should end. Even if it is a third team, it will rise. Now, we are new. We are new teams. The Easterns is no longer that old team from Korsten. That is how I see it, that those teams should have been preserved even if they played at the lower leagues, they will grow … What I'm trying to say is that, we lost that chance when we allowed our teams to be wiped off. And then we allowed schools like Cowan, Newell, Healdtown, go down, schools like Nathaniel Nyaluza in Grahamstown.[49]

Unity thus dictated that Kwaru and Zwiru merge. However, Spring Rose refused to be part of the merger, insisting on remaining separate and independent. But all the other clubs – St Cyprian's, Orientals, African Bombers, Cruel Tigers, Park Rovers and Union – joined up to form one Kwaru rugby club. The whittling away of old black clubs also drove away allegiances and their support bases. Mpumelelo 'Sbhidla' Majola pointed out that, 'Black people left. You were not able to listen to any instructions when your own club was finished. The challenge was that names had to be expunged.'[50]

The merger of non-racial and establishment sports, with all the apparent good intentions, often meant the marginalisation of non-racial sports players in the new, post-apartheid dispensation. And, of course, many of these at the helm felt nothing but disdain, if not utter contempt, for black players who came from the non-racial sports fold. In the name of racial transformation of South African rugby – and contrary to the spirit of the move – they often selected for the Springboks those black players who had played in apartheid state-sponsored black teams over those who had played in non-racial rugby.

A harrowing and poignant story highlighting this prejudice is that of Andile Nyembezi. The son of Soyisile Nyembezi, also a non-racial rugby player in Port Elizabeth, Andile grew up in a family and culture of non-racial rugby, with his father playing for Easterns. As Andile put it, 'So, I grew up surrounded by and under the influence of rugby within non-racial sport. I came to consciousness during the call for "there can be no normal sport in an abnormal society", until such time that apartheid was disbanded.'[51]

Completing his primary and high school education in Port Elizabeth, from the early 1980s he, like his father, played for Easterns. In the rugby school system, he played in PE West. In the zonal school system, he played for Thamsanqa High School, with PE West comprising Thamsanqa, Cowan, Newell, Mzontsundu and Thembalethu high schools.[52]

From the school zonal system, Nyembezi progressed to Eastern Province, playing his first game for them in 1987. He also put on his first blazer for SA Schools in the same year. The following year, he was invited to the South African Schools Sports Association (SASSA) under SARU. His team had become affiliated to SARU, against the hardened, anti-non-racial sports liberation of his high school principal. Explaining his position on non-racial sports, Nyembezi maintained that:

> We wanted non-racial sport, because our parents came from that side. We maintained that we cannot, when we play, play for ninety minutes, and then the very same people we played with in that ninety minutes game in town shoot down our brothers in a state of emergency in the township. That motivated us to stand against our school principals, and say that we were not going to do that. We protested and joined the Kwaru forces.[53]

By the time of unity, Nyembezi explained that Kwaru had all the players who had made it a legendary rugby union: Norman Xhoxho, Zola Yeye, Gerald 'Gailer' Majola, Bhabha Nolokhwe and Themba Ludwaba. However, they had now advanced in age and, as he put it, were 'dragging their feet'[54] against the strength of young white players.

And so it was that Andile Nyembezi was selected, recruited by Allister Coetzee in 1994 to join the PE Harlequins. He was subsequently selected to play for the Junior Springboks, and toured Scotland, Ireland and Wales with them. At that time, he was also on the B side of the Eastern Province – not on the A side, because, 'Racism still reigned then. There were dynamics that prevented us from getting into it. They came up with all manner of objections.'[55]

After proving his skills and prowess in the trials in Bellville, Cape Town, in 1995, Nyembezi made the B side of the Springbok team scheduled to tour Scotland, Ireland and Wales. He also went on to play against Argentina, and was then earmarked to be the first black Springbok player to play in the 1995 Rugby World Cup. As he relayed:

> And then they called my father, and then I was earmarked that I was going to be the first black Springbok in 1995. But, because whites were stubborn at that time, I was thrown out the window. They said, no, Chester Williams was better, he was black. We do not know where these people come from. They come from non-racial sport that we don't know anything about, and we don't even recognise that. Chester Williams used to play against us. Chester Williams was a member of the Leopards, *mos*. They used to play with whites there in Cape Town. Whites were on this side, they were in the Leopards.[56]

Nyembezi's and Qeqe's Kwaru's stories thus became narratives of defeat in the face of the illusion of unity, mergers and a new, post-apartheid sports dispensation. But 'the mighty Kwaru' refused to submit to that disillusionment. It had not died. Kwaru, casting its shadow long after its demise, produced Siya Kolisi, the first black Spingbok captain. Coming from one of Kwaru's affiliate second-division rugby clubs, African Bombers, Kolisi catapulted himself – and, with him, Kwaru – into the zenith of Springbok rugby which Nyembezi had lost back in 1995:

> This is where Siya Kolisi learned to play rugby. Dan Qeqe Stadium. Zwide township. Port Elizabeth. Out on the pitch, lush grass has carpeted the stony patches and buried the thorns, but everywhere else there are signs of the long, hard season just past. A crossbar slants into the ground. The skeleton of a scrum machine lies abandoned in the dead ball area. Litter drifts. Wires dangle from the floodlights, and snatches of music and the muffled barking of dogs blow in the breeze. This is the proud home of the African Bombers Rugby Football Club, and Siya Kolisi is glad to be back.[57]

The long shadow of Qeqe's Kwaru also produced not only Solly Tyibilika, the first black Springbok to score a try, but also gave South Africa its black Springbok managers, Zola Yeye and Mzwandile 'Stokololo' Stick. And so, in many ways, the demise of Kwaru at unity, at the dawn of a new, post-apartheid South African dispensation, had not been a true death. Qeqe's Kwaru's legacy lives on as the tale of the glory of South African rugby, perhaps now a normal sport in a normal society.

With the creation of the new, post-apartheid political structures, Qeqe was elected onto Port Elizabeth's TLC – the ultimate recognition of his political and civic contributions to the formation of a new South Africa. Indeed, it had been a long, uncertain and sometimes confusing journey for Qeqe, taking him from the New Brighton Native Advisory Board, later transitioning into the Port Elizabeth Joint Bantu Advisory Board, the Port Elizabeth Action Committee, PEBCO, other ad hoc civic and business entities, working with the ANC underground, into the post-apartheid TLC.

The TLC heralded a new future for Port Elizabeth. As chronicled at its opening, 'A chapter in Port Elizabeth history closed yesterday when the last committee meeting of the whites-only Port Elizabeth City Council – which first sat in 1861 – was held.'[58] Continuing, it was reported, 'But there were no tears as the seven-member Community Services Committee disposed of its official business in just over half-an-hour, paving the way to a new all-race administration.'[59]

Qeqe was elected from a list of 24 representing the ANC Alliance[60] from across the Port Elizabeth branches.[61] The other 26 individuals were chosen for their specific skills, or for wider and more equitable representation. Other prominent Port Elizabethans included on the list were Glen Goosen (Port Elizabeth's One City Management Committee chairman), Mike Nzotoyi (housing head of the South African National Civic Organisation (SANCO)), Rory Riordan (ANC local government secretary) and Mcebisi Xundu (Anglican Church archdiocesan and chairman of the Mzingisi Development Trust).[62]

Others elected from outside the ANC Alliance were Errol Heynes (a human resources employee), Dr Ronnie van Wyk (a sociologist at the then University of Port Elizabeth) and Moki Cekisani (a former Black People's Convention detainee and president of the Foundation for Sports in Africa). Also elected to the TLC was Benedicta Godolozi, the mother of Qaqawuli Godolozi of the PEBCO Three who had been disappeared in the 1980s, while Henry Fazzie, the then SANCO chairman and a veteran anti-apartheid activist, was elected to represent Zwide I branch.[63]

The democratic representation of the new, post-apartheid dispensation provided a historic opportunity for the election of women for the first time in 16 years in Port Elizabeth's local government. One of the six women elected to the TLC on a list of 50 non-statutory councillors on the ANC Alliance ticket was Jennifer Bowler.[64] Serving on Port Elizabeth's ANC One City task group since September 1991, Bowler was advertising and public relations manager at Gentyre.

Some of the teething problems were concerned with transition and the constitution of the governing body, centred mainly on differences of opinion regarding the number of councillors that should constitute the body,[65] resulting in a tussle between choosing a city council of 80 or one of 100. Eventually, the TLC settled for a city council of 80,[66] with a minimum salary of R2 000 per month.[67]

One of the major issues Qeqe took a stand against in his capacity as a TLC member was the make-up of the Eastern Cape province from the three regional entities in existence at the time.[68] It was reported that 'Port Elizabeth sports administrator and civic leader Dan Qeqe yesterday spoke out in favour of a separate region for the Eastern Province'.[69] Qeqe had pointed out that he would sign a petition calling for a referendum on the issue. He argued that the demarcation of the region had been a rushed process, thus producing more disadvantages than advantages in the process.

He had insisted that Bisho was too far away to be the capital city of the Eastern Cape province, while Umtata would be a worse option. To him, dividing the greater Eastern Cape province did not translate into neglect of the former homelands. He was quoted as saying, 'We are not overlooking this. These areas must be a priority. Preference must be given to the supply of clean water to these areas and to other needs.'[70] In effect, he regarded the then status quo of the regional separation between Ciskei, Transkei and the Border region as a 'beautiful setup'.[71]

Soon after Qeqe announced that he was launching a petition to campaign for retaining the regional status quo of the Eastern Cape province, it was announced that Qeqe had been 'persuaded to stop campaigning for separate regions in the Eastern Cape'.[72] The announcement was made by Mr Speedo Nondumo, the co-ordinator of the Port Elizabeth–Uitenhage Business Professional Grievances Forum, of which Qeqe was a member. Qeqe had made his turnabout following a meeting of the forum, and assured everyone that he had withdrawn the petition campaign in the interest of maintaining stability within the forum.

Mr Nondumo pointed out that Qeqe had started the petition campaign in his individual capacity, but that the forum had a duty to restrain him from pursuing the exercise. Nondumo said, 'Mr Qeqe had now disassociated himself from the campaign for a separate region and is appealing to people not to come to him to sign the petition.'[73] The forum had also consulted with the Eastern Cape MPs regarding views expressed by some members of the forum on the matter.

However, Qeqe's close friend, Judge Somyalo, pointed out that

Qeqe's position on the make-up of the Eastern Cape province may have been driven by some other motive he had not officially expressed at the time. It was mainly his disdain for the bureaucracy of the Transkei government, which could potentially infuse corruption into the financial and organisational management of the new Eastern Cape provincal government, especially considering its long-held tradition in these practices. Somyalo stated:

> He was one of the people who was of the view that in PE, in the Eastern Cape, should not include Transkei. I don't know if it was from the point of view that Transkei was a Bantustan, or because it would inhibit growth in the region, PE, the old Eastern Cape, you know, PE and other places. In retrospect, one would say he would have improved right, because when you look at the political situation today, you find about a lot of bad things that have happened, and they originated from the Transkei area … A lot of wrong there happened during the reign of Matanzima, there in Transkei, you see? … And that made us dysfunctional even in our territories. He was of the view that it should be a separate province.[74]

In the 1990s, Qeqe had reached a pinnacle in his farming activities, receiving an award from a progressive farmers' association in the Greenbushes area. But owning a farm in Port Elizabeth and managing it as a black man had been a rocky and tumultuous journey. He had bought the farm through Ronnie Watson.[75]

In running and managing the farm, he had encountered a legion of challenges from the white farming community, many of them racist. However, with his characteristic perseverance, by the late 1980s he had eventually won their hearts and confidence. His nephew, McKenzie Sloti, remembered Qeqe's early forays into farming and the challenges he had encountered:

> Oh, that should be, if I'm right, it should be in the '80s, in the early '80s. He had a smallholding there, a big one, about 3.8 hectares. Even there, he took his farming to a higher level. At that time, he was the only black person among those whites. They gave him some problems. They didn't like him, because he was black. Because of

> his attitude, he didn't give up. DDQ was a fighter. He remained there until he got along with the whites, and they accepted him eventually. As a result, he ended up as one of the members of the farmers' association there at Greenbushes. He was a strong member of the association, because he did a lot of things there.[76]

The 1990s also saw Qeqe's greatest loss, the passing away of his wife, Rose Nonyameko Qeqe. Regarded as the 'ever smiling and friendly Mrs Rose Nonyameko Qeqe',[77] she died in 1994 at the age of 60, having battled with diabetes ever since she was diagnosed in 1962.[78] She had undergone two surgeries, leaving her wheelchair-bound following a leg amputation.[79] Qeqe had consistently cared for her, taking her along with him on trips, even in her wheelchair-bound state.

Her funeral was big: '[One] of the biggest, most colourful and moving funerals seen in Port Elizabeth's townships in many years. A horse-drawn cart carrying her coffin was draped in the green and white colours of the Spring Rose Rugby Football Club. The coffin was also draped with the club's flag.'[80] At the funeral, her friend, Mrs Isabella Mabengeza, honoured her in a tribute that stated, 'Mrs Qeqe was a very persevering person as her vernacular name Nonyameko, meant. She was dignified and proved that behind every successful man there is a woman.'[81] Bidding his wife farewell, Qeqe said, 'Nyamie, you were a hero and now you are going to be the first to rest in the special Hero's Acre where we have a double plot – because you also made me a hero.'[82]

His wife's death profoundly affected Dan Qeqe. It made him sad,[83] but it also transformed him into a man of strong Christian faith, intensely and consistently dedicated to prayer. Mrs Jumartha Majola, a neighbour, witnessed this transformation, recalling, 'He would wake up in the morning, and come and get us to prayer. My children would say, "Hey, there's Baas Dan coming, we are going to pray now. We are going to pray now." It was not like him. We didn't know him as a prayerful person. It was not like him.'[84]

Baas Dan was buried on a rainy day in 2005.[85] It was, perhaps, a parting of the heavens, a welcome home and a grand departure for a man who had meant many things and everything to Port Elizabeth, the Eastern Cape province, and South Africa. His was a funeral where

'ANC and PAC people mix with no rancor, with genuinely fraternal affection'.[86] So ebullient was the ambience of the funeral that there was '[no] need for a sound system that evening as speaker after speaker, minister after minister, delivered thunderbolt messages with magnificent power'.[87]

Truly, he was a Baas Dan, a Dan Qeqe with magnificent power. His sense of magnificence came in big, monumental, accidental, bold, scheming, strategic, and simple and practical ways. He left an indelible imprint on the architecture and memorial landscape which no other national hero from Port Elizabeth had been able to do. In so many ways, therefore, a chronicle of his life and times is a direct replica of the people's biography of Port Elizabeth.

His is the story of the city reflected in a precise form, of how the people of the city grappled with the politics and the social environment and institutions that had shaped them. Equally, it is a reflection of how he and the people of Port Elizabeth moulded and changed the direction of the social and political environments and institutions they had inherited. No Qeqe biographer can talk of his life and times without reflecting on his intimacy with the city and its people. The corollary also holds true. No social historian of twentieth-century Port Elizabeth can possible comprehensively narrate the city's history without including the significant contribution of the life and work of Dan Qeqe.

Contemporaries of Dan Qeqe remember him in varied ways. But all these variations converge in the magnificence of his transformative life. Crosby 'Winky' Ximiya singles out for emulation the sense of exceptional leadership and responsibility that he displayed. He pointed out that, 'We lost a great man in Mr Qeqe. There's a lot, in people like us, we learnt from him, in terms of responsibility, in being a leader … So, he was quite exemplary in whatever he did.'[88]

It was this sense of wanting to emulate his exceptional qualities that his son, Mpumelelo, highlights as his most precious legacy – one he left everyone, even beyond the Qeqe family. As he put it:

> He never cheated us. He taught us humanity. He taught us compassion. And now, we need to be role models, and our children, when we talk to them, you are these people you are now because of

> your grandfather. You are Qeqes, do you understand me? Everyone draws from Baas Dan.[89]

Illuminating this legacy of Dan Qeqe, who came from the 'smaller house', of the younger wife in a polygamous family, his nephew in Fort Beaufort, Mncedi Mali, holds precious how he catapulted the Qeqe name to prominence. As he put it, that man who was as short as his father 'lifted to prominence the family name. Dan Qeqe filled his father's shoes. You see, *mos*, on the walls, it is written "Qeqe". This Qeqe on the walls comes from the smaller house.'[90] Another contemporary in non-racial sports liberation, Alan Zinn, singled out Qeqe's compassion and sense of humanity. To Zinn, he was 'a holistic human being, you know? He was a holistic man. And he had understanding. He had compassion. He would listen.'[91]

One of his protégés in rugby and sports administration, Mveleli Ncula, emphasised Qeqe's love for his community – a selfless love. As Ncula put it, 'I think what should really come out here was his, the love of the local communities. He was very, very strong there. He loved dearly his community ... He always wanted people to be successful in whatever they were doing.'[92] Others, such as Thozamile Botha, admired how Qeqe skilfully cohered politics, civic affairs and sports to mould the Port Elizabeth he wanted, and the improvements he wanted to see in the black communities of the city. As he expressed it:

> He was known as a businessman. He was also known as a sportsman, a sports administrator. And he used both sports and business to advance the struggles of the black man ... So, I would like Dan Qeqe to be remembered as a committed, as one of the most committed black business[men], contributing to the struggle for the liberation of the black man in the Port Elizabeth city, in the Eastern Cape, but in particular in Port Elizabeth, because often there's very little written about Port Elizabeth, and said about the struggles that were fought in this city.[93]

It is filling up this lacuna in the telling of South African history that Mkhuseli Jack and Valence Watson see the importance of Qeqe's life and works. Jack postulated this point thus:

> [History] now, it's time now for researchers to go back and pick up the pieces and make the true story that is going to be the final South African story. And that final South African story will be made by characters. And these characters, some of them, Dan Qeqe is one of them. This is critical in my view, and it is important.[94]

Watson's perception of this lacuna-filling mandate in the telling of a comprehensive South African history is thus:

> And my recollection of Dan Qeqe can be only be positive, irrespective of one or two hiccups that he had in his life with Kwaru. I'm talking about, because, in the bigger scheme of things, Dan Qeqe was, I think in my view, not given the prominence maybe in the new South Africa that he should have. And that goes for many, many activists. History has not shown them to true lights, and to the extent to which they were. They did a huge and positive contribution to this country.[95]

Even in the vast errors of his ways, Qeqe's arch nemeses in sports liberation – Nyondo, Ngcaphe, and to some extent, Songongo – respectfully commented on his overarching, positive contribution to the development of black people and communities in Port Elizabeth. Speaking at Qeqe's memorial service in 2005, Nyondo had this to say of him:

> This man that is lying here today, nobody worked harder than him in causing the non-racial rugby to flourish. And nobody worked harder than him in rugby in any other way … and this Qeqe laying here, I respected him all the time, and I'm still respecting him to this day, despite the fact that we had mega difficulties and differences.[96]

On his contributions, Ngcaphe noted that:

> To me, Qeqe was very, very good in rugby. Qeqe made a very big contribution in rugby. Qeqe made his resources available. Qeqe would assist anyone who was in need, you know? Qeqe was hardworking. He was down-to-earth as a person, not haughty like

> the educated people … So, in that respect, Qeqe was very good. He made a big contribution in building that field.[97]

Trenchantly critical of Qeqe's flaws in non-racial rugby and in the demise of Kwaru, Songongo pointed out, 'Do you know, if we were to stand in front of God and answer for the sins on the mess of black people's rugby in Port Elizabeth, a person who would field a lot of questions, in my opinion, would be Qeqe.'[98] And yet, in the same breath, Songongo admitted, 'It is his impact on the circumstances around him that resonated with the people, because of Qeqe's impact. He was a good man. To him, if you're wrong, you're wrong. If you are wrong, you are wrong. I know Qeqe that way, as an elder.'[99]

Looking to the future, Ray Mali, Gerald Majola, Themba Ludwaba and Thando Manana (a former Springbok player from Port Elizabeth nurtured early at the Dan Qeqe Stadium) fondly remembered him for how his non-racial rugby fight stood the future of the next generation of black rugby players in good stead. Ludwaba pointed out that 'our principles of non-racial [sport], and I think what Qeqe was saying was that, he wants, at the end of the day, that we compete with the white people.'[100] For Ray Mali, Qeqe's legacy still needs to be unfolded and celebrated in living projects that make meaningful and dynamic connections between sports, education, scholarship and community development.[101]

Manana recalled Dan Qeqe mentoring a youth who had reached his pinnacle in rugby:

> And I have to say, he's one of the guys I've looked up [to] as someone who, if I would say he was still alive, he would be mentoring me, to become what he wanted me to be … Funny enough, when I became a prominent rugby player, playing for Eastern Province, he was very much aware. He was looking at my progress. It was no surprise when I was selected for the Springboks, that he was one of the first people to come and welcome me at the PE Airport, alongside Edwin Ncula and other prominent administrators at the time.[102]

Ngconde Balfour remembered Qeqe for his humility and wished that 'we would have him again, so that we could learn from him'.[103] And for

Judge Lex Mpati, his entire life orbiting around sport and politics was wholesome. As he expressed it:

> Why should be there be something highlighted and some others don't, because his whole life was, you know, in it, call it 'sport and politics'. His whole life, so I don't think there's any specific fact, other than, of course, his contribution to Kwaru joining SARU, a non-racial body … So, being part of that decision to join SARU is to me one of the major things that he would have done.[104]

To Mthobi Tyamzashe, the authoritarian aspect of his personality conveyed a leadership acumen sorely needed at the time. As he noted:

> To me, he was authoritarian when he needed to be … To me, he struck me as that kind of guy that, if you're writing his epitaph, a person lying there was modest. Decisive, he was, because that autocratic thing means he is decisive. He didn't leave things to chance. And he believed in himself.[105]

To Vusi Pikoli, Qeqe was magnanimous, benevolent, and ready to pay the ultimate sacrifice for the struggle of the black person.[106] But to Mrs Majola, Qeqe's commitment to taking care of her family after her husband's death in 1971 nearly brought her to tears. It was her lasting, most endearing tribute to the humanitarian Qeqe:

> But what I wanted to stress was the twilight, was how Baas Dan was in this family. He was a father. He was nothing but a father in my home. He handled everything. The matter of Thozi's skipping the country, he handled it himself, so that I would not know about it, I would not get affected. How would I not get so severely affected by this as a mother who was widowed? I never felt that. Even their rites of passage to manhood, he took them himself to the mountain … In everything, he takes a lead.[107]

And yet, in all his contradictions, he was also magnanimous – a peacemaker, volatile, authoritarian and humble all rolled into one package, one attribute flowing into the other in a matter of seconds.

Judge Mpati recounted an anecdote epitomising the unfathomable, contradictory character that he was:

> In Adcock Stadium in Port Elizabeth, I think Western Province was playing Eastern Province. And we were sitting in the main stand. And Dan Qeqe, as we were walking up here, I think he had gone to the bathroom. He was walking up the stairs, you know, towards where we were sitting, as he was sitting with us there. A youngster from that side of him threw a bottle, you know, to the bottom. I think he was trying to throw it to the field. Man! Dan got hold of him, and gave him a huge klap! Nqwah! He said, 'Don't do that! Don't do that!' And then he came and sat with us … And that was just the end of it. He gave him a huge klap. I mean, you could hear it from afar. Nqwah! and sat down, as if nothing had happened.[108]

And from that volatility and turbulence, the ecstasy and endless possibilities of his life and times, Qeqe rests.

NOTES

Introduction

1 Interview 11: Qeqe family: Port Elizabeth (Ms Phumla Qeqe, Mr Mpumelelo Qeqe, Ms Sinazo Vabaza and Mr Thembelani Vabaza), 24 March 2019, New Brighton, Port Elizabeth (translated from isiXhosa), pp. 1–125.

2 'Record gate taken', *Evening Post*, 8 September 1975.

3 'Rugby union defies ruling', *Evening Post*, 19 June 1974. See also 'Kwaru not to quit Saru', *Evening Post*, 12 October 1974; Interview 10: Mr Silas Nkanunu, 23 March 2019, New Brighton, Port Elizabeth (partly translated from isiXhosa), pp. 1–24; Interview 2: Mr Mveleli Ncula, 10 March 2019, Rowallan Park, Port Elizabeth, pp. 1–19; and Interview 27: Advocate Amon Nyondo, 17 October 2019, Summerstrand, Port Elizabeth, pp. 1–74.

4 Booley, A. *Forgotten Heroes: A History of Black Rugby, 1880–1992*. Manie Booley Publications, Cape Town, 1998.

5 Ibid.

6 Interview 19: Mr Vusi and Mrs Nozuko 'Girlie' Pikoli, 24 August 2019, Faerie Glen, Pretoria (partly translated from isiXhosa), pp. 1–61. See also Interview 21: Judge Lex Mpati, 26 August 2019, Erasmuskloof, Pretoria, pp. 1–35. Radio Xhosa had broadcast non-racial rugby games from the early 1970s, but as the state tightened its restrictions on non-racial sports, these had all but ceased by the late 1970s.

7 Interview 13: Mr Gerald Majola, 26 March 2019, Newton Park, Port Elizabeth, pp. 1–56.

8 Ref. No.: AAS 213, *Ivan Peter Youth Club Accession (1970–1978)*, Donor: Mrs J Majola, Centre for African Studies, UNISA, Pretoria.

9 Interview 10: Mr Silas Nkanunu. See also Interview 16: Mr Ngconde

Balfour, 8 April 2019, Alice (partly translated from isiXhosa), pp. 1–17.

10 Interview 20: Mr Mthobi Tyamzashe, 26 August 2019, Menlyn, Pretoria, p. 15.

11 Badela, M. 'Rugby Union kicked out: Blacks' stand on non-racial sport', *Evening Post*, 31 May 1975. See also 'Kwaru not to quit Saru'.

12 'Badela back in office', *Evening Post*, 6 May 1975.

13 Ludwaba's rugby nickname, in isiXhosa, means 'the one who runs or sprints in big strides'.

14 Interview 26: Mr Themba Ludwaba, 17 October 2019, New Brighton, Port Elizabeth, pp. 1–17.

15 Booley, *Forgotten Heroes*.

16 Ibid.

17 Ibid, p. 244.

18 Interview 21: Judge Lex Mpati. Mpati, then based in Grahamstown, had been a SARU official.

19 Interview 20: Mr Mthobi Tyamzashe, 26 August 2019, Menlyn, Pretoria, (partly translated from isiXhosa), pp. 1–37.

20 Ibid.

21 Booley, *Forgotten Heroes*.

22 Ibid, p. 144.

23 Ibid.

24 Ibid.

25 Ibid.

26 Ibid.

27 Ibid.

28 Ibid, p. 258.

29 Ibid.

30 Interview 2: Mr Mveleli Ncula. See also Interview 11: Qeqe family: Port Elizabeth.

31 Interview 29: Mr Barry Sinuka, 18 October 2019, New Brighton, Port Elizabeth (translated from isiXhosa), pp. 1–23.

32 Booley, *Forgotten Heroes*.

33 Ibid, p. 19.

34 Ref. No.: AAS218, *RJ Scholtz Accession (1954–1979)*, Donor: RJ Scholtz, Centre for African Studies, UNISA, Pretoria.

35 'Record gate taken'.

36 Interview 32: Mr Dan Ngcaphe, 29 October 2019, Zwide, Port Elizabeth (translated from isiXhosa), pp. 1–45.

37 'Record gate taken'.

Chapter 1: The History of Black Rugby (1820–1955)

1 Rogers, A. 'Try me, says PE's Dan: Qeqe throws Pamensky cricket gauntlet', *Herald*, 13 January 1976.

2 Ibid.

3 Mveleli Ncula was appointed CEO of SA Rugby by the then Minister of Sport, Culture and Recreation, Makhenkesi Stofile, from 2001 to 2013. In 2009, he was appointed a member of the National Lotteries Sports Committee. In 2014, he became a member of the sports committee of the National Lotteries Commission, and retains this position still. He played for Easterns before the founding of Kwaru, and was elected match secretary for the KwaZakhele Rugby Union (Kwaru) in its Action Committee (1977–1989).

4 Interview 2: Mr Mveleli Ncula, 10 March 2019, Rowallan Park, Port Elizabeth, p. 18.

5 'Minutes of General Meeting of the South African Council on Sport' (9 February 1980, Kimberley), 'Reggie Feldman Accession', National Heritage and Cultural Studies [NAHECS], University of Fort Hare, Alice.

6 Rogers, 'Try me, says PE's Dan'.

7 Ibid.

8 *Official Year Book of South Africa*, 1974, cited in Booth, D., & Nauright, J. *Embedded Identities: Sport and Race in South Africa*, cited in, Nauright, J.; Cobley. A.G. & Wiggins, D.K. (eds) (2014) *Beyond C.L.R. James: Shifting Boundaries of Race and Ethnicity in Sport*, (University of Arkansas Press, Fayetteville).

9 Booth and Nauright, *Embedded Identities.*

10 Ramphal, SS. 'International Sports Against Apartheid', *Ufama: A Journal of South African Studies*, 13, 2/3 (1994), p. 62.

11 Wilkins, I and Strydom, H. *The Super-Afrikaners: Inside the Broederbond*. Jonathan Ball Publishers, Johannesburg, 1978, p. 244.

12 Nongogo, P. 'The Struggle to Deracialise South African Sport: A Historical Overview', Unpublished PhD thesis, University of Pretoria, 2015.

13 Eben Donges was Minister of Interior in 1956.

14 Nongogo, 'The Struggle to Deracialise South African Sport'.

15 Ibid, pp. 64–65.

16 Du Plessis, C. '"Divided We Stand!": The Origins of Separation in South African Rugby, 1861–1899', Unpublished MA thesis, Department of History, University of Pretoria, 2017, p. 14.

17 Nongogo, 'The Struggle to Deracialise South African Sport'.

18 Ibid.

19 Ibid, p. 66.

20 Ibid.

21 Du Plessis, '"Divided We Stand!"'.

22 Ibid, p. 48.

23 Kaur, T and Akindes, G. 'Sporting Subalternities and Social Justice: Rethinking South African Sports Studies', *Acta Academia*, 50, 2, 2018, pp. 1–11, https://dx.doi.org.org/10.18 820/24150479/aa50:2.intro, pp. 1–2.

24 Black, DR and Nauright, J. *Rugby and the South African Nation: Class, Politics and Power in the Old and New South Africas*. Manchester University Press, UK, 1998. See also Ministry: Sport and Recreation, Republic of South Africa, Pretoria, 7 November 2008, https://www.pmg.org.za (accessed 14 October 2021).

25 Matomela, T. 'History of Black Rugby', Unpublished, 2021.

26 Allen, D. 'Beating Them at their Own Game: Rugby, the Anglo-Boer War and Afrikaner Nationalism, 1899–1948', *International Journal of the History of Sport* (2013), pp. 37–57.

27 Ibid, p. 48.

28 'The Early History of Rugby in South Africa', South African History Online, https://www.sahistory.org.za/article/early-history-rugby-south-africa (accessed 17 July 2021). See also Nongogo, 'The Struggle to Deracialise South African Sport' and Allen, 'Beating Them at their Own Game'.

29 Mayosi, T. 'Rediscovering the Heritage and Culture of Black Rugby and Challenging Ignorance', https://www.ubumbo.org.za/2020/09/10/rediscovering-the-heritage-and-culture-of-black-rugby-and-challenging-ignorance (accessed 19 July 2021).

30 Odendaal, A, 'Even the White Boys Call Us "Boys!": Early Organisations in Port Elizabeth with Particular Reference to the African and American Working Men's Union in the 1890s', Unpublished paper presented at the conference 'Port Elizabeth's Place in South African History and Historiography', Vista University, Port Elizabeth, 24–25 September 1992.

31 Ibid, p. 1.

32 Ibid.

33 Nongogo, 'The Struggle to Deracialise South African Sport'.

34 Matomela, 'History of Black Rugby'.

35 Ibid.

36 Booley, A. *Forgotten Heroes: A History of Black Rugby, 1880–1992*. Manie Booley Publications, Cape Town, 1998.

37 Ibid.

38 Matomela, 'History of Black Rugby'.

39 Du Plessis, '"Divided We Stand!"', p. 2.

40 Ibid.

41 Interview 25: Mr Thami Songongo, 16 October 2019, Uitenhage, Nelson Mandela Bay Metropolitan Municipality (translated from isiXhosa), p. 13.

42 Winter Rose Rugby Football Club, https://www.sahistoryonline.org.za.archive/winter-rose-rugby-football-club-est.1890 (accessed 14 October 2021).

43 Ibid.

44 Booley, *Forgotten Heroes*.

45 Lily White Rugby Football Club, https://www.sahistory.org.za/default/files/archive-files/lily_white rugby_football_club.

46 Eastern Rugby Football Club, https://www.m.facebook.com/pages/category/Sport-Club/Eastern-Rugby-Football-Club-207073763519938.

47 Ibid.

48 Ibid.

49 'The Early History of Rugby in South Africa'.

50 'Fingo: A Public History Project dedicated to preserving the past, celebrating the present, and imagining the future of the Fingo Village Township, Grahamstown', in *Black Rugby in Fingo Village and Grahamstown*, http://fingovillage.blogspot.com/2007/05/black-rugby-in-fingo-village-and-Grahamstown.

51 Ibid.

52 Ibid.

53 Booley, *Forgotten Heroes*.

54 Ibid. See also Harmans, B. 'Formation of the Spring Rose Rugby Club, Port Elizabeth, South Africa', (Nelson Mandela Metropolitan University, *The Herald*, and *Weekend Post*).

55 Gaca, NW. 'The Rise and Fall of Rugby in a South African Township: The Case of Mdantsane, Eastern Cape', Unpublished MSocSci thesis, Institute of Social and Economic Research, University of Fort Hare, Alice.

56 Winter Rose Rugby Football Club.

57 Ibid.

58 Baines, GF. 'New Brighton, Port Elizabeth, c. 1903–1953: Its Legitimacy

and Legacy', Unpublished paper presented to the Fifth Triennial Workshop at the University of the Witwatersrand, Johannesburg, February 1990. See also Baines, GF. 'New Brighton, Port Elizabeth, c. 1903–1953: A History of an Urban African Community', Unpublished PhD thesis, Department of History, University of Cape Town, 1994.

59 Boshoff, G. 'Black Legend: Makaya Jack', https://www.sarugbymag.co.za/black-legend-makaya-jack/ (accessed 19 July 2021).

60 These were: Union Rugby Football Club, Eastern Rugby Football Union, Spring Rose Rugby Football Club, Fabs Rugby Football Union, St Cyprian's Rugby Football Union, Wallabies Rugby Football Union, Butcher Birds Rugby Football Union, Park Rovers Rugby Football Union, Walmer Wales Rugby Football Union, Orientals Rugby Football Union and African Bombers Rugby Football Union.

61 Booley, *Forgotten Heroes*. See also Mayosi, 'Rediscovering the Heritage and Culture of Black Rugby and Challenging Ignorance'.

62 Matomela, 'History of Black Rugby'.

63 Gaca, 'The Rise and Fall of Rugby in a South African Township'.

64 Matomela, 'History of Black Rugby'.

65 Gaca, 'The Rise and Fall of Rugby in a South African Township', p. 43.

66 Ibid, p. 44.

67 Ibid.

68 Ibid.

69 Botha, T. 'The History of Non-Racial Black Rugby in Port Elizabeth and the Influence of Community Politics on the Sport: The Conversation with a Stranger', Unpublished paper, 2019, pp. 1–53.

70 This covered Fort Beaufort, Alice, Middledrift, Adelaide, Bedford, Seymour and King William's Town.

71 Chief M Zinto played for the Eastern Province Bantu Rugby Union in the 1950s.

72 Interview 2: Mr Mveleli Ncula, p. 13.

73 Interview 13: Mr Gerald Majola, 26 March 2019, Newton Park, Port Elizabeth (partly translated from isiXhosa), pp. 13–14.

74 Clan name, short for Dlangamandla.

75 Interview 9: Messrs Mpumelelo 'Sbhidla' Majola and Lucky 'Coach' Mange, 22 March 2019, New Brighton, Port Elizabeth (translated from isiXhosa), pp. 3–4.

76 Interview 25: Mr Thami Songongo (translated from isiXhosa), pp. 14–15.

Chapter 2: The History of Black Rugby (1956–1971)

1 'Baas Dan Mbona' Qeqe: Obituary (2005, Port Elizabeth). See also Jimmy Matyu, Resume: DDQ (2005, Port Elizabeth), Unpublished, and prepared in tandem with the obituary of Dan Qeqe in 2005.

2 Booley, A. *Forgotten Heroes: A History of Black Rugby, 1882–1992.* Manie Booley Publications, Cape Town, 1998.

3 Interview 25: Mr Thami Songongo, 16 October 2019, Uitenhage, Nelson Mandela Bay Metropolitan Municipality (translated from isiXhosa), p. 4.

4 Interview 31: Mr Harold and Mrs Sheila Wilson, 24 October 2019, Bethelsdorp, Port Elizabeth, pp. 1–48. See also Interview 7: Mr Lucky 'Coach' Mange, 21 March 2019, New Brighton, Port Elizabeth (translated from isiXhosa), pp. 1–30); Interview 9: Messrs Mpumelelo 'Sbhidla' Majola and Lucky 'Coach' Mange, New Brighton, Port Elizabeth (translated from isiXhosa), pp. 1–142.

5 Interview 18: Mr Ray Mali, 10 April 2019, Winterstrand, East London, p. 1.

6 Interview 23: Mr Joe Maboyisi Mahala Mbiza, 14 October 2019, East London (translated from isiXhosa), p. 13.

7 Eastern Province Rugby Union rugby team, photo credit: Barry Sinuka.

8 This was a championship trophy sponsored by cigarette company, President Giants.

9 Interview 29: Mr Barry Sinuka, 18 October 2019, New Brighton, Port Elizabeth (translated from isiXhosa), pp. 1–30. See also Interview 25: Mr Thami Songongo; Matomela, T. 'History of Black Rugby', Unpublished, 2021.

10 Eastern Province Bantu Rugby Union team, President Giants Cup, Umtata, 1957, photo credit: Barry Sinuka.

11 Interview 29: Mr Barry Sinuka (translated from isiXhosa), p. 4.

12 Interview 27: Advocate Amon Nyondo, 17 October 2019, Summerstrand, Port Elizabeth, p. 11.

13 Matomela, 'History of Black Rugby'.

14 Ibid.

15 Interview 29: Mr Barry Sinuka.

16 Interview 25: Mr Thami Songongo (translated from isiXhosa), p. 45.

17 Ibid (translated from isiXhosa), p. 18.

18 Matomela, 'History of Black Rugby'.

19 Booley, *Forgotten Heroes.*

20 Interview 29: Mr Barry Sinuka (translated from isiXhosa), pp. 14–15.

21 Ibid.

22 Interview 25: Mr Thami Songongo (translated from isiXhosa), p. 46.
23 Interview 27: Advocate Amon Nyondo.
24 Interview 23: Mr Joe Mbiza.
25 Interview 29: Mr Barry Sinuka (translated from isiXhosa), p. 13.
26 Matomela, 'History of Black Rugby'.
27 Odendaal, A. *The Story of an African Game*. David Philip Publishers, Cape Town, 2003.
28 Booley, *Forgotten Heroes*.
29 Interview 25: Mr Thami Songongo (translated from isiXhosa), p. 19.
30 Matomela, 'History of Black Rugby'.
31 Booley, *Forgotten Heroes*.
32 Matomela, 'History of Black Rugby'.
33 Interview 29: Mr Barry Sinuka (translated from isiXhosa), p. 21.
34 Nongogo, P. 'The Struggle to Deracialise South African Sport: A Historical Overview', Unpublished PhD thesis, Department of Sport and Leisure Studies, University of Pretoria, 2015.
35 Ibid.
36 Ibid, p. 24.
37 Ibid.
38 Stofile, MA. 'SADET Project: Sport – Site of Struggle', Unpublished, 2011.
39 Nongogo, 'The Struggle to Deracialise South African Sport'.
40 Wilkins, I and Strydom, H. *The Super-Afrikaners: Inside the Afrikaner Broederbond*, Jonathan Ball Publishers, Johannesburg, 1978.
41 Booley, *Forgotten Heroes*.
42 Ibid, p. 22.
43 SACOS In Perspective, 'Reggie Feldman Accession', Box No. 4, National Heritage and Cultural Studies Centre [NAHECS], University of Fort Hare, Alice.
44 Ibid.
45 Ibid.

Chapter 3: Qeqe Begins (1929–1950s): The Roots

1 Interview 17: Qeqe family: Fort Beaufort (Mr Mncedi Mali, Mr Nqaba Mali and Mr Weaver Qeqe), 9 April 2019, Fort Beaufort (translated from isiXhosa), pp. 1 – 56.
2 Ibid.
3 Sutton, K. 'Keith Sutton's profile of boy who made good', *Weekend Post*, 4 April 1986.

4 In Western languages, Vleikop Qeqe was Mncedi Mali's great-uncle. However, such delineations do not exist in isiXhosa. Great-uncles are grouped and addressed as 'grandfathers', not making any distinction between them.

5 Interview 17: Qeqe family: Fort Beaufort (translated from isiXhosa), p. 42.

6 Interview 15: Messrs Kolekile Kwatsha and Keke Pemba, 27 March 2019, New Brighton, Port Elizabeth (translated from isiXhosa), p. 16.

7 McKenzie Sloti is the son of Dan Qeqe's elder sister, Tobhiya, from the senior wife's house. Dan Qeqe raised and educated McKenzie and his brother, Mzwandile, in Port Elizabeth, when Tobhiya passed away in Fort Beaufort.

8 Interview 3: Mr McKenzie Sloti, 10 March 2019, Kabega, Port Elizabeth (translated from isiXhosa), p. 2.

9 Ref. No.: VELC/4, *Victoria East Local Council: Supplementary Estimates*, 25 July 1929, King William's Town Archival Depot, King William's Town, p. 1)

10 Ibid.

11 Ref. No.: VELC/4, *Victoria East Local Council: Estimates of Expenditure 1928*, 5 May 1929, King William's Town Archival Depot, King William's Town, p. 1.

12 Ref. No.: NA 31/360 A, *Victoria East Local Council: Estimates for the year 1930*, 26 February 1930, King William's Archival Depot, King William's Town, p. 3.

13 Interview 17: Qeqe family: Fort Beaufort. See also Interview 11: Qeqe family: Port Elizabeth (Ms Phumla Qeqe, Mr Mpumelelo Qeqe, Mr Thembelani Vabaza and Ms Sinazo Vabaza), 24 March 2019, New Brighton, Port Elizabeth (translated from isiXhosa), pp. 1–125.

14 These are primarily located in the King William's Town Archival Depot.

15 These are Alice, Fort Beaufort, Hogsback, Seymour, Balfour, Bedford and Middledrift, towns that currently fall under the Nkonkobe Municipality.

16 File No. 122/366, *General Circular No. 366 of 1940, Re: Succession to Native Chieftainship*, Department of Native Affairs, King William's Town Archival Depot, King William's Town.

17 Ref. N/A. 1/35, ELB.LP. *Re: Recognised Chiefs in the Ciskei*, The Chief Native Commissioner, Cape, 8 December 1930, King William's Town Archival Depot, King William's Town.

18 Ref. No. 2/11, *Re: Recognition of Bonyoti Qasana as a Chief*, Assistant

Native Commissioner, East London, 8 October 1930, King William's Town Archival Depot, King William's Town.

19 Writing to Mr Lister, the School Inspector of Bantu Education in King William's Town on 11 April 1956, the Chief Native Affairs Commissioner lists the recognised chiefs of Ciskei as Archie Velile Sandile (Paramount Chief of the Rarabe); Siseko Kama (Chief of the AmaGqunukhwebe); JN Makinana (Chief of the AmaNdlambe); Zimlindile Siwani (Chief of the Imidushane); Mabikwe Toise (Chief of the AmaToise); Ninus Mhlambiso (Acting Chief of the Hlubis); Nonight Jali (Chieftainess of the Imi-Qhayi); James Matomela (Chief of the Amabele of Peddie); Ndaba Njokweni (Chief of the AmaZizi); Justice Mabandla (Chief of the AmaBele of Alice); Manzezulu Mtirara (Sub-Chief of the Hala); Zwelixolile Mpangele (Sub-Chief of the Gcina); Mgwebi Wulana (Chief of the Amanzinzi); Slingsby Kwatsha (Chief of the AmaHlubi); and Davidson Mavuso (Sub-Chief of the AmaBele). Ref. N.1/1/2, EJHY/AHE, *Recognised Chiefs: Ciskei*, Correspondence from the Chief Native Commissioner, Private Bag 426, King William's Town, to Mr Lister, School Inspector, Bantu Education, King William's Town, 11 April 1956, King William's Town Archival Depot, King William's Town.

20 Ref. No. N.1/1/2, From Chief Bantu Affairs Commissioner, Private Bag 426, King William's Town, 23 September 1959, King William's Town Archival Depot, King William's Town.

21 Ibid.

22 Interview 17: Qeqe family: Fort Beaufort (translated from isiXhosa), pp. 43–44.

23 Interview 11: Qeqe family: Port Elizabeth.

24 'Baas Dan Mbona' Obituary (2005), Port Elizabeth. 'Mbona' is Dan Qeqe's clan name.

25 Interview 17: Qeqe family: Fort Beaufort.

26 Interview 11: Qeqe family: Port Elizabeth.

27 Ibid.

28 Ibid.

29 Interview 17: Qeqe family: Fort Beaufort.

30 Raymond Mhlaba was a prominent member of the African National Congress (ANC) who was born and spent his childhood in Fort Beaufort. Moving on to Port Elizabeth for work, he became one of the leading activists in the ANC's Defiance Campaign in the 1950s, and was elected to the New Brighton Native Advisory Board in the early 1950s. With Nelson Mandela, Govan Mbeki, Walter Sisulu and others, he was

arrested in the early 1960s and spent the next 27 years on Robben Island until his release in 1990.

31 Orie, T. 'Raymond Mhlaba and the Genesis of the Congress Alliance: A Political Biography', Unpublished MA thesis, Department of History, University of Cape Town, 1993.

32 The jurisdiction of the Victoria East Local Council then comprised Cathcart, Seymour, Jamestown, Doordrecht, Middledrift, Barkley East, Hanover, Alice, Tarkastad, Queenstown, Stutterheim, Seymour, Alice, King William's Town, etc.

33 Ref. No.: VELC/2, *Victoria East Local Council: Estimates of Revenue and Expenditure for 1932*, King William's Town Archival Depot, King William's Town, p. 1.

34 This is a reference to the main Tyume River in the Lovedale/Alice areas.

35 Ref. No.: VELC/23/4/2, *Proposed Native District Nurse for Victoria East: Suggestions for working out the Scheme*, King William's Town Archival Depot, King William's Town.

36 Ibid, p. 2.

37 Ibid.

38 Interview 17: Qeqe family: Fort Beaufort, 9 April 2019 (Messrs Mncedi Mali, Nqaba Mali and Weaver Qeqe) (translated from isiXhosa), pp. 48–49.

39 Ibid, pp. 37–38.

40 Interview 11: Qeqe family: Port Elizabeth, 24 March 2019, New Brighton, Port Elizabeth (Ms Phumla Qeqe, Mr Mpumelelo Qeqe, Mr Thembelani Vabaza and Ms Sinazo Vabaza) (translated from isiXhosa), pp. 1–125.

41 'Baas Dan Mbona' Qeqe: Obituary (2005).

42 Sutton, 'Keith Sutton's profile of boy who made good'.

43 Interview 3: Mr McKenzie Sloti, 10 March 2019, Kabega, Port Elizabeth (translated from isiXhosa), p. 2.

44 Interview 17: Qeqe family: Fort Beaufort (translated from isiXhosa), pp. 39–40.

45 Ibid, pp. 46–47.

46 Bhiza is Dan Qeqe's elder brother from his father's first wife.

47 A street in New Brighton, in the old McNamee section of the township.

48 Interview 11: Qeqe family: Port Elizabeth (translated from isiXhosa), pp. 30–31.

49 Owing to the fire that broke out during the riots in September 1977 following the murder of Steve Biko, the archival material of Healdtown

High School was torched. It was thus not possible to access Dan Qeqe's school files at Healdtown.

50 Interview 3: Mr McKenzie Sloti.

51 Sutton, 'Keith Sutton's profile of boy who made good'.

52 Interview 17: Qeqe family: Fort Beaufort (translated from isiXhosa), p. 29.

53 Sutton, 'Keith Sutton's profile of boy who made good'.

54 Cheapline was a nickname of one of Ngwehlathi Bazi's sons.

55 Interview 15: Messrs Kolekile Kwatsha and Keke Pemba, 27 March 2019, New Brighton, Port Elizabeth (translated from isiXhosa), p. 16.

56 Ibid (translated from isiXhosa), p. 14.

57 Ibid.

58 Sutton, 'Keith Sutton's profile of boy who made good'.

59 Interview 15: Messrs Kolekile Kwatsha and Keke Pemba (translated from isiXhosa), p. 1.

60 Interview 17: Qeqe family: Fort Beaufort (translated from isiXhosa), p. 25.

61 Interview 3: Mr McKenzie Sloti. Unfortunately, many of the official archives were destroyed during the fire that burnt down much of the school. This had been sparked by the September 1977 riots, following the murder of Steve Biko.

62 Interview: Mrs Nomasomi Penina Gxasheka, 20 September 2021.

63 Ibid.

64 Ibid.

65 https://www.sahistory.org.za/people/jjr-jolobe#:~:text=James%20Ranisi%20Jolobe (accessed 26 October 2021). For more on Reverend JJR Jolobe, see also Hunter, CFD. 'Some Aspects of the African Missionary Policy of the Presbytery of Adelaide/Port Elizabeth with Special Reference to the Origin and Development of the New Brighton Presbyterian Mission Church, 1898–1962', Unpublished PhD thesis, Rhodes University, Grahamstown, 1983.

66 Baines, GF. 'New Brighton, Port Elizabeth, c. 1903–1953: A History of an Urban African Community', Unpublished PhD thesis, Department of History, University of Cape Town, 1994. See also Baines, G. 'The New Brighton Native Advisory Board, c. 1923–1952: Its Legitimacy and Legacy', Unpublished paper presented to the Fifth Triennial History Workshop at the University of the Witwatersrand, Johannesburg, February 1990.

67 Ibid.

68 Interview 14: Mrs Jumartha Milase Majola, 26 March 2019, New Brighton, Port Elizabeth (translated from isiXhosa), pp. 2–3.

69 'Baas Dan Mbona' Qeqe: Obituary (2005).

70 Personal communication with Phumla Qeqe, 26 October 2021.

71 Interview: Mrs Nomasomi Penina Gxasheka, 25 October 2021.

72 Interview 3: Mr McKenzie Sloti.

73 Interview 25: Mr Thami Songongo, 16 October 2019, Uitenhage, Nelson Mandela Bay Metropolitan Municipality (translated from isiXhosa), pp. 1–63.

74 Interview 14: Mrs Jumartha Milase Majola.

Chapter 4: Qeqe in Port Elizabeth (1950s–1971)

1 Sutton, K. 'Keith Sutton's profile of boy who made good', *Weekend Post*, 4 April 1986.

2 Interview 3: Mr McKenzie Sloti (translated from isiXhosa), p. 4.

3 Ibid (translated from isiXhosa), pp. 4–5.

4 Ibid. See also Interview 3: Mr McKenzie Sloti.

5 Interview 17: Qeqe family: Fort Beaufort (translated from isiXhosa), p. 40.

6 Interview 15: Messrs Kolekile Kwatsha and Keke Pemba (translated from isiXhosa), p. 3.

7 Ibid.

8 Interview 31: Mr Harold and Mrs Sheila Wilson, 24 October 2019, Bethelsdorp, Port Elizabeth, pp. 1–46.

9 Ibid.

10 Ibid.

11 Interview 35: Judge Cecil 'Doc' Somyalo, 6 November 2019, Summerstrand, Port Elizabeth (partly translated from isiXhosa), pp. 1–39.

12 Ibid (translated from isiXhosa), p. 9.

13 Ibid (translated from isiXhosa), p. 10.

14 Ibid.

15 Orie, T. 'Port Elizabeth in the 1940s–1950s: The Tripartite Alliance?', Unpublished paper presented at the conference 'Port Elizabeth in South African History and Historiography', Vista University, Port Elizabeth, 24–25 September 1992.

16 Orie, T. 'Raymond Mhlaba and the Genesis of the Congress Alliance: A Political Biography', Unpublished MA thesis, Department of History, University of Cape Town, 1993; see also Baines, G. 'The New Brighton Advisory Board, c. 1923–1952: Its Legitimacy and Legacy',

Unpublished paper delivered at the Fifth Triennial History Workshop of the University of the Witwatersrand, Johannesburg, February 1990; Interview 15: Messrs Kolekile Kwatsha and Keke Pemba.

17 Interview 1: Mr Crosby 'Winky' Ximiya, 5 March 2019, South End, Port Elizabeth, pp. 1–16.

18 Report No. 13/1952, *Report by Town Clerk to Native Affairs Committee* (Special Meeting: 15 December 1952), City of Port Elizabeth, Town Clerk's Department, Port Elizabeth Archives, Port Elizabeth.

19 Ibid, p. 11.

20 These are distinct from the members of the New Brighton Native Advisory Board nominated by the township's registered residents, and approved by the Port Elizabeth Council. See Ref. No.: AAS218, *RJ Scholtz Accession* (1954–1979), UNISA Documentation Centre for African Studies, University of South Africa, Pretoria. See also Baines, GF. 'New Brighton, Port Elizabeth, c. 1903–1953: A History of an Urban African Community', Unpublished PhD thesis, Department of History, University of Cape Town, 1994; Baines, 'The New Brighton Advisory Board'.

21 Ref. No.: AAS218, Port Elizabeth Municipality: Native Advisory Board Regulations: Special Meetings, 4 June 1954 (PN 468/1954, *RJ Scholtz Accession* (1954–1979)), UNISA Documentation Centre for African Studies, University of South Africa, Pretoria, p. 5.

22 Baines, 'New Brighton, Port Elizabeth, c. 1903–1953: A History of an Urban African Community'.

23 Harmans, B. (2006) *Rugby: Formation of the Spring Rose Rugby Club* (St George's Park History, Port Elizabeth, South Africa) (accessed 24 June 2019). http://www.nmbt.co.za/listing/st_georges_park_html#~text=Established%20in%201860%2C%20St%20George'scricket%20club%in%South%20Africa/, accessed 24/06/2019.

24 Booley, A. *Forgotten Heroes: A History of Black Rugby, 1882–1992.* Manie Booley Publications, Cape Town, 1998.

25 Interview 17: Qeqe family: Fort Beaufort, 9 April 2019 (Messrs Mncedi Mali, Nqaba Mali and Weaver Qeqe), Fort Beaufort (translated from isiXhosa), pp. 1–56.

26 Ibid, p. 37.

27 PP Mati also served on the executive committee of the Spring Rose Rugby Football Club in 1959, along with Wilson F Ximiya and Dan Qeqe. See, 'Baas Dan Mbona' Qeqe: Obituary (2005), New Brighton,

Port Elizabeth.

28 Baines, 'The New Brighton Advisory Board, c. 1923–1952: Its Legitimacy and Legacy'.

29 Report No. 13/1952, p. 11.

30 Ibid.

31 Ibid.

32 Ibid.

33 Ibid, p. 12.

34 Ibid.

35 Report No. 13/1952, p. 12.

36 Ibid.

37 BAO/C100/6/5279 Vol. 1 – C100/6/5289, Correspondence from Department of Labour, Pretoria, to The Secretary for Native Affairs, 6 January 1925, National Archives of South Africa, Pretoria.

38 Baines, 'New Brighton Advisory Board: c. 1923–1952: Its Legitimacy and Legacy', p. 1.

39 Ballantine, C. *Marabi Nights: Early South African Jazz and Vaudeville*, Johannesburg, 1993, p. 92. Cited in Baines, 'New Brighton Advisory Board: c. 1923–1952: Its Legitimacy and Legacy'.

40 Report No. 13/1952, p. 1.

41 Ibid.

42 Christopher, AJ. 'Apartheid Planning in South Africa: The Case of Port Elizabeth', *The Geographic Journal*, 153, 2, 1987.

43 Baines, 'New Brighton Advisory Board, c. 1923–1952: Its Legitimacy and Legacy'.

44 Report No. 13/1952.

45 Ibid, pp. 3–4.

46 Maylam, P. 'Explaining the Apartheid City: 20 Years of South African Urban Historiography', *Journal of Southern African Studies*, 21, 1, 1995.

47 Ref. No. 87/293 (B), Correspondence between the Secretary for Public Works, Pretoria, to Secretary for Native Affairs, in *Re: Steel drawers for Tax Cards: Native Commissioner, Port Elizabeth*, 24 October 1949, National Archives of South Africa, Pretoria.

48 DE's Ref. PEH 166, Ref. No. 1/23/5, 9 April 1956, *Report on premises situated at Veeplaats (Bioscope) proposed to be hired for the purpose of Issuing of Reference Books to Natives: Port Elizabeth District*, National Archives of South Africa, Pretoria.

49 Ref. No.: 5/1529, N. 1/23/5, *Re: Issue of Reference Books to Natives in Port Elizabeth District*, 10 April 1956. Correspondence from Native

Commissioner, Port Elizabeth, to The District Representative, Public Works Department, Port Elizabeth, National Archives of South Africa, Pretoria.

50 By his own admission, Dan Qeqe had served on the New Brighton Native Advisory Board and its successor, the Port Elizabeth Joint Bantu Advisory Board, from 1964 to 1977. See Sutton, K. 'Keith Sutton's profile of boy who made good'. See also Interview 1: Mr Crosby 'Winky' Ximiya, 5 March 2019, South End, Port Elizabeth (partly translated from isiXhosa), pp. 1–15; Interview 3: Mr McKenzie Sloti, 10 March 2019, Kabega, Port Elizabeth (translated from isiXhosa), pp. 1–46; Interview 13: Mr Gerald Majola, 26 March 2019, Newton Park, Port Elizabeth, pp. 1–56); and Interview 19: Mr Vusi and Mrs Nozuko 'Girlie' Pikoli.

51 Interview 1: Mr Crosby 'Winky' Ximiya, p. 2.

52 Ibid.

53 Ref. No.: AAS218, *RJ Scholtz Accession* (1954–1979), Donor: RJ Scholtz, UNISA Documentation Centre for African Studies, University of South Africa, Pretoria.

54 Interview 4: Mr Thozamile Botha, 11 March 2019, North End, Port Elizabeth, p. 5.

55 Booley, *Forgotten Heroes*.

56 Ref. No.: AAS218, *RJ Scholtz Accession* (1954–1979), UNISA Documentation Centre for African Studies, University of South Africa, Pretoria.

57 Interview: Mrs Nomasomi Penina Gxasheka.

58 Maylam, 'Explaining the Apartheid City: 20 Years of South African Urban Historiography'.

59 Interview 15: Messrs Kolekile Kwatsha and Keke Pemba (translated from isiXhosa), p. 13.

60 Cited in Baines, 'The New Brighton Advisory Board, c. 1923–1952: Its Legitimacy and Legacy': Walter Nobatana (elected 1910); John Yokwe (nominated 1910); Charles Mtimka (elected 1911); J Rula (elected 1914); N Stokwe (elected 1914); P Nguna (elected 1914); Z Teya (elected 1914); J Ngqolombe (elected 1916); P Funde (nominated 1916); Reverend JW Gqamlana (nominated 1917); M Dubula (elected 1919); Prince Nikiwe (elected 1922); AF Pendla (elected 1925); JM Dippa (elected 1927); Reverend J Limba (elected 1932); M Zibonda (elected 1933); AZ Tshiwula (elected 1935); Reverend JJ Jolobe (nominated 1936); WW Jabavu (elected 1938); J Ntshinga (elected 1938); T Zokufa (elected 1940); Reverend GB Molefe (nominated 1940); TN Ranuga (elected

1943); PJB Kwaza (elected 1943); IM Mfuku (elected 1944); PM Sandla (elected 1944); AO Malakane (elected 1944); Reverend D Mbopa (nominated 1944); WW Mabija (elected 1946); A Nkaphuka (elected 1946); WB Ntshekisa (nominated 1946); M Nkosinkulu (elected 1947); J Marwanqa (nominated 1947); DL Mtiya (elected 1949); TJ Tladi (elected 1949) and WM Norongo (elected 1950).

61 Baines, 'New Brighton Advisory Board, c. 1923–1952: Its Legitimacy and Legacy'.

62 Mrs Nozuko Pikoli was born and grew up in Veeplaas, Port Elizabeth. She left for exile to continue with her African National Congress (ANC) work in Lesotho, Zambia and Zimbabwe. See also Pikoli, V and Wiener, M. *My Second Initiation: The Memoir of Vusi Pikoli*. Picador Africa, Johannesburg, 2013.

63 Interview 19: Mr Vusi and Mrs Nozuko 'Girlie' Pikoli, 24 August 2019, Faerie Glen, Pretoria (partly translated from isiXhosa), p. 11.

64 Tarrow, S. *Power in Movement: Social Movements and Contentious Politics*. Cambridge University Press, Cambridge, 1998, p. 71.

65 Botha, T. 'The History of Non-Racial Black Rugby in Port Elizabeth and the Influence of Community Politics on the Sport: The Conversation with a Stranger', Unpublished paper, 2018, pp. 16–17.

66 Badela, M. 'Advisory board may end', *Evening Post*, 13 October 1977. See also 'Qeqe not to go to Pretoria', *Evening Post*, 24 August 1976.

67 Ref. No.: AAS218, *RJ Scholtz Accession* (1954–1979), UNISA Documentation Centre for African Studies, University of South Africa, Pretoria.

68 Ibid.

69 Interview 19: Mr Vusi and Mrs Nozuko 'Girlie' Pikoli.

70 Ref. No.: AAS215, Letter from Reverend Molefe, Union Theological Seminary, New York, to Dr Thomas Jesse Jones, Phelps-Stokes Foundation, New York City, 21 February 1939, *JG Molefe Accession* (1939–1974), UNISA Documentation Centre for African Studies, University of South Africa, Pretoria.

71 Ref. No.: AAS215, Letter from Charles T Loram, 5 June 1939, to Mr George Molefe, Union Theological Seminary, New York, *JG Molefe Accession* (1939–1974), UNISA Documentation Centre for African Studies, University of South Africa, Pretoria.

72 Baines, 'The New Brighton Advisory Board, c. 1923–1952: Its Legitimacy and Legacy?'.

73 Molefe, GB. 'How to Consolidate the Principles of Christianity Amongst the Native People With a View to Raising the Tone of Native Society',

Unpublished paper: Address by Reverend GB Molefe, Natal Missionary Conference, Thursday, 2 July 1936, pp. 55–58.

74 Ibid.

75 Ibid, p. 38.

76 Ibid.

77 Ref. No.: AAS214, *Active Social Organiser, JHE Ntshinga Accession*, Bantu Benevolent and Welfare Society (1941–1968), UNISA Documentation Centre for African Studies, University of South Africa, Pretoria. See also Baines, 'New Brighton, Port Elizabeth, c.1903–1953: A History of an Urban African Township'; Baines, 'New Brighton Advisory Board, c. 1923 – 1952: Its Legitimacy and Legacy'.

78 Ref. No.: AAS214, *Active Social Organiser*.

79 Ibid.

80 Ref. No.: AAS214, Letter from JHE Ntshinga, President: Bantu Benevolent and Welfare Society, New Brighton, to The Chief: Bantu Affairs Commissioner, 17 September 1968, *JHE Ntshinga Accession*, Bantu Benevolent and Welfare Society (1941–1968), UNISA Documentation Centre for African Studies, University of South Africa, Pretoria.

81 Ref. No.: AAS214, Constitution: Bantu Benevolent and Welfare Society, *JHE Ntshinga Accession*, Bantu Benevolent and Welfare Society (1941–1968), UNISA Documentation Centre for African Studies, University of South Africa, Pretoria, p. 1.

82 Maylam, 'Explaining the Apartheid City: 20 Years of South African Urban Historiography', pp. 33–34 (emphasis added).

Chapter 5: The Accidental Birth of the KwaZakhele Rugby Union (1950s–1971)

1 Interview 24: Sipho McDonald Tanana, 14 October 2019, Vincent Park, East London, p. 4.

2 Interview 32: Mr Dan Ngcaphe, 29 October 2019, Zwide, Port Elizabeth (translated from isiXhosa), p. 9.

3 Ibid, p. 5.

4 Ibid, pp. 5–6.

5 White, CS. 'The Rule of Brigadier Oupa Gqozo in Ciskei: 4 March 1990 to 22 March 1994', Unpublished MA thesis, Rhodes University, Grahamstown, 2008.

6 Booley, A. *Forgotten Heroes: A History of Black Rugby, 1882–1992*. Manie Booley Publications, Cape Town, 1998.

7 Wilson's Three-X Mints advert, (undated).
8 Interview 14: Mrs Jumartha Milase Majola, 26 March 2019, New Brighton, Port Elizabeth (translated from isiXhosa), pp. 1–48.
9 He went on to play for Kwaru in the 1970s and early 1980s.
10 A chief of amaJingqi, member of the New Brighton Cricket Club and later high school principal, he descended from Chief Maqoma in the nineteenth century, as did Dan Qeqe. He went on to become a member of the Ciskei Legislative Assembly, along with Wilson F Ximiya and AZ Lamani, following the elections of 1973.
11 'Kokie' The Great – Eric Majola: Obituary (1971), New Brighton, Port Elizabeth.
12 See also Booley, *Forgotten Heroes*.
13 Interview 23: Mr Joe Maboyisi Mahala Mbiza, 14 October 2019, Mdantsane, East London (translated from isiXhosa), p. 12.
14 Interview 13: Mr Gerald Majola, 26 March 2019, Newton Park, Port Elizabeth (partly translated from isiXhosa), p. 3.
15 Interview 25: Mr Thami Songongo, 16 October 2019, Uitenhage, Nelson Mandela Bay Metropolitan Municipality (translated from isiXhosa), pp. 1–2.
16 Interview 13: Mr Gerald Majola.
17 Booley, *Forgotten Heroes*, p. 109.
18 Ibid.
19 Interview 20: Mr Mthobi Tyamzashe, 26 August 2019, Menlyn, Pretoria, pp. 1–2.
20 Interview 18: Mr Ray Mali, 10 April 2019, Winterstrand, East London, p. 20.
21 Ibid.
22 Interview 35: Judge Cecil 'Doc' Somyalo, 6 November 2019, Summerstrand, Port Elizabeth (partly translated from isiXhosa), p. 16.
23 Ibid (partly translated from isiXhosa), p. 17.
24 Binney, A. *The Political and Social Thought of Kwame Nkrumah*. Palgrave McMillan, New York, 2011.
25 Odendaal, A. *The Story of an African Game*. David Philip Publishers, Cape Town, 2003.
26 'Major crisis forces union', *Herald*, 9 June 1977.
27 'Mayor may intervene in rugby crisis', *Evening Post*, 2 October 1971.
28 Interview 25: Mr Thami Songongo (translated from isiXhosa), p. 22.
29 Interview 27: Advocate Amon Nyondo, 17 October 2019, Summerstrand, Port Elizabeth, pp. 12–13.

30 Interview 29: Mr Barry Sinuka, 18 October 2019, New Brighton, Port Elizabeth (translated from isiXhosa), pp. 10–11.

31 Booley, *Forgotten Heroes*, p. 109.

32 Ibid.

33 Interview 25: Mr Thami Songongo (translated from isiXhosa), p. 40.

34 Interview 29: Mr Barry Sinuka (translated from isiXhosa), p. 13.

35 Odendaal, *The Story of an African Game*.

36 Matomela, T. 'History of Black Rugby', Upublished, 2021.

37 Booley, *Forgotten Heroes*.

38 Ibid.

39 Interview 7: Mr Lucky 'Coach' Mange, 21 March 2019, New Brighton, Port Elizabeth (translated from isiXhosa), p. 6.

40 Interview 29: Mr Dan Ngcaphe, 29 October 2019, Zwide, Port Elizabeth (translated from isiXhosa), pp. 1–45. See also Interview 27: Advocate Amon Nyondo, Interview 25: Mr Thami Songongo, Interview 7: Mr Lucky 'Coach' Mange, and Interview 9: Messrs Mpumelelo 'Sbhidla' Majola and Lucky 'Coach' Mange, 22 March 2019, New Brighton, Port Elizabeth (translated from isiXhosa), pp. 1–142.

41 Interview 27: Advocate Amon Nyondo, p. 15.

42 Odendaal, *The Story of an African Game*.

43 Booley, *Forgotten Heroes*, p. 113.

44 Odendaal, *The Story of an African Game*.

45 https://www.sahistoryonline.co.za (accessed 11 November 2019).

46 Booley, *Forgotten Heroes*. See also Interview 29: Mr Barry Sinuka.

47 Booley, *Forgotten Heroes*, p. 19.

48 Interview 32: Mr Dan Ngcaphe (translated from isiXhosa), p. 8.

49 Interview 29: Mr Barry Sinuka (translated from isiXhosa), p. 2.

50 Botha, T. 'The History of Non-Racial Black Rugby in Port Elizabeth and the Influence of Community Politics on the Sport: The Conversation with a Stranger', Unpublished paper, 2018, pp. 1–53.

51 Ibid, pp. 17–18.

52 Interview 25: Mr Thami Songongo (translated from isiXhosa), p. 17.

53 Ibid (translated from isiXhosa), pp. 17–18.

54 Sutton, K. 'Keith Sutton's profile of boy who made good', *Weekend Post*, 4 April 1986.

55 Interview 31: Mr Harold and Mrs Sheila Wilson, 24 October 2019, Bethelsdorp, Port Elizabeth, pp. 16–17.

56 Interview 2: Mr Mveleli Ncula, 10 March 2019, Rowallan Park, Port Elizabeth, p. 2.

57 Botha, 'The History of Non-Racial Black Rugby in Port Elizabeth', p. 25.

58 Dall, N. 'South Africa's History of Black Rugby Dates Back More Than a Century', https://www.ozy.com/news-and-polities/south-africas-history-of-black-rugby-goes-back-more-than-a-century/232242/ (accessed 17 July 2021). See also Nongogo, P. 'The Struggle to Deracialise South African Sport: A Historical Overview', Unpublished DPhil thesis, Department of Sport and Leisure Studies, University of Pretoria, 2015.

59 Ref. No.: AAS218, Port Elizabeth Municipality, Port Elizabeth Joint Bantu Advisory Board Minutes: 1954, 1970, 1971, 1977. *RJ Scholtz Accession* (1954–1979), UNISA Documentation Centre for African Studies, University of South Africa, Pretoria.

60 Ref. No.: AAS218, Port Elizabeth Municipality, Port Elizabeth Joint Bantu Advisory Board Minutes: 1970, 1971. *RJ Scholtz Accession* (1954–1979), UNISA Documentation Centre for African Studies, University of South Africa, Pretoria.

61 Cited in Molapo, RR. 'Sports, Festivals and Popular Politics: Aspects of the Social and Popular Culture in Langa Township, 1945–70', Unpublished MA thesis, Faculty of Arts, University of Cape Town, 1994, p. 52.

62 'Mayor may intervene in rugby crisis', *Evening Post*, 2 October 1971.

63 Ibid.

64 Ref. No.: AAS218, Port Elizabeth Municipality: Port Elizabeth Joint Bantu Advisory Board Minutes: 1971 – Dissensions within the Port Elizabeth African Rugby Board, *RJ Scholtz Accession* (1954–1979), UNISA Documentation Centre for African Studies, University of South Africa, Pretoria, p. 33.

65 Massey, D. *Under Protest: The Rise of Student Resistance at the University of Fort Hare*, Hidden Histories Series, UNISA Press, Pretoria, 2010, p. 21.

66 Booley, *Forgotten Heroes*.

67 Interview 9: Messrs Mpumelelo 'Sbhidla' Majola and Lucky 'Coach' Mange, 22 March 2019, New Brighton, Port Elizabeth (translated from isiXhosa), pp. 1–142.

68 Interview 18: Mr Ray Mali, p. 15.

69 Interview 9: Messrs Mpumelelo 'Sbhidla' Majola and Lucky 'Coach' Mange, pp. 54–55.

70 Interview 25: Mr Thami Songongo (translated from isiXhosa), pp. 43–44.

71 Salvatore, N. 'Biography and Social History: An Intimate Relationship', *Labor History*, 87 (2004), pp. 189–90.

Chapter 6: 'Up Kwaru!'

1 Victoria East covered the peri-urban towns of Alice, Middledrift, Hogsback, Seymour, Fort Beaufort, Adelaide, Bedford and Somerset East.

2 Stofile, MA. Victoria East Rugby Union – Presidential Address by Outgoing President, MA Stofile (81/04/03, Unpublished), Reverend MA Stofile Private Papers, Alice, Eastern Cape, p. 1.

3 Interview 18: Mr Ray Mali, 10 April 2019, Winterstrand, East London, p. 14.

4 Ibid.

5 Booley, A. *Forgotten Heroes: A History of Black Rugby, 1882–1992.* Manie Booley Publications, Cape Town, 1998, p. 122.

6 Ibid.

7 Stofile, Victoria East Rugby Union – Presidential Address, p. 2.

8 Booley, *Forgotten Heroes.*

9 Interview 20: Mr Mthobi Tyamzashe, 26 August 2019, Menlyn, Pretoria, p. 4.

10 Interview 19: Mr Vusi and Mrs Nozuko 'Girlie' Pikoli, 24 August 2019, Faerie Glen, Pretoria (partly translated from isiXhosa), p. 35.

11 Ibid.

12 Interview 35: Judge Cecil 'Doc' Somyalo, 6 November 2019, Summerstrand, Port Elizabeth (translated from isiXhosa), p. 3.

13 Interview 21: Judge Lex Mpati, 26 August 2019, Erasmuskloof, Pretoria, p. 15.

14 Ibid, p. 13.

15 South African Rugby Union (SARU): Official Rhodes and SA Cup Winners Mailing List; Constitution: 1989, Reverend MA Stofile Private Papers, Alice, Eastern Cape.

16 Ibid.

17 Interview 16: Mr Ngconde Balfour, 8 April 2019, Alice, Eastern Cape (translated from isiXhosa), p. 3.

18 Ibid.

19 From 1971, right up to the coup of the Mono Badela's Kwaru executive committee led by the Qeqe-aligned Action Committee, the Kwaru executive committee comprised the following members: Arthur Sipho Mono Badela (president), Wilkinson Maku (vice-president), Newman Grawana (treasurer), Samuel Nghona (general secretary), Bruce Mahonga (assistant secretary), Daliwonga Siwisa (recording secretary), Koks Mtwa (match secretary); Lawrence Jack (chairman), Thomas

Sullo and Morris Peta (trustees), Sipho Nozewu and Thomas Sullo and Hamilton Madikana (senior selectors), Morris Peta and James Mtonga and Zweli Wabana (junior selectors) and Sipho Nozewu (coach). See 'Badela Back in Office', *Evening Post*, 8 May 1975.

20 MCH 63-3-30-194, Ref. No.: SACOS/INT/1989.26, 9 February 1989, Sam Ramsamy Collection, Mayibuye Archives, University of the Western Cape (UWC), Robben Island, Cape Town: Correspondence between SACOS General Secretary CR Clarke to Sam Ramsamy: SAN-ROC Executive Chairman, London, on Mohammed Agherdien being among six coaches to undertake a 'three-week coaching stint' in London, departing on 19 February 1989. Agherdien was also a member of the SARU Directorate of Coaching; see South African Rugby Union (SARU): Official Rhodes and SA Cup Winners Mailing List; Constitution: 1989, Reverend MA Stofile, Private Papers, Alice, Eastern Cape.

21 Interview 9: Messiers Mpumelelo 'Sbhidla' Majola and Lucky 'Coach' Mange, 22 March 2019, New Brighton, Port Elizabeth (translated from isiXhosa), p. 29.

22 Ibid (translated from isiXhosa), p. 24.

23 Ibid (translated from isiXhosa), p. 25.

24 Ibid (translated from isiXhosa), p. 28.

25 Ibid.

26 Interview 36: Mr Archie Mkele, 8 November 2019, Summerstrand, Port Elizabeth (partly translated from isiXhosa), p. 3.

27 Interview 9: Messrs Mpumelelo 'Sbhidla' Majola and Lucky 'Coach' Mange, p. 29.

28 Interview 33: Mr Valence Watson I, 1 November 2019, Mill Park, Port Elizabeth, p. 2.

29 Interview 25: Mr Thami Songongo, 16 October 2019, Uitenhage, Nelson Mandela Bay Metropolitan Municipality (translated from isiXhosa), pp. 3–4.

30 Interview 18: Mr Ray Mali, pp. 13–14.

31 Interview 25: Mr Thami Songongo (translated from isiXhosa), pp. 2–3.

32 Interview 2: Mr Mveleli Ncula, 10 March 2019, Rowallan Park, Port Elizabeth, p. 15.

33 Gaca, NW. 'The Rise and Fall of Rugby in a South African Township: The Case Study of Mdantsane, Eastern Cape', Unpublished MSocSci thesis, Fort Hare Institute of Social and Economic Research, University of Fort Hare, Alice, 2018.

34 Ibid.

35 Interview 9: Messrs Mpumelelo 'Sbhidla' Majola and Lucky 'Coach' Mange.

36 Interview 5: Mr Alan Zinn, 11 March 2019, Summerstrand, Port Elizabeth, p. 10.

37 Ibid, pp. 4–5.

38 Ibid, p. 5.

39 Interview 2: Mr Mveleli Ncula, p. 15.

40 Interview 13: Mr Gerald Majola, 26 March 2019, Newton Park, Port Elizabeth (partly translated from isiXhosa), pp. 1–56.

41 Ibid, p. 48.

42 Vuyokazi Nkanjeni, 'Rugby "road" needs major work', *Weekend Post*, 19 March 2016.

43 See also Booley, *Forgotten Heroes*.

44 Interview 9: Messrs Mpumelelo 'Sbhidla' Majola and Lucky 'Coach' Mange (translated from isiXhosa), p. 18.

45 Interview 36: Mr Archie Mkele (translated from isiXhosa), p. 1.

46 Interview 32: Mr Dan Ngcaphe, 29 October 2019, Zwide, Port Elizabeth (translated from isiXhosa), p. 1.

47 Khaya Majola was Eric Majola's son and Gerald Majola's elder brother. He became a national cricket champion in his own right. See also Odendaal, A. *The Story of an African Game*. David Philip Publishers, Cape Town, 2003. For a more personal reference, see Pikoli, V and Wiener, M. *My Second Initiation: The Memoir of Vusi Pikoli*. Picador Africa, Johannesburg, 2013.

48 Ibid (translated from isiXhosa), p. 41.

49 Ibid (translated from isiXhosa), p. 42.

50 Ibid (translated from isiXhosa), p. 40.

51 Ibid (translated from isiXhosa), p. 39.

52 'Rugby match yields R500', *Evening Post*, Evening Post School Fund, 18 September 1973.

53 Interview 19: Mr Vusi and Mrs Nozuko 'Girlie' Pikoli, p. 12.

54 Interview 13: Mr Gerald Majola (partly translated from isiXhosa), pp. 20–21.

55 'Report angered fans – Qeqe', *Herald*, 31 July 1978.

56 Ibid.

57 Ibid.

58 'Kwaru fans storm official's car', *Indaba*, 9 June 1978.

59 Interview 33: Valence Watson I, p. 14.

60 Interview 34: Valence Watson II, p. 10.

61 Ibid, p. 10.

62 Botha, T. 'The History of Non-Racial Black Rugby in Port Elizabeth and

the Influence of Community Politics on the Sport: The Conversation with a Stranger', Unpublished paper, 2018, pp. 1–53. See also Interview 34: Valence Watson II, pp. 1–28; Williamson, K. *Brothers to Us: The Story of a Remarkable Family's Fight Against Apartheid*, Penguin, Australia, 1997.

63 Ibid, p. 1.

64 Williamson, K. *Brothers to Us*, p. 49.

65 Ibid, p. 42.

66 Pottinger, B. 'Mixed rugby club head alleges harassment by authorities', *Evening Post*, 29 June 1979. See also 'Qeqe: Racism isolating sport', *Evening Post*, 30 March 1979.

67 Interview 34: Mr Valence Watson II, p. 2.

68 Truth and Reconciliation Commission (TRC) 1996, https://www.justice.gov.za/trc/hrvtrans/hrvpe1/day1.htm (accessed 18 August 2020).

69 Ibid.

70 Ibid.

71 Interview 32: Mr Dan Ngcaphe, p. 10.

72 Berger, G. 'Mono Badela – South African journalistic legend', South African History Online (SAHO), https://www.sahistory.org.za/people/mono-badela (accessed 18 August 2020).

73 Ibid.

74 Ibid.

75 Barron, C. 'South Africa: Mono Badela: A Journalist Persecuted for Fighting Apartheid', *Sunday Times*, 17 November 2002, https://allafrica.com/stories/200211170016.html/ (accessed 18 August 2020).

76 'Black writers' meeting banned', *Herald*, 10 June 1978.

77 'Reporter's home raided', *Herald*, 16 June 1978.

78 'Community Council bans Post', *Weekend Post*, 19 July 1979.

79 Ibid.

80 Truth and Reconciliation Commission (TRC) 1996.

81 Lodge, T and Swilling, M. 'Year of the Amabuthu', *Africa Report* (March–April 1986), pp. 4–7.

82 Ibid.

83 CIS Files: OP GBS 22/3/4/3/6 Agenda and Minutes, Vol. 2, August 1984 – May 1985, Professor Janet Cherry Private Papers, Lovemore Park, Port Elizabeth.

84 See 12/4/85, OP GBS exec, in CIS Files: OP GBS 22/3/4/3/6 Agenda and Minutes, Vol. 2, August 1984 – May 1985, Professor Janet Cherry

Private Papers, Lovemore Park, Port Elizabeth.

85 Ref. No.: EC 0217/96.

86 See 19/4/85, Special GVS GOS, in CIS Files: OP GBS 22/3/4/3/6 Agendas and Minutes, Vol. 2, August 1984 – May 1985, Professor Janet Cherry Private Papers, Lovemore Park, Port Elizabeth.

87 See 1/8/85 – OP GBS, in CIS Files: OP GBS 22/8/4/3/6 – Agendas and Minutes (65/3/1/), Vol. 3, May 1985 – September 1985, Professor Janet Cherry Private Papers, Lovemore Park, Port Elizabeth.

88 Ibid. See also 12/8/85, CIS Files: OP GBS 22/8/4/3/6 – Agendas and Minutes (65/3/1/), Vol. 3, May 1985 – September 1985, Professor Janet Cherry Private Papers, Lovemore Park, Port Elizabeth.

89 Interview 34: Mr Valence Watson II, p. 11.

90 'Mayor may intervene in rugby crisis', *Evening Post*, 2 October 1971.

91 Ibid.

92 Ibid.

93 Molapo, RR. 'Sports, Festivals and Popular Politics: Aspects of the Social and Political Culture in Langa Township, 1945–70', Unpublished MA thesis, Faculty of Arts, University of Cape Town, 1994, p. 52.

94 See also Booley, *Forgotten Heroes*.

95 'Kwaru not to quit Saru', *Evening Post*, 12 October 1974.

96 Interview 21: Judge Lex Mpati, p. 14.

97 'Rugby union defies ruling', *Evening Post*, 19 June 1974.

98 Ibid.

99 Ibid.

Chapter 7: Building *e*Dan Qeqe

1 Mono Badela, 'Rugby Union kicked out', *Evening Post*, 31 May 1975.

2 Ibid.

3 Interview 18: Mr Ray Mali, 10 April 2019, Winterstrand, East London, p. 14.

4 Interview 24: Mr Sipho McDonald Tanana, 14 October 2019, Vincent Park, East London, pp. 1–26.

5 Ibid, p. 14.

6 Interview 10: Mr Silas Nkanunu, 23 March 2019, New Brighton, Port Elizabeth (partly translated from isiXhosa), p. 6.

7 Interview 27: Advocate Amon Nyondo, 17 October 2019, Summerstrand, Port Elizabeth, p. 29.

8 Interview 31: Mr Harold and Mrs Sheila Wilson, 24 October 2019, Bethelsdorp, Port Elizabeth, p. 27.

9 Interview 2: Mr Mveleli Ncula, 10 March 2019, Rowallan Park, Port Elizabeth, pp. 1–19.

10 Interview 13: Mr Gerald Majola, 26 March 2019, Newton Park, Port Elizabeth, p. 12.

11 Case No.: 430/82, Date: 28/3/82, *In the Supreme Court of South Africa (East Cape Local Division), Held at Grahamstown, In the matter between, KwaZakhele Rugby Union + 2 Applicants, and, Amon Mbulaleki Nyondo + 2 Respondents, Before The Honourable Mr Justice Stewart*, Port Elizabeth Archives, Greenacres, Port Elizabeth, p. 5.

12 Sutton, K. 'Keith Sutton's profile of boy who made good', *Weekend Post*, 4 April 1986.

13 Dan Mbane was also a member of the Port Elizabeth Joint Bantu Advisory Board, along with Dan Qeqe, Reverend George B Molefe, Reverend JJR Jolobe, Wilson F Ximiya, AZ Lamani, AT Yeko and AS Mpondo. See Ref. No.: AAS218, Port Elizabeth Municipality: Port Elizabeth Joint Bantu Advisory Board: Minutes, *RJ Scholtz Accession* (1954–1979), UNISA Documentation Centre for African Studies, University of South Africa, Pretoria.

14 Interview 31: Mr Harold and Mrs Sheila Wilson, p. 27.

15 Interview 2: Mr Mveleli Ncula, p. 2.

16 Interview 10: Mr Silas Nkanunu.

17 See DE's Ref. PEH 166, Ref. No. 1/23/5, 9 April 1956, *Report on premises situated at Veeplaats (Bioscope) proposed to be hired for the purpose of Issuing of Reference Books to Natives: Port Elizabeth District*, National Archives of South Africa, Pretoria. See also Ref. No. 87/293 (B), Correspondence between the Secretary for Public Works, Pretoria, to Secretary for Native Affairs, in *Re: Steel drawers for Tax Cards: Native Commissioner, Port Elizabeth*, 24 October 1949, National Archives of South Africa, Pretoria.

18 Interview 13: Mr Gerald Majola (partly translated from isiXhosa), p. 15.

19 Baines, GF. 'New Brighton, Port Elizabeth, c. 1903–1953: A History of an Urban African Community', Unpublished PhD thesis, Department of History, University of Cape Town, 1994. See also Baines, G. 'The New Brighton Advisory Board, c. 1923–1952: Its Legitimacy and Legacy', Paper delivered at the Fifth Triennial History Workshop, University of the Witwatersrand, Johannesburg, February 1990; Maylam, P. 'Explaining the Apartheid City: 20 Years of South African Urban Historiography', *Journal of Southern African Studies*, 21, 1, March 1995.

20 Interview 19: Mr Vusi and Mrs Nozuko 'Girlie' Pikoli, 24 August 2019,

Faerie Glen, Pretoria (partly translated from isiXhosa), pp. 15–16.

21 Interview 11: Qeqe family: Port Elizabeth (Ms Phumla Qeqe, Mr Mpumelelo Qeqe, Mr Thembelani Vabaza and Ms Sinazo Vabaza), 24 March 2019, New Brighton, Port Elizabeth (translated from isiXhosa), pp. 33–34.

22 Ibid (translated from isiXhosa), p. 34.

23 Interview 14: Mrs Jumartha Milase Majola, 26 March 2019, New Brighton, Port Elizabeth (translated from isiXhosa), p. 36.

24 Interview 27: Advocate Amon Nyondo, p. 30.

25 Interview 32: Mr Dan Ngcaphe, 29 October 2019, Zwide, Port Elizabeth (translated from isiXhosa), pp. 4–5.

26 Interview 25: Mr Thami Songongo, 16 October 2019, Uitenhage, Nelson Mandela Bay Municipality (translated from isiXhosa), p. 36.

27 Interview 28: Mr Moki Cekisani, 18 October 2019, Walmer, Port Elizabeth, p. 4.

28 Untitled, *Evening Post*, c. 1975.

29 Ibid.

30 Interview 32: Mr Dan Ngcaphe (translated from isiXhosa), pp. 5–6.

31 Interview 8: Mr Mkhuseli Jack, 21 March 2019, Summerstrand, Port Elizabeth, p. 2.

32 'Frustration of non-racial rugby attacked', *Evening Post*, March 1975.

33 Untitled, *Evening Post*, c. 1975; 'Frustration of non-racial rugby attacked'.

34 Ibid.

35 Ibid.

36 Ibid.

37 Interview 3: Mr McKenzie Sloti, 10 March 2019, Kabega, Port Elizabeth (translated from isiXhosa), p. 36.

38 Interview 9: Messrs Mpumelelo 'Sbhidla' Majola and Lucky 'Coach' Mange (translated from isiXhosa), pp. 56–57.

39 Interview 14: Mrs Jumartha Milase Majola (translated from isiXhosa), p. 7.

40 Interview 4: Mr Thozamile Botha, 11 March 2019, North End, Port Elizabeth, p. 9.

41 Untitled, *Evening Post*, c. 1975.

42 Interview 11: Qeqe family: Port Elizabeth (translated from isiXhosa), pp. 41–43.

43 Interview 13: Mr Gerald Majola (partly translated from isiXhosa), p. 27.

44 Interview 19: Mr Vusi and Mrs Nozuko 'Girlie' Pikoli, p. 15.

45 Interview 2: Mr Mveleli Ncula, p. 2.
46 Interview 11: Qeqe family: Port Elizabeth (translated from isiXhosa), p. 44.
47 Ibid (translated from isiXhosa), p. 21.
48 Interview 32: Mr Dan Ngcaphe.
49 'Record gate taken', *Evening Post*, 8 September 1975.
50 Ibid.
51 Ibid.
52 Ibid.
53 Ibid.
54 Interview 27: Advocate Amon Nyondo, pp. 36–7.
55 Interview 32: Mr Dan Ngcaphe (translated from isiXhosa), pp. 6–7.
56 Interview 20: Mr Mthobi Tyamzashe, 26 August 2019, Menlyn, Pretoria, p. 15.
57 Ibid.
58 Interview 2: Mr Mveleli Ncula, p. 3.
59 Interview 11: Qeqe family: Port Elizabeth.
60 Interview 33: Mr Valence Watson I, 1 November 2019, Mill Park, Port Elizabeth, p. 7.
61 Interview 9: Messrs Mpumelelo 'Sbhidla' Majola and Lucky 'Coach' Mange (translated from isiXhosa), p. 55.
62 Ibid (translated from isiXhosa), pp. 55–6.
63 Interview 33: Mr Valence Watson I.
64 'Stadium ban on Kwaru lifted', *Herald*, 18 February 1977.
65 'Only one tap for 50 000 mourners', *Evening Post*, 29 April 1985.
66 Ibid.
67 Interview 14: Mrs Jumartha Milase Majola (translated from isiXhosa), pp. 8–9.
68 Ibid.
69 Ibid.
70 Matyu, J. 'Qeqe threat to fly to NZ over water cut', *Evening Post*, 21 May 1985.
71 'Kwaru in the money', *Evening Post*, 20 October 1978.
72 Ibid.
73 Matyu, J, 'Qeqe denies any Kwaru debt to Ecab', *Evening Post*, 26 April 1983.
74 Ibid.
75 Matyu, 'Qeqe threat to fly to NZ over water cut'.

Chapter 8: The First Implosion (1977) …

1 Interview 32: Mr Dan Ngcaphe, 29 October 2019, Zwide, Port Elizabeth (translated from isiXhosa), p. 13.

2 Ronnie Madinda was a Kwaru player who had firmly aligned himself with the Qeqe Action Committee faction as the story of the first implosion unfurled.

3 Skosana, BT. 'Kwaru and Saru have been harmed' (Letter to the Editor), *Evening Post*, 16 June 1977.

4 'Kwaru leaders resign posts', *Evening Post*, 13 June 1977.

5 This is one of the instances in which Kwaru's involvement in sports and social matters became overtly political, attracting the attention of the Security Branch. Through the Eastern Province Council on Sport (EPCOS), a provincial affiliate of SACOS, Kwaru had got involved in an affiliation dispute in boxing. This conflict, which eventually came to the attention of the Security Branch because of the alleged involvement of PEBCO (and invariably Kwaru officials), was fought between the mother body, the Eastern Province Boxing Control Board and its non-racial affiliate, the Eastern Province Boxing Unity. Eventually, Kwaru assisted the non-racial boxing body to break away and stage its tournaments at the Dan Qeqe Stadium. For more details, see South African Council on Sport (SACOS): Meeting Minutes – 11 March 1980, National Heritage and Cultural Studies Centre, University of Fort Hare, Alice.

6 Interview 27: Advocate Amon Nyondo, 17 October 2019, Summerstrand, Port Elizabeth, p. 40.

7 Interview 32: Mr Dan Ngcaphe (translated from isiXhosa), p. 18.

8 Ibid, pp. 38–40.

9 'Committee running Kwaru now', *Herald*, 14 June 1977.

10 'Kwaru leaders resign posts', *Evening Post*, 13 June 1977.

11 Ibid.

12 Ibid.

13 'Committee running Kwaru now'.

14 Ibid.

15 Interview 32: Mr Dan Ngcaphe (translated from isiXhosa), p. 14.

16 Ibid (translated from isiXhosa), p. 15.

17 Ibid (translated from isiXhosa), p. 13.

18 Xayimpi, N. 'Kwaru executive ousted', *Herald*, 9 June 1977.

19 'Major crisis faces union', *Herald*, 8 June 1977.

20 Agherdien, Y. 'Attempt to oust Kwaru executive', *Herald*, 13 June 1977.

21 'Kwaru unrest mystery grows', *Herald*, 8 June 1977.

22 'Kwaru leaders resign posts'.
23 'Committee running Kwaru now'.
24 Agherdien, 'Attempt to oust Kwaru executive'.
25 Botha, T. 'The History of Non-Racial Black Rugby in Port Elizabeth and the Influence of Community Politics on the Sport: The Conversations with a Stranger', Unpublished paper, 2018, p. 37.
26 'Kwaru leaders resign posts'.
27 'Kwaru unrest mystery grows'.
28 Agherdien, 'Attempt to oust Kwaru executive'.
29 Interview 35: Judge Cecil 'Doc' Somyalo, 6 November 2019, Summerstrand, Port Elizabeth (translated from isiXhosa), p. 31.
30 Ibid (translated from isiXhosa), pp. 31–32.
31 Interview 10: Mr Silas Nkanunu, 23 March 2019, New Brighton, Port Elizabeth (translated from isiXhosa), p. 4.
32 Interview 35: Judge Cecil 'Doc' Somyalo (translated from isiXhosa), pp. 34–35.
33 Ibid (translated from isiXhosa), p. 34.
34 Interview 32: Mr Dan Ngcaphe (translated from isiXhosa), p. 16.
35 'Kwaru leaders resign posts'.
36 Ibid.
37 Interview 27: Advocate Amon Nyondo.
38 Ibid (translated from isiXhosa.
39 Jali, B. 'Point of View' (Letter to the Editor), *Evening Post*, 22 September 1977.
40 'No hard feelings he says', *Daily Dispatch*, 14 June 1979.
41 Interview 33: Valence Watson I, p. 13.
42 Xayimpi, 'Kwaru executive ousted'.
43 Agherdien, 'Attempt to oust Kwaru executive'.
44 Interview 27: Advocate Amon Nyondo, p. 40.
45 Interview 32: Mr Dan Ngcaphe. See also Interview 9: Messrs Mpumelelo 'Sbhidla' Majola and Lucky 'Coach' Mange, 22 March 2019, New Brighton, Port Elizabeth (translated from isiXhosa), pp. 1–142.
46 Interview 32: Mr Dan Ngcaphe (translated from isiXhosa), pp. 20–21.
47 Agherdien, 'Attempt to oust Kwaru executive'.
48 Skosana, 'Kwaru and Saru have been harmed'.
49 Interview 27: Advocate Amon Nyondo, p. 38.
50 Ibid, p. 47.
51 Interview 24: Mr Sipho McDonald Tanana, 14 October 2019, Vincent Park, East London, p. 16.

52 Ibid.

53 Interview 25: Mr Thami Songongo, 16 October 2019, Uitenhage, Nelson Mandela Bay Metropolitan Municipality (translated from isiXhosa), pp. 43–44.

54 Ibid (translated from isiXhosa), pp. 46–47.

55 Personal communication during fieldwork research in March–April and October–November 2019.

56 Berger, G. 'Mono Badela: South African journalistic legend', South African History Online (SAHO), 2002, https//www.sahistory.org.za/people/mono-badela (accessed 15 November 2019).

57 Interview 31: Mr Harold and Mrs Sheila Wilson, 24 October 2019, Bethelsdorp, Port Elizabeth, p. 32.

58 Ibid.

59 Interview 33: Valence Watson I, p. 15.

60 'Committee running Kwaru now'.

61 Botha, 'The History of Non-Racial Black Rugby in Port Elizabeth', p. 40.

Chapter 9: … and the Second Implosion (1982)

1 'Call for release of Qeqe', *Evening Post*, 17 October 1977.

2 Pikoli, V and Wiener, M. *My Second Initiation: The Memoir of Vusi Pikoli*. Picador Africa, Johannesburg, 2013.

3 He joined the PAC upon its founding in 1959. Following the Sharpeville massacre, he was imprisoned on Robben Island from 1961 to 1964.

4 Interview 19: Mr Vusi and Mrs Nozuko 'Girlie' Pikoli, 24 August 2019, Faerie Glen, Pretoria (partly translated from isiXhosa), pp. 8–9.

5 Ibid (translated from isiXhosa), p. 86.

6 Lodge, T and Nasson, B. *All, Here and Now: Black Politics in South Africa in the 1980s*. Ford Foundation: Foreign Policy Association, New York, 1991. See also Pikoli and Wiener, *My Second Initiation: The Memoir of Vusi Pikoli*.

7 See CIS Files: OP GBS 22/3/4/3/6 Agenda and Minutes, Vol. 2, August 1984 – May 1985; 12/4/85 – OP GBS exec, 1/8/85, CIS Files: OP GBS 22/8/4/3/6 Agenda and Minutes – (65/3/1), Vol. 3, May 1985 – September 1985; 19/4/85, Special GVS GOS, TRC 1996, Professor Janet Cherry Private Papers, Lovemore Park, Port Elizabeth.

8 Ibid (translated from isiXhosa), pp. 98–99. For more on 'amabutho', see Lodge, T and Swilling, M. 'The Year of Amabuthu', *Africa Report*, March–April 1986.

9 Ibid, p. 19.

10 Interview 2: Mr Mveleli Ncula, 10 March 2019, Rowallan Park, Port Elizabeth, p. 8.

11 Ibid.

12 Ibid (translated from isiXhosa), pp. 22–23.

13 Ibid, p. 45.

14 Ibid (translated from isiXhosa), pp. 8–9.

15 Interview 28: Mr Moki Cekisani, 18 October 2019, Walmer, Port Elizabeth, pp. 1–10.

16 Interview 13: Mr Gerald Majola, 26 March 2019, Newton Park, Port Elizabeth (partly translated from isiXhosa), pp. 49–50.

17 Ibid (translated from isiXhosa), p. 28.

18 Interview 36: Mr Archie Mkele, 8 November 2019, Summerstrand, Port Elizabeth (translated from isiXhosa), p. 9.

19 Interview 20: Mr Mthobi Tyamzashe, 26 August 2019, Menlyn, Pretoria, pp. 20–21.

20 Interview 21: Judge Lex Mpati, 26 August 2019, Erasmuskloof, Pretoria, p. 11.

21 Interview 16: Mr Ngconde Balfour, 8 April 2019, Alice, Eastern Cape (translated from isiXhosa), pp. 4–5.

22 Interview 20: Mr Mthobi Tyamzashe (from communication around the interview, and not documented in the interview transcript).

23 Interview 31: Mr Harold and Mrs Sheila Wilson, 24 October 2019, Bethelsdorp, Port Elizabeth, pp. 1–48.

24 Interview 27: Advocate Amon Nyondo, 17 October 2019, Summerstrand, Port Elizabeth, pp. 1–74.

25 Ibid, pp. 7–12.

26 Victoria East Soccer Union: Articles of Constitution; Fort Hare Rugby Football Club: Articles of Constitution; Fort Hare Ring-Tennis Club: Articles of Constitution; Volleyball Club of the University of Fort Hare: Articles of Constitution; and Red Lions Rugby Football Club: Articles of Constitution, Reverend MA Stofile Private Papers, Alice.

27 Ibid.

28 Interview 27: Advocate Amon Nyondo. See also Massey, D. *Under Protest: The Rise of Student Resistance at the University of Fort Hare*, Hidden Histories Series, University of South Africa Press, 2010.

29 Matyu, J. 'Ciskei Government banishes two more Kadru officials', *Evening Post*, 9 September 1981. See also Interview 27: Advocate Amon Nyondo.

30 Interview 27: Advocate Amon Nyondo, pp. 20–21.

31 Ibid.

32 Case No.: 430/82, Date: 28/3/82, *In the Supreme Court of South Africa (Eastern Cape Local Division), In the matter between: KwaZakhele Rugby Union + 2 Applicants and Amon Mbulaleko Nyondo + 2 Respondents, Before the Honourable Mr Justice Stewart*, Port Elizabeth Archives, Greenacres, Port Elizabeth.

33 Interview 32: Mr Dan Ngcaphe.

34 Case No.: 430/82, Date: 28/3/82.

35 Interview 27: Advocate Amon Nyondo, p. 51.

36 Known as '*i*club *yamagoduka*', or 'the club of migrant labourers', Fabs Rugby Football Club comprised players from the rural and peri-urban towns in and around Ciskei and the Border region. The acronym 'FABS' stood for Fort Beaufort, Alicedale, Bedford and Seymour. See also Interview 2: Mr Mveleli Ncula, 10 March 2019, Rowallan Park Port Elizabeth, pp.1–19; and Interview 19: Mr Vusi and Mrs Nozuko 'Girlie' Pikoli, 24 August 2019, Faerie Glen, Pretoria (translated from isiXhosa), pp. 1–61.

37 Interview 32: Mr Dan Ngcaphe.

38 Ibid.

39 Notice of Motion 430/82, File No.: M430/82 (emphasis in original), Port Elizabeth Archives, Greenacres, Port Elizabeth.

40 Interview 32: Mr Dan Ngcaphe (translated from isiXhosa), p. 24.

41 Interview 33: Mr Valence Watson I, 1 November 2019, Mill Park, Port Elizabeth (partly translated from isiXhosa), pp. 15–16.

42 Notice of Motion 430/82. File No.: M430/82.

43 Ibid (emphasis in original), pp. 5–6.

44 Interview 32: Mr Dan Ngcaphe (translated from isiXhosa), p. 28.

45 Matyu, J. 'Pledge given to support Kwaru', *Evening Post*, 22 February 1982; 'Union decides to keep the Dan Qeqe', *Herald*, 1 April 1982; and 'SARU to explain Kwaru's same-field rugby match rivalry', *Herald*, 8 April 1982.

46 Interview 27: Advocate Amon Nyondo, p. 56.

47 Interview 16: Mr Ngconde Balfour (translated from isiXhosa), p. 6.

48 Ibid, p. 48.

49 Interview 27: Advocate Amon Nyondo, pp. 33–41.

50 Ibid.

51 Ibid, p. 41.

52 Ibid, p. 46.

53 Case No.: 798/82, File No.: M430/82, *In the Supreme Court of South*

Africa, EC; In the matter: KwaZakhele Rugby Union versus (1) Amon Mbulaleki Nyondo, (2) Fani James; (3) L. Mhlambiso, Port Elizabeth Archives, Greenacres, Port Elizabeth.

54 Interview 27: Advocate Amon Nyondo.

55 Matyu, 'Pledge given to support Kwaru executive'.

56 Ibid.

57 Ibid.

58 Interview 27: Advocate Amon Nyondo, p. 56.

59 Interview 21: Judge Lex Mpati, p. 5.

60 'SARU to explain Kwaru's same-field rugby match rivalry'.

61 Ibid.

62 Interview 32: Mr Dan Ngcaphe (translated from isiXhosa), pp. 29–30.

63 Case No.: 1075/82, *In the Supreme Court of South Africa (South Eastern Cape Local Division; Port Elizabeth, 7 May 1982), (KwaZakhele Rugby Union – Applicant and Skumbuzo Sidney Mgengo – 1st Respondent; NDS Quza – 2nd Respondent; D Sqwebu – 3rd Respondent; DV Peta – 4th Respondent; M Ngcaphe – 5th Respondent; D Menemene – 6th Respondent; L Nghona – 7th Respondent; L Mhlambiso – 8th Respondent*, Port Elizabeth Archives, Greenacres, Port Elizabeth.

64 Interview 27: Advocate Amon Nyondo, p. 56.

65 Ibid, p. 54.

66 Interview 32: Mr Dan Ngcaphe (translated from isiXhosa), p. 40.

67 Case No.: 430/82, *In the Supreme Court of South Africa (Eastern Cape Division), Grahamstown, Sunday, 28 March 1982, Before the Honourable Mr Justice Stewart*, Port Elizabeth Archives, Greenacres, Port Elizabeth.

68 Interview 27: Advocate Amon Nyondo, p. 27.

69 Benjamin T Skosana was a Kwaru player who had openly expressed his opposition to the first implosion, the first to have made reference, in documented form to the 'Badela coup'. He expressed his views in a letter to the editor of, and which was published in, the *Evening Post* as 'Kwaru and Saru have been harmed' on 6 June 1977.

70 Interview 36: Mr Archie Mkele, p. 13.

71 Case No.: 1075/82, p. 7.

72 Interview 32: Mr Dan Ngcaphe (translated from isiXhosa), p. 30.

73 Interview 13: Mr Gerald Majola (translated from isiXhosa), p. 41.

74 Interview 27: Advocate Amon Nyondo, pp. 63–64.

75 Interview 13: Mr Gerald Majola. See also Interview 9: Messrs Mpumelelo 'Sbhidla' Majola and Lucky 'Coach' Mange; Interview 25: Mr Thami Songongo; Interview 26: Mr Themba Ludwaba; and

Interview 32: Mr Dan Ngcaphe.

76 Interview 16: Mr Ngconde Balfour (translated from isiXhosa), p. 5.

77 Interview 13: Mr Gerald Majola, p. 26.

78 Interview 25: Mr Thami Songongo, 16 October 2019, Uitenhage, Nelson Mandela Bay Metropolitan Municipality (translated from isiXhosa), p. 55.

Chapter 10: Qeqe and Port Elizabeth in the 1970s

1 Interview 35: Judge Cecil 'Doc' Somyalo, 6 November 2019, Summerstrand, Port Elizabeth (translated from isiXhosa), p. 39.

2 Interview 14: Mrs Jumartha Milase Majola, 26 March 2019, New Brighton, Port Elizabeth (translated from isiXhosa), p. 38.

3 Interview 35: Judge Cecil 'Doc' Somyalo.

4 Interview 24: Mr Sipho McDonald Tanana, 14 October 2019, Vincent Park, East London, pp. 1–26.

5 Bentley, K. 'Street committees are our democracy', *Post Focus*, *Weekend Post*, 7 April 1986.

6 Interview 22: Ambassador Phumelele 'Stone' Sizani, 16 September 2019 (Written responses: Berlin, Germany, 16 September 2019), p. 2.

7 Interview 24: Mr Sipho McDonald Tanana (translated from isiXhosa), p. 24.

8 Ibid.

9 Interview 16: Mr Ngconde Balfour, 8 April 2019, Alice (translated from isiXhosa), pp. 1–17.

10 Interview 2: Mr Mveleli Ncula, 10 March 2019, Rowallan Park, Port Elizabeth, p. 14.

11 Sizwe Kondile, who had become Chris Hani's driver in Lesotho, was killed in Hani's attempted assassination there. For reference, see Hani, L. *Being Chris Hani's Daughter*, MFBooks, Johannesburg, 2017.

12 Interview 11: Qeqe family: Port Elizabeth (Ms Phumla Qeqe, Mr Mpumelelo Qeqe, Mr Thembelani Vabaza and Ms Sinazo Vabaza), 24 March 2019, New Brighton, Port Elizabeth (translated from isiXhosa), pp. 1–124.

13 Ibid, p. 79.

14 Interview 8: Mr Mkhuseli Jack, 21 March 2019, Summerstrand, Port Elizabeth, p. 3.

15 Lodge, T and Nasson, B. *All, Here and Now: Black Politics in South Africa in the 1980s*. Ford Foundation: Foreign Policy Association, New York, 1991.

16 Truth and Reconciliation CSI Files (1992 – 1994): (GBS 516/5),

(22/3/2/15) – Terrorisme – Binnebring van lyke van Terroriste; OP GBS 22/8/4/3/6 – Agendas and Minutes (65/3/1); OP GBS (22/3/4/3/6) – Agendas and Minutes, Vol. 2, August 1984 – May 1985); OP GBS 22/8/4/3/6 – Agendas and Minutes – (65/3/1), Vol. 3, May 1985 – September 1985, Vol. 4, September 1985 – March 1986; OP GBS 65/3/1 (22/8/4/3/6) – Minutes, Vol. 2 – September 1988 – December 1988, Professor Janet Cherry Private Papers, Lovemore Park, Port Elizabeth)

17 Jack, M. *To Survive and Succeed: From Farm Boy to Businessman*. Kwela Books, Cape Town, 2018.

18 'Baas Dan Mbona' Qeqe: Obituary (2005), Port Elizabeth.

19 Interview 17: Qeqe family: Fort Beaufort (Messrs Mncedi Mali, Nqaba Mali and Weaver Qeqe), 9 April 2019, KwaDubu, Fort Beaufort (translated from isiXhosa), pp. 1–56.

20 'Chiefs for election service', *Herald*, 15 December 1972.

21 Ibid.

22 Interview 18: Mr Ray Mali, 10 April 2019, Winterstrand, East London, pp. 1–35.

23 Interview 15: Messrs Kolekile Kwatsha and Keke Pemba, 27 March 2019, New Brighton, Port Elizabeth (translated from isiXhosa), pp. 1–45.

24 Interview 18: Mr Ray Mali, p. 9.

25 Peires, J. *The Implosion of Transkei and Ciskei*.

26 Interview 11: Qeqe family: Port Elizabeth. See also Interview 9: Messrs Mpumelelo 'Sbhidla' Majola and Lucky 'Coach' Mange, 22 March 2019, New Brighton, Port Elizabeth (translated from isiXhosa), pp. 1–142.

27 Interview 18: Mr Ray Mali, p. 7.

28 Interview 24: Sipho McDonald Tanana. See also Interview 18: Mr Ray Mali.

29 Peires, *The Implosion of Transkei and Ciskei*.

30 Evans, L. 'Resettlement and the Making of the Ciskei Bantustan, c. 1960–1976', *Journal of Southern African Studies*, 40, 1 2014, pp. 21–40.

31 White, CS. 'The Rule of Brigadier Oupa Gqozo in Ciskei: 4 March 1990 to 22 March 1994', Unpublished MA thesis, Rhodes University, Grahamstown, 2008.

32 Ref. No. GO 8/2/1, 5 July 1979, *Survey: Ciskeian Xhosa*, East Cape Administration Board, correspondence from LC Koch, Director: East Cape Administration Board, to Mr H du Toit T Hefer, The Secretary: Ciskei Commission, Silverton.

33 Interview 2: Mr Mveleli Ncula.

34 Interview 31: Mr Harold and Mrs Sheila Wilson, 24 October 2019, Bethelsdorp, Port Elizabeth, p. 34.

35 Interview 19: Mr Vusi and Mrs Nozuko 'Girlie' Pikoli, 24 August 2019, Faerie Glen, Pretoria (partly translated from isiXhosa), pp. 28–29.

36 Baines, GF. 'New Brighton, Port Elizabeth, c.1903–1953: A History of an Urban African Community', Unpublished PhD thesis, Department of History, University of Cape Town, 1994, p. 160.

37 Ibid. See also Report No. 13/1952, City of Port Elizabeth, Town Clerk's Department, Report by Town Clerk to Native Affairs Committee (Special Meeting: 15 December 1952).

38 Ibid, pp. 20–21.

39 'School building fund mounts', *Herald*, 17 November 1979.

40 Ibid.

41 Hunter, CFD. 'Some Aspects of the African Missionary Policy of the Presbytery of Adelaide/Port Elizabeth with Special Reference to the Origin and Development of the New Brighton Presbyterian Missionary Church, 1898–1962', Unpublished PhD thesis, Rhodes University, Grahamstown, 1983.

42 Ibid, p. 85.

43 Ibid.

44 Ibid.

45 Ref. No.: AAS215, Letter from Reverend Molefe, Union Theological Seminary, New York, to Dr. Thomas Jesse Jones, Phelps–Stokes Foundation, New York City, 21 February 1939, *JG Molefe Accession* (1939–1974), UNISA Documentation Centre for African Studies, University of South Africa, Pretoria.

46 Ibid.

47 Hunter, 'Some Aspects of the African Missionary Policy'.

48 'Cement floor school rejected', *Herald*, 15 December 1973.

49 Interview 19: Mr Vusi and Mrs Nozuko 'Girlie' Pikoli, p. 26.

50 Interview 9: Messrs Mpumelelo 'Sbhidla' Majola and Lucky 'Coach' Mange (translated from isiXhosa), pp. 11–12.

51 Badela, M. 'BAAB failure on schools attacked', *Evening Post*, 23 October 1975.

52 Ibid.

53 'Cement floor school rejected'.

54 Ibid.

55 Ibid.

56 Ibid.

57 Ibid.

58 Ibid.

59 Ibid.

60 Interview 3: Mr McKenzie Sloti, 10 March 2019, Kabega, Port Elizabeth (translated from isiXhosa), pp. 1–46.

61 Interview 9: Messrs Mpumelelo 'Sbhidla' Majola and Lucky 'Coach' Mange (translated from isiXhosa), p. 12.

62 Interview 8: Mr Mkhuseli Jack, p. 2.

63 Interview 3: Mr McKenzie Sloti (translated from isiXhosa), pp. 8–9.

64 'School building fund mounts'.

65 Baines, 'New Brighton, Port Elizabeth, c. 1903–1953'.

66 Ref. No.: AAS218, Port Elizabeth Municipality: Port Elizabeth Joint Bantu Advisory Board Minutes, 01/10/70–30/09/71, *RJ Scholtz Accession* (1954–1979), UNISA Documentation Centre for African Studies, University of South Africa, Pretoria, p. 8.

67 Ibid, p. 12.

68 French, KJ. 'James Mpanza and the Sofasonke Party in the Development of Local Politics in Soweto', Unpublished MA thesis, University of the Witwatersrand, Johannesburg, 1983.

69 Interview 3: Mr McKenzie Sloti (translated from isiXhosa), p. 5.

70 Interview 9: Messrs Mpumelelo 'Sbhidla' Majola and Lucky 'Coach' Mange (translated from isiXhosa), pp. 8–9.

71 Interview 2: Mr Mveleli Ncula. See also Interview 9: Messrs Mpumelelo 'Sbhidla' Majola and Lucky 'Coach' Mange; Interview 11: Qeqe family: Port Elizabeth; Interview 14: Mrs Jumartha Milase Majola; Interview 17: Qeqe family: Fort Beaufort; and Interview 19: Mr Vusi and Mrs Nozuko 'Girlie' Pikoli.

72 Interview 35: Judge Cecil 'Doc' Somyalo (translated from isiXhosa), p. 5.

73 Ibid.

74 Interview 35: Judge Cecil 'Doc' Somyalo (translated from isiXhosa), p. 6.

75 Interview 14: Mrs Jumartha Milase Majola (translated from isiXhosa), p. 24.

76 Interview 3: Mr McKenzie Sloti. See also Interview 14: Mrs Jumartha Milase Majola.

77 Ibid.

78 Ibid.

79 Ibid.

80 Badela, M. 'Upset by increases', *Evening Post*, 9 August 1979.

81 Ibid.

82 Ibid.

83 'Move to increase bus fares will be opposed – Qeqe', *Herald*, 1974.

84 Ibid.

85 Ibid.

86 Ibid.

87 Badela, M. 'Police locked children up', *Evening Post*, 29 January 1977.

88 Ibid.

89 Ibid.

90 Ibid.

91 'The Struggle Ahead for Soweto: Conversations with a Ghetto Leader', https://www.thecrimson.com/article/1979/11/1/the-struggle-ahead-for-soweto-pidr/ (accessed 11 November 2020).

92 'Nthato Motlana's memories of Joburg', https://www.joburg.org.za/play_Pages/Play%20in%20Joburg%20Vibe/links/people%20of%20the%20City/Links/Nthato-Motlana27s-memories-of-Joburg.aspx (accessed 11 November 2020).

93 Ibid.

94 Badela, M. [title unclear], *Evening Post*, 22 September 1976.

95 Badela, M. 'Advisory Board may end', *Evening Post*, 13 October 1977.

96 [Title unclear].

97 [Title unclear], *Evening Post*, 12 October 1977.

98 'Koch: we will have community councils', *Herald*, 28 October 1977. See also 'Detainee freed', *Herald*, 15 December 1977.

99 Ibid.

100 Badela, 'Advisory Board may end'.

101 [Title unclear], *Evening Post*, 12 October 1977.

102 Badela, 'Advisory Board may end'. David Mbane was also a businessman who owned a butchery in Veeplaas. This was where Kwaru players, its administrators and SARU's president, Abdul Abbas, had gathered after the final SA Cup Final match between Kwaru and Tygerberg, and officially named the stadium the 'Dan Qeqe Stadium.' See also Interview 27: Advocate Amon Nyondo, 17 October 2019, Summerstrand, Port Elizabeth, pp. 1–74); Interview 32: Mr Dan Ngcaphe, 29 October 2019, Zwide, Port Elizabeth (translated from isiXhosa), pp. 1–45.

103 'Police hold Qeqe', *Herald*, 17 October 1977.

104 'Call for release of Qeqe', *Herald*, 17 October 1977.

105 Ibid.

106 'Police detain Qeqe', *Herald*, 15 October 1977.

107 A. Qeqe, 'Character of detainee', *Evening Post*, 3 December 1977.
108 Ibid.
109 'Black Sash on detainees', *Herald*, 29 October 1977.
110 Ibid.
111 Ibid.
112 'Police hold Qeqe'.
113 Interview 11: Qeqe family: Port Elizabeth (translated from isiXhosa), p. 82.
114 Ibid (translated from isiXhosa), pp. 8 –82.
115 'Qeqe's home raided', *Herald*, 19 October 1977.
116 'Four in family held', *Herald*, 20 October 1977. See also 'Four members of Qeqe family held', *Herald*, 21 October 1977.
117 Interview 14: Mrs Jumartha Milase Majola (translated from isiXhosa), pp. 14–15.
118 'Qeqe's home raided'; 'Four in family held'.
119 Interview 11: Qeqe family: Port Elizabeth (translated from isiXhosa), p. 74.
120 Ibid.
121 Mrs Qeqe visited husband', *Herald*, 3 November 1977.
122 'Four members of Qeqe family held'. See also 'Four in family held'.
123 Ibid.
124 Personal communications.
125 Interview 3: Mr McKenzie Sloti.
126 Ibid (translated from isiXhosa), pp. 14–15.
127 Interview 11: Qeqe family: Port Elizabeth (translated from isiXhosa), pp. 27–28.
128 Ibid.
129 Interview 14: Mrs Jumartha Milase Majola (translated from isiXhosa), p. 34.
130 Ref. No.: AAS213, *Ivan Peter Youth Club Accession* (1976–1977), UNISA Documentation Centre for African Studies, University of South Africa, Pretoria.
131 Ibid.
132 Ref. No.: AAS213, Charlton Andrews, 'Rugby player's widow', *Ivan Peter Youth Club Accession* (1976–1977), UNISA Documentation Centre for African Studies, University of South Africa, Pretoria.
133 Ref. No.: AAS213, Constitution: Ivan Peter Youth Club, *Ivan Peter Youth Club Accession* (1976–1977), UNISA Documentation Centre for African Studies, University of South Africa, Pretoria.
134 Ref. No.: AAS213, Youth Week: 1977, *Ivan Peter Youth Club Accession* (1976–1977), UNISA Documentation Centre for African Studies,

University of South Africa, Pretoria.

135 Interview 1: Mr Crosby 'Winky' Ximiya, 5 March 2019, South End, Port Elizabeth, p. 11.

136 See also Williamson, K. *Brothers to Us: The Story of a Remarkable Family's Fight Against Apartheid*. Penguin, Australia, 1997.

137 Interview 19: Mr Vusi and Mrs Nozuko 'Girlie' Pikoli (translated from isiXhosa), p. 42.

138 This is in reference to Silas Nkanunu.

139 Pikoli, V and Wiener, M. *My Second Initiation: The Memoir of Vusi Pikoli*. Picador Africa, Johannesburg, 2013, p. 45.

140 By 1977, Wridge Qeqe was a local township councillor in Zwelitsha. He ran again in 1977 for a seat in the Zwelitsha Township Council. See 'Voters' roll battle won by Mr Qeqe', *Indaba*, 30 September 1977.

141 Ibid (translated from isiXhosa), pp. 43–44.

142 Interview 20: Mr Mthobi Tyamzashe, 26 August 2019, Menlyn, Pretoria, pp. 14–15.

143 Ibid, p. 30.

Chapter 11: Qeqe and Port Elizabeth in the 1980s

1 Interview 11: Qeqe family: Port Elizabeth (Ms Phumla Qeqe, Mr Mpumelelo Qeqe, Mr Thembelani Vabaza and Ms Sinazo Vabaza), 24 March 2019, New Brighton (translated from isiXhosa), pp. 1–124.

2 Lodge, T and Swilling, M. 'The Year of the Amabuthu', *Africa Report*, March–April 1986, p. 4.

3 Ibid, p. 60.

4 Riordan, R. 'Eastern Cape: Life on the Low Road', *Optima*, 36, 2, 1988.

5 Ibid.

6 Ibid.

7 Ibid.

8 Ref: OTP/017/0134/3, (31/05/80), *An Interview with Comrade Oliver Tambo – President of the African National Congress of South Africa* (31.05.80), Unpublished, OR Tambo Collection, National Heritage and Cultural Studies [NAHECS], University of Fort Hare, Alice, p. 3.

9 Ref: OTP/017/0134/2, *Message to the People of South Africa by Comrade President Oliver Tambo on the Occasion of the 68th Anniversary of the African National Congress of South Africa, January 8th, 1980*, Unpublished, OR Tambo Collection, National Heritage and Cultural Studies [NAHECS], University of Fort Hare, Alice, p. 5.

10 Ref: OTP/017/0134/3, *An Interview with Comrade Oliver Tambo –*

President of the African National Congress of South Africa, p. 3.

11 Swilling, M. 'UDF and Local Government in South Africa', *Monitor*, 1988, pp. 44–50.

12 Riordan, 'Eastern Cape: Life on the Low Road'.

13 Ibid.

14 Ref: OTP/038/0336/4, *Radio Freedom Broadcast of the Secretary-General to the People of South Africa on the Occasion of June 26, 1982*, Unpublished, OR Tambo Collection, National Heritage and Cultural Studies [NAHECS], University of Fort Hare, Alice.

15 Interview 4: Mr Thozamile Botha, 11 March 2019, North End, Port Elizabeth, p. 10.

16 Interview 35: Judge Cecil 'Doc' Somyalo, 6 November 2019, Summerstrand, Port Elizabeth (translated from isiXhosa), pp. 26–27.

17 Interview 8: Mr Mkhuseli Jack, 21 March 2019, Summerstrand, Port Elizabeth, pp. 5–6.

18 Interview 13: Mr Gerald Majola, 26 March 2019, Newton Park, Port Elizabeth (translated from isiXhosa), p. 30.

19 Pottinger, B. 'PE police detain black leaders', *Herald*, 11 January 1980.

20 Allen, B and Viljoen, A. 'PE Police moves: Botha, top PEBCO men questioned', *Herald*, 11 January 1980.

21 'Why black leaders are being held', *Herald*, 12 January 1980.

22 Ibid.

23 Allen and Viljoen, 'PE Police moves: Botha, top PEBCO men questioned'.

24 Ibid.

25 Interview 4: Mr Thozamile Botha, p. 11.

26 Swilling, 'UDF Local Government in South Africa'.

27 Ibid.

28 'Why black leaders are being held'.

29 'Qeqe detained – now four are held', *Herald*, 16 January 1980.

30 Ibid.

31 Ibid.

32 Lange, P. 'Detained Pebco leaders may know fate today', *Herald*, 20 January 1980.

33 Ibid.

34 Pottinger, B. 'Pebco men now held under Terror Act', *Herald*, 23 January 1980.

35 Ibid.

36 Ibid.

37 Ibid.

38 Lange, P. 'Detention of black trio strongly condemned', *Herald*, 24 January 1980.
39 Ibid.
40 Ibid.
41 Ibid.
42 Ibid.
43 'Pebco aid for families', *Herald*, 29 January 1980.
44 Ibid.
45 'Pebco branch's elections', *Weekend Post*, 14 February 1980.
46 Interview 35: Judge Cecil 'Doc' Somyalo (translated from isiXhosa), pp. 22–23.
47 Interview 11: Qeqe family: Port Elizabeth (translated from isiXhosa), pp. 86–87.
48 Interview 31: Mr Harold and Mrs Sheila Wilson, 24 October 2019, Bethelsdorp, Port Elizabeth, p. 38.
49 Pottinger, B. 'Qeqe freed after 14 days in detention', *Herald*, 29 January 1980.
50 Ibid.
51 Ibid.
52 Ibid.
53 'Pebco official welcomes Qeqe release', *Herald*, 30 January 1980.
54 Ibid.
55 Interview 11: Qeqe family: Port Elizabeth (translated from isiXhosa), p. 90.
56 'Call for action on Pebco men's detention', *Weekend Post*, 29 January 1980.
57 Ibid.
58 'Bannings put Pebco men out of work', *Herald*, 28 February 1980.
59 'Four Port Elizabeth men on banned list', *Herald*, 21 March 1980.
60 Ibid.
61 Ibid.
62 'Remand for Qeqe', *Herald*, 18 March 1980.
63 'Brief appearance', *Herald*, 11 March 1980.
64 Interview 11: Qeqe family: Port Elizabeth (translated from isiXhosa), p. 84.
65 Interview 35: Judge Cecil 'Doc' Somyalo (translated from isiXhosa), pp. 23–24.
66 Interview 3: Mr McKenzie Sloti (translated from isiXhosa), p. 27.
67 Ibid.
68 Ibid.
69 Interview 35: Judge Cecil 'Doc' Somyalo (translated from isiXhosa), p. 24.

70 Matyu, J. 'Complaints over electricity subsidy', *Evening Post*, 23 July 1984.

71 Ibid.

72 Ibid.

73 Ibid.

74 Boutall, D. 'Qeqe slams electricity rebates for PE Africans', *Herald*, 27 March 1984.

75 Ibid.

76 Ibid.

77 Ibid.

78 Matyu, J. 'Power failure in PE township', *Evening Post*, 19 April 1982.

79 Ibid.

80 Ibid.

81 Bam, T. 'Another township power cut', *Herald*, 10 June 1982.

82 Ibid.

83 Ibid.

84 'Big crowd attend wedding in PE', *Weekend Post*, 26 April 1984.

85 Ibid.

86 Ibid.

87 Interview 11: Qeqe family: Port Elizabeth (translated from isiXhosa), p. 20.

88 MaCheapie was the nickname of Cheapline, the son of Ngwehlathi Bazi, Qeqe's maternal uncle, who was a prominent businessman in New Brighton from the 1930s to the 1970s. See also Interview 15: Messrs Kolekile Kwatsha and Keke Pemba, 27 March 2019, New Brighton, Port Elizabeth (translated from isiXhosa), pp. 1–35.

89 Interview 14: Mrs Jumartha Milase Majola, 26 March 2019, New Brighton, Port Elizabeth (translated from isiXhosa), pp. 41–43.

90 'Eastern Cape mourns death of Mrs Qeqe', *Herald*, 26 August 1994.

91 Personal communication with Ms Phumla Qeqe and Mr McKenzie Sloti, February 2021.

92 Interview 14: Mrs Jumartha Milase Majola, 26 March 2019, New Brighton, Port Elizabeth (translated from isiXhosa), p. 17.

93 Matyu, J. 'Homage paid to Nyamie', *Evening Post*, 5 September 1994.

94 Interview 20: Mr Mthobi Tyamzashe, 26 August 2019, Menlyn, Pretoria, p. 17.

95 Interview 13: Mr Gerald Majola, 26 March 2019, Newton Park, Port Elizabeth (translated from isiXhosa), pp. 44–45.

96 Ref. No.: AAS218, Port Elizabeth Municipality: Port Elizabeth Joint Bantu Advisory Board: Minutes – 01/10/1970 – 30/09/71, Keeping

of Animals in Townships, *RJ Scholtz Accession* (1954–1979), UNISA Documentation Centre for African Studies, University of South Africa, Pretoria, p. 41.

97 Saliso, M. 'Discharge over pigs opposed', *Weekend Post*, 17 August 1982.

98 Ref. No.: AAS218, Port Elizabeth Municipality: Port Elizabeth Joint Bantu Advisory Board Minutes – 01/10/1970 – 30/09/71, Keeping of Animals in Townships.

99 Ibid, p. 41.

100 Ibid.

101 Interview 11: Qeqe family: Port Elizabeth (translated from isiXhosa), pp. 24–25.

102 Ibid. See also Interview 3: Mr McKenzie Sloti, 10 March 2019, Kabega, Port Elizabeth (translated from isiXhosa.

103 Ford, short for 'Fordville', named after a Ford vehicle-assembly plant located nearby, was a site-and-build-yourself, upmarket suburb of New Brighton. It was set up in 1983/4, following President PW Botha's policy on urban black house ownership, and was meant to consolidate a black middle class to create a buffer between the local state and the rest of the poor, working-class black people.

104 Interview 3: Mr McKenzie Sloti (translated from isiXhosa), p. 22.

105 Matyu, J. 'Qeqe threat to fly to NZ over water cut', *Evening Post*, 21 May 1985.

106 Interview 11: Qeqe family: Port Elizabeth.

Chapter 12: Qeqe Rests: The Legacy

1 Matyu, J. 'President's award for Qeqe', *Evening Post*, 15 August 1997.

2 'Recognition for Qeqe', *Evening Post*, 18 August 1997.

3 Ibid.

4 Matyu, 'President's award for Qeqe'.

5 Ibid.

6 Shortened reference to 'Robben Island'.

7 Interview 20: Mr Mthobi Tyamzashe, 26 August 2019, Menlyn, Pretoria, pp. 18–19.

8 Matyu, 'President's award for Qeqe'.

9 Adkins, B. 'They were outstanding: Club names top three for awards', *Herald*, 5 September 1995.

10 She is referenced in the newspaper article only by her first name.

11 Ibid.

12 Dewes, J. 'Dan Qeqe wins award', *Herald*, 22 September 1995.

13 Ibid.

14 Ibid.
15 Matyu, J. 'Better deal sought', *Evening Post*, 12 November 1993.
16 Ibid.
17 Ibid.
18 Ibid.
19 Ibid.
20 Matyu, J. 'Qeqe delighted by banquet invitation', *Evening Post*, 28 June 1991.
21 Ibid.
22 Ibid.
23 Terblanche, S. 'Qeqe tipped for top EP rugby post', *Herald*, 28 October 1994.
24 Ibid.
25 Interview 11: Qeqe family: Port Elizabeth (Ms Phumla Qeqe, Mr Mpumelelo Qeqe, Mr Thembelani Vabaza and Ms Sinazo Vabaza), 24 March 2019, New Brighton, Port Elizabeth (translated from isiXhosa), pp. 22, 23–24.
26 'Call for unity at official opening of Zwide stadium', *Herald*, 11 December 1992.
27 Ibid.
28 Ibid.
29 Case No.: 430/82, Date: 28/3/82, *In the Supreme Court of South Africa (Eastern Cape Local Division), In the matter between: KwaZakhele Rugby Union + 2 Applicants, and Amon Mbulaleki Nyondo + 2 Respondents, Before the Honourable Mr Justice Stewart*, Port Elizabeth Archives, Greenacres, Port Elizabeth, p. 5.
30 Interview 30: Mr Gerald Majola, 26 March 2019, Newton Park, Port Elizabeth (partly translated from isiXhosa), pp. 1–56.
31 Ibid (translated from isiXhosa), pp. 47–48.
32 Interview 25: Mr Thami Songongo, 16 October 2019, Uitenhage, Nelson Mandela Bay Metropolitan Municipality (translated from isiXhosa), p. 56.
33 Ref.: MCH63, The Harare Initiative, 15 November 1988, (With compliments of the South African Rugby Union), Sam Ramsamy Collection, Mayibuye Archives/Robben Island, University of the Western Cape [UWC], p. 9.
34 Ibid.
35 MCH63-30-4-203, *South African Rugby Board: Report Released to the Cape Times*, 1990, Sam Ramsamy Collection, Mayibuye Archives/Robben Island, University of the Western Cape [UWC].

36 MCH63-30-4-211, African National Congress, London, to: Mr John MacG K Kendal-Carpenter, London, 31 October 1988, Sam Ramsamy Collection, Mayibuye Archives/Robben Island, University of the Western Cape [UWC].

37 MCH63-30-4-207, *Statement by Dr D H Craven on Behalf of Rugby*, 01/06/1990, Sam Ramsamy Collection, Mayibuye Archives/Robben Island, University of the Western Cape [UWC].

38 Ibid.

39 MCH63, The Harare Initiative, p. 6.

40 Ibid.

41 MCH63, South African Rugby Union, *To: All Affiliated Units, Clubs and Officials: Press Statement Released by the President, Mr E.S. Patel, On Behalf of the South African Rugby Union on the 26th October 1988*, Sam Ramsamy Collection, Mayibuye Archives/Robben Island, University of the Western Cape [UWC].

42 MCH63-30-3-197, Media Release, 22/2/90, Sam Ramsamy Collection, Mayibuye Archives/Robben Island, University of the Western Cape [UWC].

43 MCH63-30-4-202, Correspondence from NSC General Secretary, M Tyamzashe, to: Secretary: International Rugby Board, Mr KA Rowlands, 6 December 1990, Sam Ramsamy Collection, Mayibuye Archives/Robben Island, University of the Western Cape [UWC], p. 1.

44 MCH63-30-4-221, National Olympic and Sports Congress of South Africa (NSC), Sports Moratorium (c. 1991), Sam Ramsamy Collection, Mayibuye Archives/Robben Island, University of the Western Cape [UWC], p. 3.

45 Interview 9: Messrs Mpumelelo 'Sbhidla' Majola and Lucky 'Coach' Mange, 22 March 2019, New Brighton, Port Elizabeth (translated from isiXhosa), p. 88.

46 'Comrades destroy 'Ibhayi ID cards'', *Weekend Post*, 3 October 1986.

47 Lodge, T and Swilling, M. 'The Year of Amabuthu', *Africa Report*, March–April 1986 (emphasis in original), p. 5.

48 Interview 33: Mr Valence Watson I, 1 November 2019, Mill Park, Port Elizabeth, p. 5.

49 Interview 18: Mr Ray Mali, 10 April 2019, Winterstrand, East London, p. 29.

50 Interview 9: Messrs Mpumelelo 'Sbhidla' Majola and Lucky 'Coach' Mange (translated from isiXhosa), p. 95.

51 Interview 30: Mr Andile Nyembezi, 18 October 2019, Algoa Park, Port

Elizabeth (translated from isiXhosa), p. 2.

52 Ibid.

53 Ibid (translated from isiXhosa), p. 6.

54 Ibid (translated from isiXhosa), p. 7.

55 Ibid.

56 Ibid (translated from isiXhosa), p. 8.

57 'African Bomber: The True Story of Siya Kolisi', https://www.sablenetwork.com/resources/siya-kolisi-true-story.pdf (accessed 19 April 2021).

58 Bentley, K. 'The end of an era: PE set to enter a new age on May 16 when all races will run city', *Herald*, 6 May 1994.

59 Ibid.

60 This comprised the South African Communist Party (SACP), the Congress of South African Trade Unions (COSATU) and the South African National Civic Organisation (SANCO).

61 Bentley, K. 'PE's historic City Council', *Herald*, c. 1994.

62 Ibid.

63 Ibid.

64 Bentley, K. 'Women join new council', *Herald*, c. 1994.

65 Morris, L. '1993 sees end of white domination in PE', *Herald*, 1 December 1993.

66 Bentley, K. 'ANC plan for City Council of 80', *Herald*, 29 December 1993.

67 'Many members of TLC have lost their interest' (Editorial), *Evening Post*, 16 May 1995.

68 Cull, P. 'Qeqe in favour of separate region', *Herald*, 13 October 1994.

69 Ibid.

70 Ibid.

71 Ibid.

72 Matyu, J. 'Qeqe backs off', *Evening Post*, 25 October 1994.

73 Ibid.

74 Interview 35: Judge Cecil 'Doc' Somyalo, 6 November 2019, Summerstrand, Port Elizabeth (translated from isiXhosa), pp. 12–13.

75 Interview 33: Mr Valence Watson I.

76 Interview 3: Mr McKenzie Sloti, 10 March 2019, Kabega, Port Elizabeth (translated from isiXhosa), pp. 16–17.

77 Matyu, J. 'Homage paid to 'Nyamie'', *Evening Post*, 5 September 1994.

78 'Eastern Cape mourns death of Mrs Qeqe', *Herald*, 26 August 1994.

79 Personal communication with Ms Phumla Qeqe and Mr McKenzie Sloti, February 2021.

80 Matyu, 'Homage paid to 'Nyamie''.
81 Ibid.
82 Ibid.
83 Interview 11: Qeqe family: Port Elizabeth.
84 Interview 14: Mrs Jumartha Milase Majola, 26 March 2019, New Brighton, Port Elizabeth (translated from isiXhosa), p. 38.
85 Riordan, R. 'My View: Singing in the rain', *Weekend Post* (c. 2005).
86 Ibid.
87 Ibid.
88 Interview 1: Mr Crosby 'Winky' Ximiya, 5 March 2019, South End, Port Elizabeth, p. 15.
89 Interview 11: Qeqe family: Port Elizabeth (translated from isiXhosa), p. 122.
90 Interview 17: Qeqe family: Fort Beaufort (Messrs Mncedi Mali, Nqaba Mali and Weaver Qeqe), 9 April 2019, Fort Beaufort (translated from isiXhosa), p. 54.
91 Interview 5: Mr Alan Zinn, 11 March 2019, Summerstrand, Port Elizabeth, p. 12.
92 Interview 2: Mr Mveleli Ncula, 10 March 2019, Rowallan Park, Port Elizabeth, p. 17.
93 Interview 4: Mr Thozamile Botha, 11 March 2019, North End, Port Elizabeth, pp. 15–16.
94 Interview 8: Mr Mkhuseli Jack, 21 March 2019, Summerstrand, Port Elizabeth, p. 8.
95 Interview 33: Mr Valence Watson I, p. 31.
96 Interview 27: Advocate Amon Nyondo, 17 October 2019, Summerstrand, Port Elizabeth (partly translated from isiXhosa), p. 71.
97 Interview 32: Mr Dan Ngcaphe, 29 October 2019, Zwide, Port Elizabeth (translated from isiXhosa), p. 43.
98 Interview 25: Mr Thami Songongo, 16 October 2019, Uitenhage, Nelson Mandela Bay Metropolitan Municipality (translated from isiXhosa), p. 63.
99 Ibid (translated from isiXhosa), p. 57.
100 Interview 26: Mr Themba Ludwaba, 17 October 2019, New Brighton, p. 17.
101 Interview 18: Mr Ray Mali.
102 Interview 12: Mr Thando Manana, 25 March 2019, Adcock Stadium, Port Elizabeth, p. 1.
103 Interview 16: Mr Ngconde Balfour, 8 April 2019, Alice (translated from isiXhosa), p. 16.

104 Interview 21: Judge Lex Mpati, 26 August 2019, Erasmuskloof, Pretoria, p. 35.

105 Interview 20: Mr Mthobi Tyamzashe, 26 August 2019, Menlyn, Pretoria, p. 36.

106 Interview 19: Mr Vusi and Mrs Nozuko 'Girlie' Pikoli, 24 August 2019, Faerie Glen, Pretoria (partly translated from isiXhosa), pp. 1–61.

107 Interview 14: Mrs Jumartha Milase Majola (translated from isiXhosa), p. 37–38.

108 Interview 21: Judge Lex Mpati, p. 34.

INDEX